Apple Pro Training Series

Compressor 3 Quick-Reference Guide

Brian Gary

Apple
Certified

Apple Pro Training Series: Compressor 3 Quick-Reference Guide
Brian Gary

Published by Peachpit Press. For information on Peachpit Press books, contact:

Peachpit Press
1249 Eighth Street
Berkeley, CA 94710
(510) 524-2178
(800) 283-9444
Fax: (510) 524-2221
http://www.peachpit.com
To report errors, please send a note to errata@peachpit.com
Peachpit Press is a division of Pearson Education

ISBN 0-321-51422-X
9 8 7 6 5 4 3 2 1
Printed and bound in the United States of America

Table of Contents

About the Author

Award-winning writer, producer, and director, Brian Gary heads Flying Chaucer Films, LLC in Los Angeles. He creates a wide variety of content for commercial, television, and theatrical release as well as the Web. He has studied with the Actors Studio in New York City in their MFA program. In 2005, he joined forces at Sennet/Sheftell Entertainment as a producer. An accomplished film and television editor, Gary tours globally speaking to audiences of Final Cut Pro editors.

1

Interface Basics

Content distribution has become both varied and multifaceted. Gone are the days when laying your final edit out to tape was the only option. Now you may find yourself producing video screeners for iPods, compressing movies for Apple TV playback, encoding high-quality trailers for the web, and creating both standard- and high-definition DVDs, in addition to tape output. Modern post-production workflows involve cross-compatibility between video and audio files in many formats and codecs, and between the hardware platforms used to create and manipulate them. Compressor shines as the digital distribution application for work inside Final Cut Studio, and for other platforms in your post-production pipeline.

Fortunately, Compressor handles all the nontape, QuickTime-compatible formats simply and efficiently. So, whether you need digital distribution or digital transfer, you'll only need to learn Compressor's interface and workflow to create the media you require.

Compressor uses five main windows to guide you through the different steps of the encoding process: the Batch window, the Preview window, the History window, the Inspector window, and the Presets window.

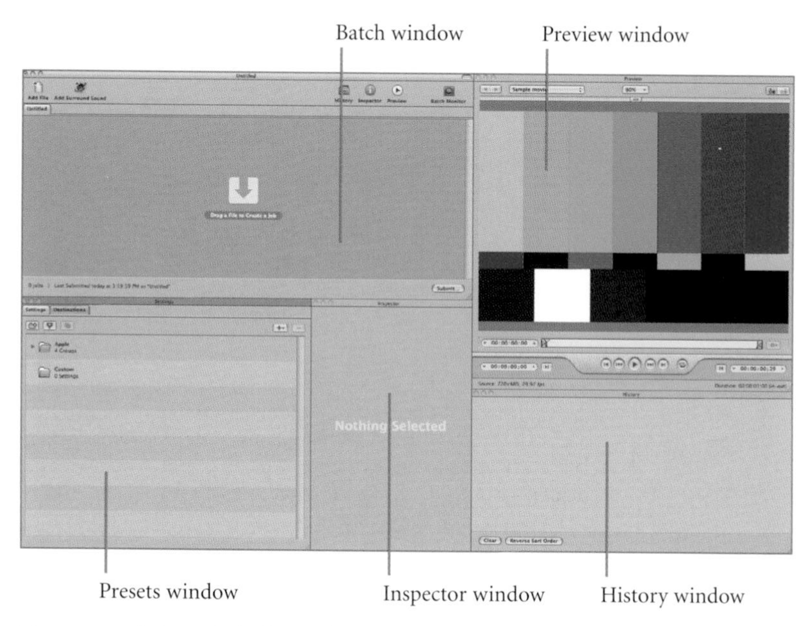
Batch window
Preview window
Nothing Selected
Presets window
Inspector window
History window

Compressor's Standard window layout

Standard Window	Function
Batch window	The vast majority of work done in Compressor starts and finishes inside the Batch window. Media is imported, targets are applied, destinations are selected, output file names are customized, and jobs are submitted to the encoder for compression.
Preview window	The Preview window compares the source media and the proposed target settings in real time. This window also lets you define the section of the source media that the encoder will process, and it lets you place chapter, podcast, and compression markers to support interactivity and compression.
History window	This window provides easy access to recent encoding jobs that can be imported back into Compressor for reference or re-submission.
Inspector window	The Inspector window serves as a portal to information and settings. The window's display changes depending on what is selected in the Presets and Batch windows. If media is selected, information regarding that media is displayed in the Inspector. If a preset or destination is selected, the settings interface is displayed.
Presets window	This window focuses on management of Settings and Destinations. Creation, organization, duplication, and deletion of both settings and destinations are easily accessible via a row of buttons. The label at the top of the window displays the name of the currently-active tab.

Batch Window

The Batch window lets you manage your encoding tasks. With a combination of main menus, shortcut menus, and buttons, the Batch window provides access to all the essential components of Compressor.

The Batch window is divided into two sections: a toolbar at the top and a lower section that contains the Batch tabs.

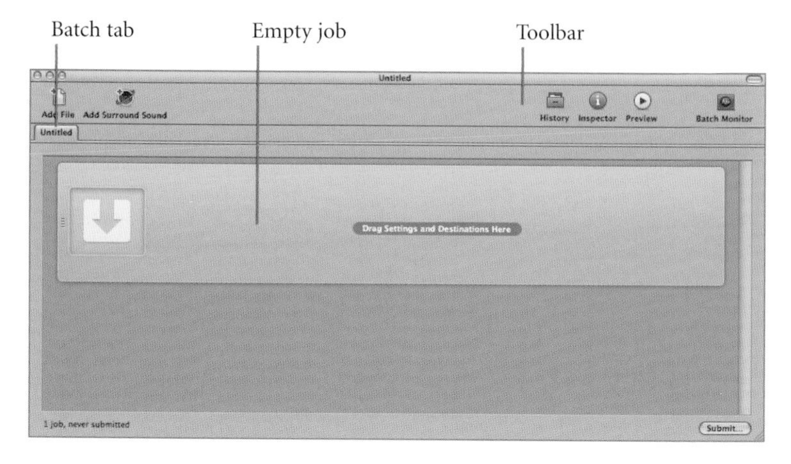
Batch tab
Empty job
Toolbar
Untitled
Add File
Add Surround Sound
History
Inspector
Preview
Batch Monitor
Drag Settings and Destinations Here
1 job, never submitted
Submit...

The Batch window toolbar gives you one-click access to the other Compressor windows. If a window is currently visible, click its button to activate it. If the window is not visible, click its button to both open and activate that window.

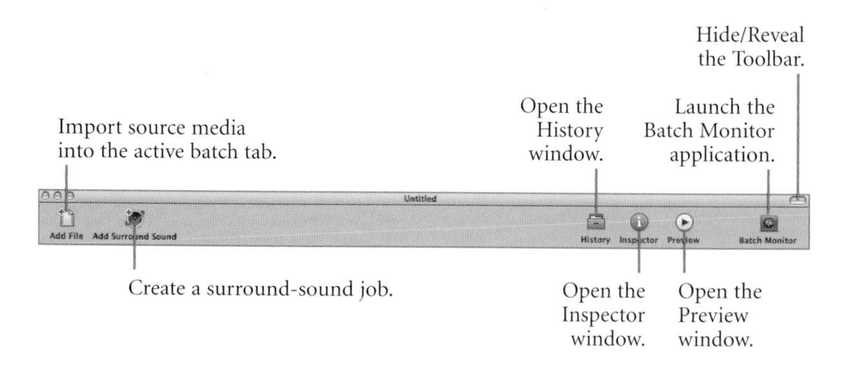
Hide/Reveal the Toolbar.
Open the History window.
Launch the Batch Monitor application.
Import source media into the active batch tab.
Untitled
Add File
Add Surround Sound
History
Inspector
Preview
Batch Monitor
Create a surround-sound job.
Open the Inspector window.
Open the Preview window.

You can customize the Toolbar by selecting the Batch window and choosing View > Customize Toolbar.

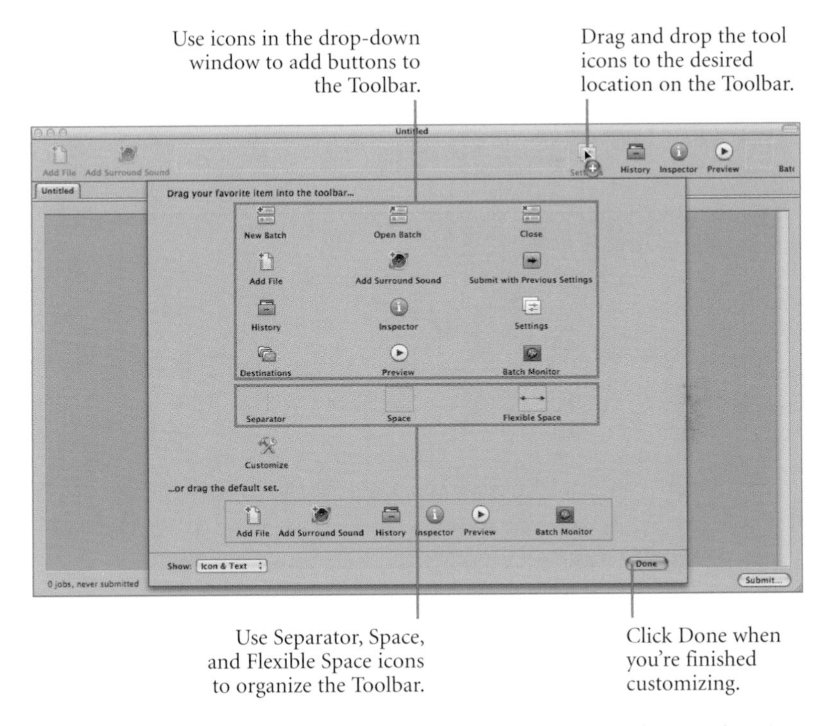
Use icons in the drop-down window to add buttons to the Toolbar.
Drag and drop the tool icons to the desired location on the Toolbar.
Untitled
History
Inspector
Preview
Drag your favorite item into the toolbar...
New Batch
Open Batch
Close
Add File
Add Surround Sound
Submit with Previous Settings
History
Inspector
Settings
Destinations
Preview
Batch Monitor
Separator
Space
Flexible Space
Customize
...or drag the default set.
Add File
Add Surround Sound
History
Inspector
Preview
Batch Monitor
Show: Icon & Text
Done
0 jobs, never submitted
Submit...
Use Separator, Space, and Flexible Space icons to organize the Toolbar.
Click Done when you're finished customizing.

Batch windows let you import source media—called *jobs*—and assign encoding tasks—called *targets*—to each job. Targets are comprised of both a setting and a destination. You can create multiple jobs, each with multiple targets, which together comprise a *batch* that you can submit to encode as one session.

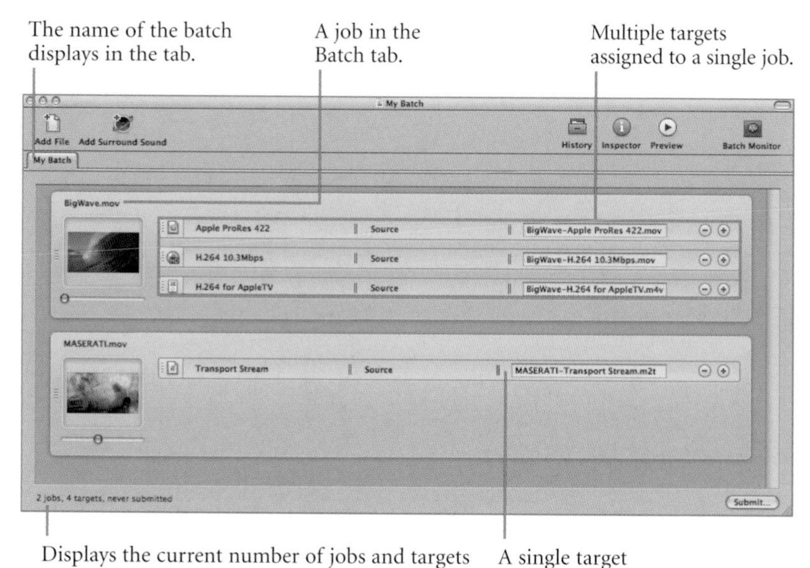
The name of the batch displays in the tab.
A job in the Batch tab.
Multiple targets assigned to a single job.
My Batch
Add File
Add Surround Sound
History
Inspector
Preview
Batch Monitor
BigWave.mov
Apple ProRes 422
Source
BigWave-Apple ProRes 422.mov
H.264 10.3Mbps
BigWave-H.264 10.3Mbps.mov
H.264 for AppleTV
BigWave-H.264 for AppleTV.m4v
MASERATI.mov
Transport Stream
MASERATI-Transport Stream.m2t
2 jobs, 4 targets, never submitted
Submit...
Displays the current number of jobs and targets in the batch and their submission status.
A single target assigned to a job.

Both jobs together make up the batch.

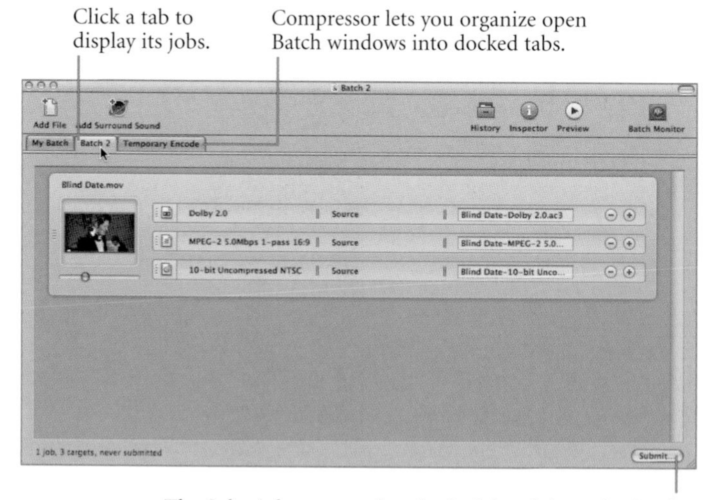
Click a tab to display its jobs.
Compressor lets you organize open Batch windows into docked tabs.
Batch 2
Add File
Add Surround Sound
History
Inspector
Preview
Batch Monitor
My Batch
Temporary Encode
Blind Date.mov
Dolby 2.0
Source
Blind Date-Dolby 2.0.ac3
MPEG-2 5.0Mbps 1-pass 16:9
Blind Date-MPEG-2 5.0...
10-bit Uncompressed NTSC
Blind Date-10-bit Unco...
1 job, 3 targets, never submitted
Submit...

The Submit button sends only the jobs of the active batch to the encoder for processing. You can continue working on other open batches and submit them when ready.

The Batch window very effectively implements shortcut menus. Both the Toolbar and Batch tabs provide context-specific menus depending on where you Control-click.

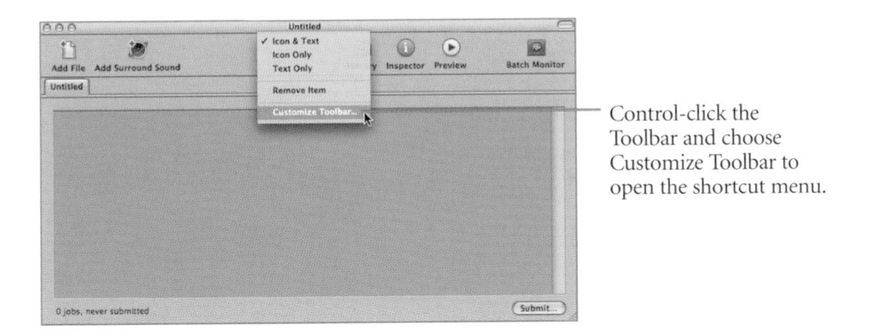
Untitled
Icon & Text
Icon Only
Text Only
Remove Item
Customize Toolbar...
Add File
Add Surround Sound
Inspector
Preview
Batch Monitor
Untitled
0 jobs, never submitted
Submit...

Control-click the Toolbar and choose Customize Toolbar to open the shortcut menu.

The Preview Window

The Preview window is divided into three areas: Display controls, Preview screen, and Timeline controls.

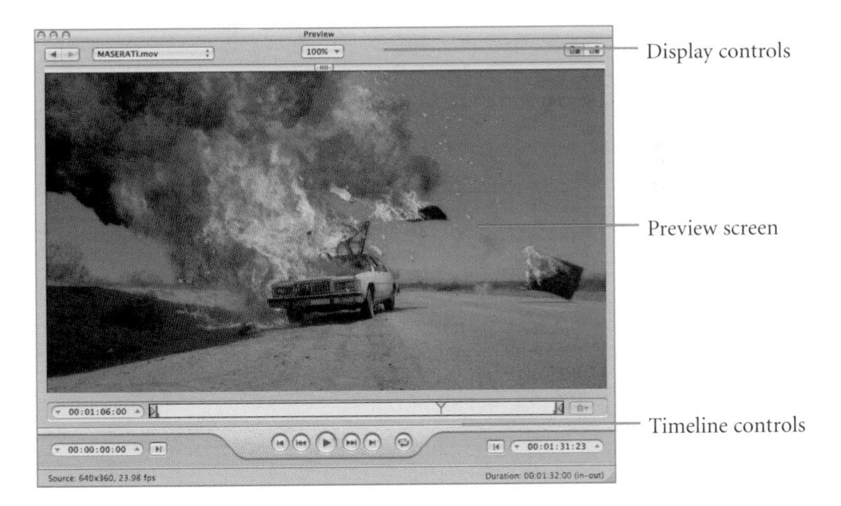
Preview
MASERATI.mov
100%
00:01:06:00
00:00:00:00
00:01:31:23
Source: 640x360, 23.98 fps
Duration: 00:01:32:00 (in-out)

Display controls

Preview screen

Timeline controls

Display Controls and Preview Screen

The Display control buttons and pop-up menus let you manage how the Preview window presents the native source media and the source media with the currently selected setting (target) applied. The Preview screen plays back the currently selected source media or applied target as a real-time preview.

The Next and Previous selection buttons navigate forward and backward through the currently available media in the Batch Window.
The Batch Item pop-up menu provides quick access to the media and targets loaded into the Batch window. It also displays the currently active item in the Preview screen.
Preview
MASERATI.mov
100%
The Source/Setting selection buttons control the aspect ratio and frame size of the Preview screen. See the following table for more information.
The Preview scale selection pop-up menu adjusts the size of the Preview window relative to the source media or output file. The menu offers three choices: 100%, 75%, or 50% (see table). You can also set whether the Preview window displays square or non-square pixels by selecting the appropriate option.

The Source/Setting selection buttons can be somewhat confusing when used in tandem with the Preview screen. The following table clarifies how to use these buttons.

You Want To:	Click This Button:
Watch playback of source media	Click the Source button. The choice in the Preview scale selection pop-up menu is relative to the source media. If your source is 720 x 480 pixels, for example, and you choose 50%, the Preview window will scale the Playback area to 360 x 240 pixels.
Crop the source media manually	Click the Source button. Note that the cropping boundaries are available only when the Source button is selected.
Watch a preview relative to the output media—that is, view a particular target in its output dimensions rather than the source's native dimensions	Click the Output button. The choice in the Preview scale selection pop-up menu is relative to the output media. If the output dimension is 320 x 240 pixels, for example, choosing 50% will scale the Playback area in the Preview window to 160 x 120 pixels.
View any manual crop settings or crop values that were applied in the Geometry pane of the Inspector	Click the Output button. The cropping boundaries will disappear, and the Source/Output information display will reflect the output frame size and rate.

Timeline Controls

During media playback, the Preview window uses standard transport controls much like those in QuickTime Player or in Final Cut Pro's Viewer and Canvas windows.

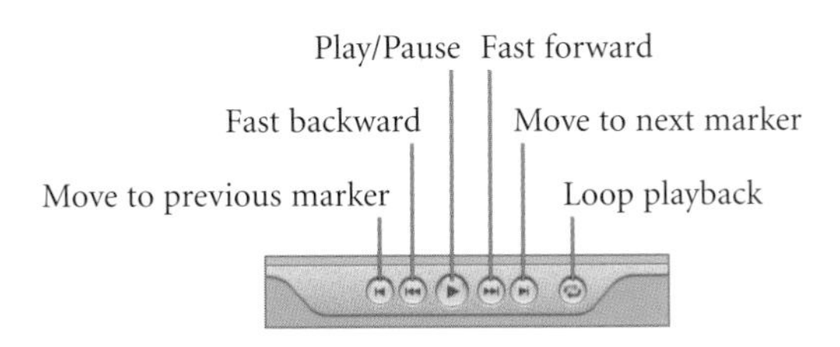
Play/Pause
Fast forward
Fast backward
Move to next marker
Move to previous marker
Loop playback

In addition to using the transport controls, you can also scrub the Timeline by dragging the playhead. For more precise control, refer to the timecode field to the left of the Timeline.

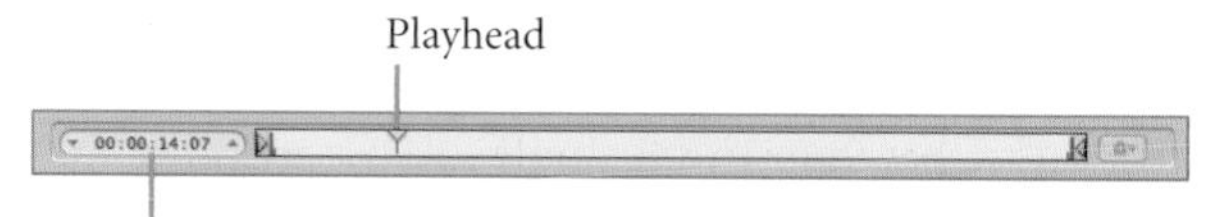
Playhead
00:00:14:07

Enter the exact frame in the timecode field or click the up and down triangles on either side to move the playhead forward or backward one frame at a time.

The Timeline also lets you set In and Out points to select a section of source media bound for encoding.

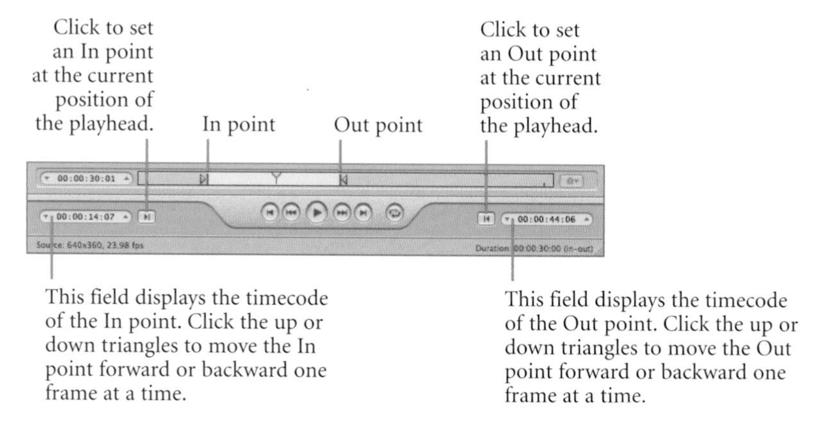
Click to set an In point at the current position of the playhead.
In point
Out point
Click to set an Out point at the current position of the playhead.
00:00:30:01
00:00:14:07
00:00:44:06
Source: 640x360, 23.98 fps
Duration: 00:00:30:00 (In-out)
This field displays the timecode of the In point. Click the up or down triangles to move the In point forward or backward one frame at a time.
This field displays the timecode of the Out point. Click the up or down triangles to move the Out point forward or backward one frame at a time.

In tandem with the playhead position, type I or O on the keyboard to set the In and Out points, respectively.

The History Window

The History window provides convenient access to recent encoding jobs and targets, allowing you to quickly re-enter them into your Compressor workflow. The History window lists the batches by date.

You can re-import an entire batch or just a single job by dragging the entry from the History window into the Batch window.

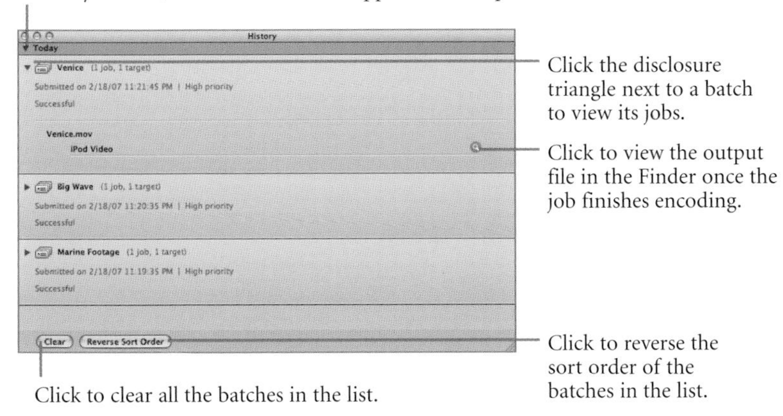
Click the disclosure triangle to see all the batches for a certain submission date. By default, more recent batches appear at the top of the list.
History
Today
Venice (1 job, 1 target)
Submitted on 2/18/07 11:21:45 PM | High priority
Successful
Venice.mov
iPod Video
Big Wave (1 job, 1 target)
Submitted on 2/18/07 11:20:35 PM | High priority
Successful
Marine Footage (1 job, 1 target)
Submitted on 2/18/07 11:19:35 PM | High priority
Successful
Clear
Reverse Sort Order
Click the disclosure triangle next to a batch to view its jobs.
Click to view the output file in the Finder once the job finishes encoding.
Click to reverse the sort order of the batches in the list.
Click to clear all the batches in the list.

The History window also displays the status of currently encoding batches.

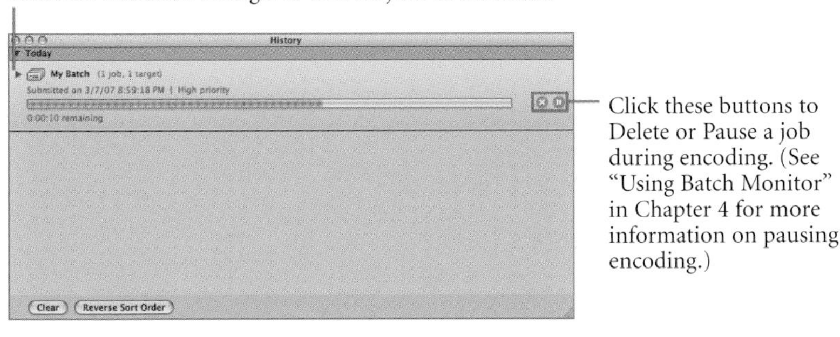
Click the disclosure triangle to view all jobs in the batch.
History
Today
My Batch (1 job, 1 target)
Submitted on 3/7/07 8:59:18 PM | High priority
0:00:10 remaining
Clear
Reverse Sort Order
Click these buttons to Delete or Pause a job during encoding. (See "Using Batch Monitor" in Chapter 4 for more information on pausing encoding.)

The Inspector Window

The Inspector window is your portal to Compressor's brain, providing access to all the inner workings and parameters that define settings and destinations. It also displays the most useful information about the imported source media.

For the Inspector to display anything, though, you have to select a job or target in the Batch window or a preset in the Presets window. If nothing is selected, the Inspector window remains blank except for a "Nothing Selected" message.

If source media is selected in the Batch window, the Inspector details the specs of the imported file.

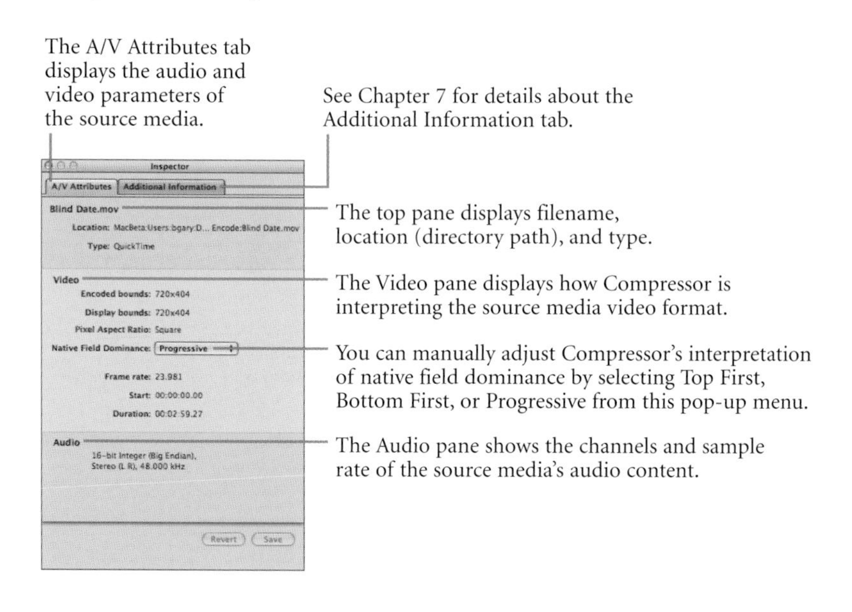
The A/V Attributes tab displays the audio and video parameters of the source media.
See Chapter 7 for details about the Additional Information tab.
Inspector
A/V Attributes
Additional Information
Blind Date.mov
Type: QuickTime
Video
Encoded bounds: 720x404
Display bounds: 720x404
Pixel Aspect Ratio: Square
Native Field Dominance: Progressive
Frame rate: 23.981
Start: 00:00:00.00
Duration: 00:02:59.27
Audio
16-bit Integer (Big Endian), Stereo (L R), 48.000 kHz
Revert
Save
The top pane displays filename, location (directory path), and type.
The Video pane displays how Compressor is interpreting the source media video format.
You can manually adjust Compressor's interpretation of native field dominance by selecting Top First, Bottom First, or Progressive from this pop-up menu.
The Audio pane shows the channels and sample rate of the source media's audio content.

In addition to displaying source media information, the Inspector provides detailed access to the stock and custom settings and destinations. Depending on which preset you've selected from the Presets window, or which target you've selected from the Batch window, the Inspector will display different interfaces that let you modify the applicable parameters. The vast majority of custom work you perform in Compressor will employ the Inspector window, and your desired output media type will dictate largely how you interact with an item's settings.

Before learning about the Inspector's details, here are some general aspects of the window that are worth knowing:

These two fields display the Name and Description of the selected preset. The generic "Selected Target" displays when a target is selected from a job in the Batch window.

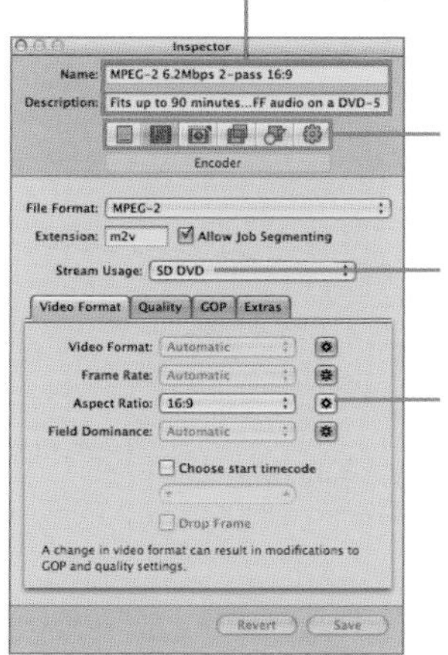
Inspector
Name: MPEG-2 6.2Mbps 2-pass 16:9
Description: Fits up to 90 minutes...FF audio on a DVD-5
Encoder
File Format: MPEG-2
Extension: m2v
Allow Job Segmenting
Stream Usage: SD DVD
Video Format
Quality
GOP
Extras
Video Format: Automatic
Frame Rate: Automatic
Aspect Ratio: 16:9
Field Dominance: Automatic
Choose start timecode
Drop Frame
A change in video format can result in modifications to GOP and quality settings.
Revert
Save

The Inspector window's appearance when working with Settings

The button bar navigates between the six panes of the Inspector window. The active pane is displayed in the field below.

The lower two-thirds of the Inspector window display settings and options based on the button selected in the button bar.

Many settings offer an Automatic option that you engage by clicking the button that corresponds with the parameter you want Compressor to control for you.

In this example, the Aspect Ratio pop-up menu is set to manual and the Field Dominance is set to automatic. Notice that when a parameter is set to automatic its pop-up menu becomes dimmed.

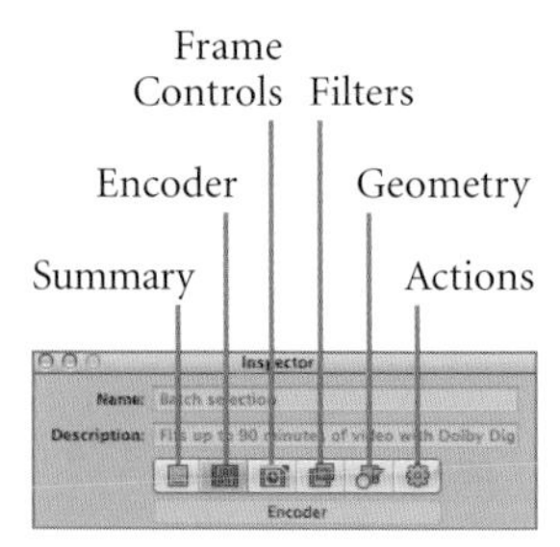
Frame Controls
Filters
Encoder
Geometry
Summary
Actions
Inspector
Name:
Description:
Encoder

A closer look at the Inspector's button bar

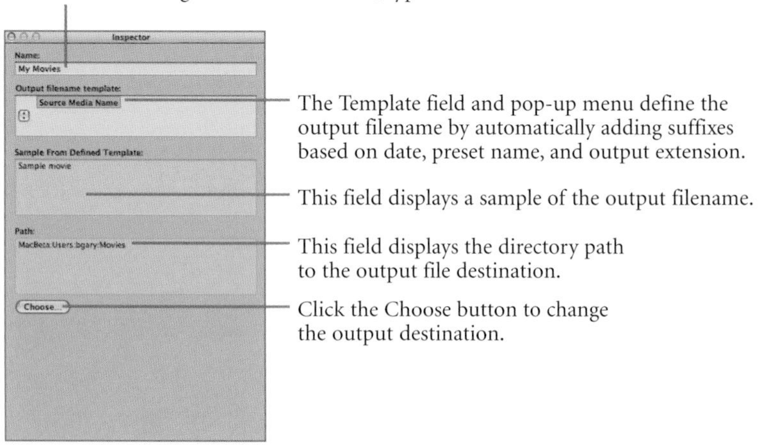
This field displays the name of the selected output file destination. When creating custom destinations, type the desired name here.
Inspector
Name:
My Movies
Output filename template:
Source Media Name
Sample From Defined Template:
Sample movie
Path:
Choose...
The Template field and pop-up menu define the output filename by automatically adding suffixes based on date, preset name, and output extension.
This field displays a sample of the output filename.
This field displays the directory path to the output file destination.
Click the Choose button to change the output destination.

The Inspector window's appearance when working with Destinations

The Presets Window

Compressor encodes for media formats ranging from DVD to Apple TV, from high-definition devices to cell phones. Each of those compression targets is governed by a setting and is output to a destination. The Presets window lets you manage the library of stock Apple settings and destinations installed with Compressor, and the library of custom settings and destinations that you create.

You access the two sections of the Presets window by selecting the Settings or Destinations tab in the upper-left corner of the window.

Settings Tab

The Settings tab displays two folders containing presets you can apply as targets to jobs in the Batch window. When Compressor is installed, all of the stock Apple presets are placed in the Apple folder; presets that you create are saved to the Custom folder.

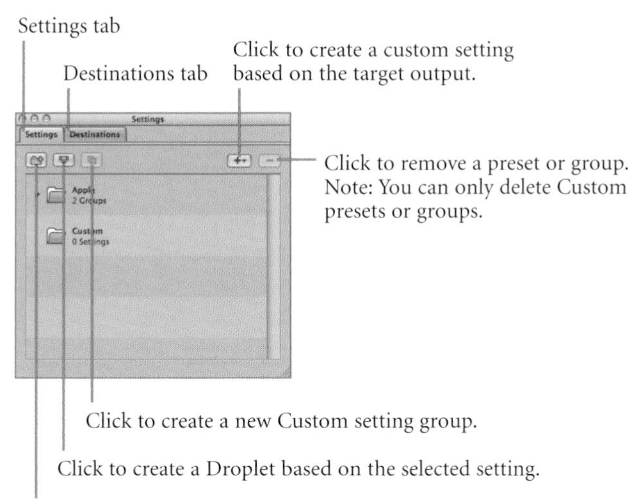
Settings tab
Destinations tab
Click to create a custom setting based on the target output.
Settings
Destinations
Click to remove a preset or group. Note: You can only delete Custom presets or groups.
Click to create a new Custom setting group.
Click to create a Droplet based on the selected setting.
Click to duplicate a selected preset or group of presets.

To view the contents of a folder, click the disclosure triangle to the left of the folder.

Destinations Tab

Each target assigned to a job in the Batch window must have a local or remote destination for the output file. The Destinations tab includes both the default Apple destinations and any custom destinations you define.

Click to duplicate the selected destination or group.

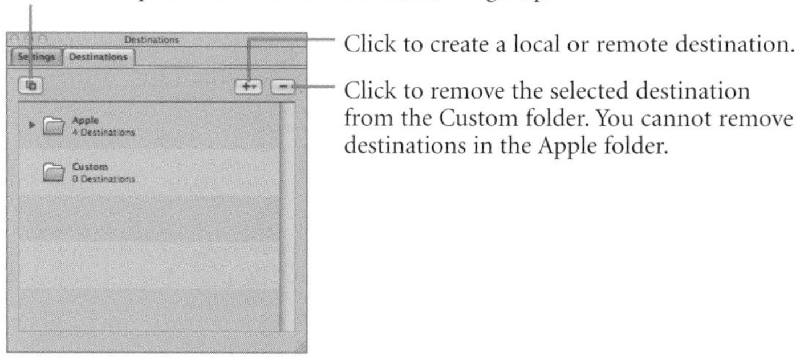
Destinations
Settings
Destinations
Apple
4 Destinations
Custom
0 Destinations
Click to create a local or remote destination.
Click to remove the selected destination from the Custom folder. You cannot remove destinations in the Apple folder.

To view the contents of a folder, click the disclosure triangle to the left of the folder.

Window Layouts

Compressor's default window layout is called Standard (see the figure on page 2) and it appears in two screen resolutions: 1440 x 900 and 1280 x 800. As a frame of reference, if you are working on a MacBook Pro and choose the Standard 1440 x 900 layout, the Compressor windows will fill your screen real estate to the edges.

> **NOTE ▸** The three Batch layouts and the two Standard layouts cannot be deleted.

Compressor also installs with a Batch layout that displays in three screen resolutions: 1440 x 900, 1280 x 800, and 1024 x 768.

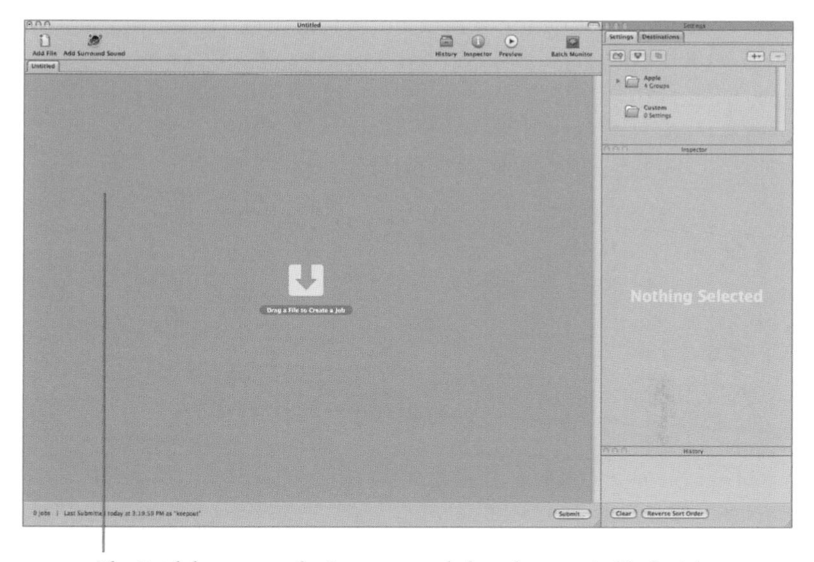
Untitled
Add File
Add Surround Sound
History
Inspector
Preview
Batch Monitor
Settings
Destinations
Apple
Custom
Inspector
Drag a File to Create a Job
Nothing Selected
History
Submit
Clear
Reverse Sort Order

The Batch layouts emphasize an expanded work area suitable for jobs in the Batch window and easy access to the Inspector window.

To use a predefined window layout, choose Window > Layouts and select the desired orientation and resolution.

In addition to the layouts that install with Compressor, you can create custom layouts and save them for future use. For example, you may find that a layout including Batch, Preview, and Presets windows works best with batches that require no setting customization.

TIP You can adjust multiple windows simultaneously by placing your cursor between two or more windows and dragging the group.

Once you have designed a window arrangement that suits your needs, choose Window > Save Layout. Name the layout and click Save.

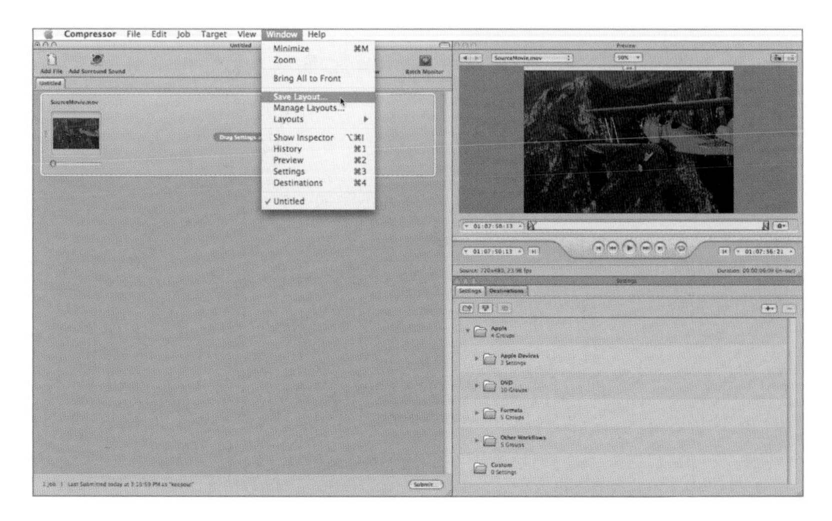
Compressor File Edit Job Target View Window Help
Minimize ⌘M
Zoom
Bring All to Front
Save Layout...
Manage Layouts...
Layouts
Show Inspector ⌥⌘I
History ⌘1
Preview ⌘2
Settings ⌘3
Destinations ⌘4
✓ Untitled

Choose Window > Manage Layouts to add or delete custom window arrangements.

You can arrange Compressor's windows with this drop-down window open. Click the Plus button to add a new layout. Name it and click Done.

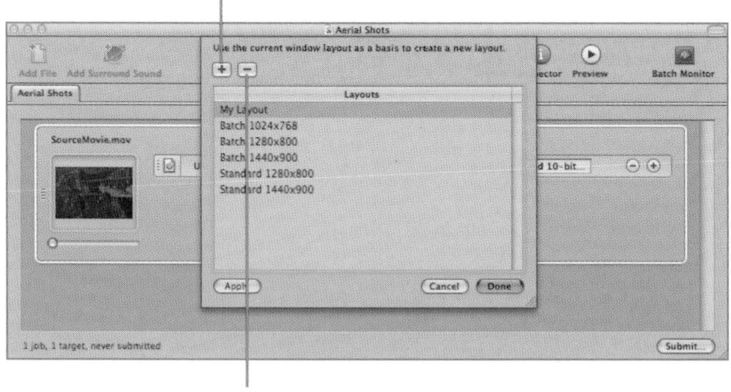
Aerial Shots
Use the current window layout as a basis to create a new layout.
Add File
Add Surround Sound
Preview
Batch Monitor
Aerial Shots
SourceMovie.mov
Layouts
My Layout
Batch 1024x768
Batch 1280x800
Batch 1440x900
Standard 1280x800
Standard 1440x900
Apply
Cancel
Done
1 job, 1 target, never submitted
Submit...

Click to remove any selected layouts from the list.

2

Importing Footage

Compressor not only delivers media from Final Cut Studio to the rest of the world, but it's also the post-production workhorse for transcoding media files from one format to another. While it can, for example, transform a Final Cut Pro sequence into MPEG-2 and Dolby Digital Professional assets that are appropriate for DVD, it can also use the Apple ProRes production codec to transcode HD camera footage into a format better suited to workflows inside Final Cut Studio.

Without source media to transcode, Compressor lies dormant. Therefore, the first step in any Compressor process is to import source media.

Footage can be imported into Compressor in two ways:

- Export media directly into Compressor from Final Cut Pro or Motion
- Import QuickTime–compatible media from a local or remote drive

Exporting from Final Cut Pro

Use the following steps to export a completed sequence from Final Cut Pro directly into Compressor:

1 In Final Cut Pro's Browser, select the sequence to export.

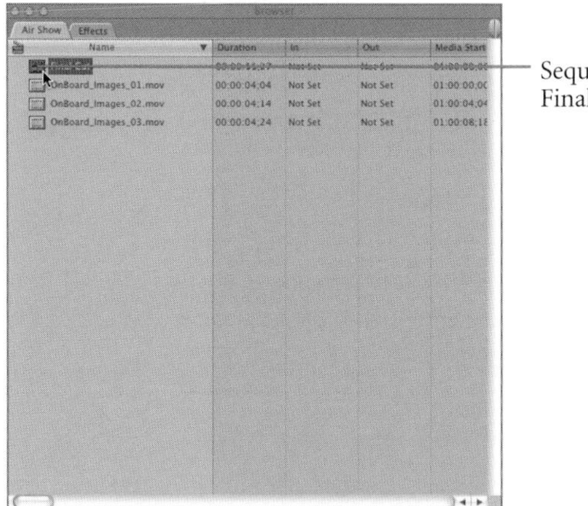
Air Show
Effects
Name
Duration
In
Out
Media Start
OnBoard_Images_01.mov
OnBoard_Images_02.mov
OnBoard_Images_03.mov
Sequence to export from Final Cut Pro's Browser

Final Cut Pro Browser window

Or, in Final Cut Pro's Timeline, select the sequence by clicking its tab.

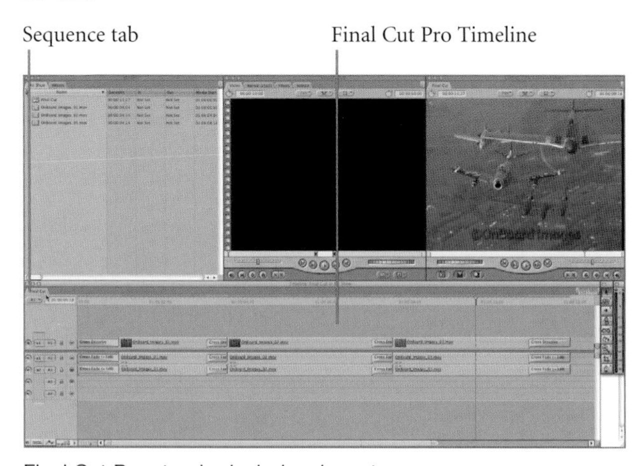
Sequence tab
Final Cut Pro Timeline

Final Cut Pro standard window layout

2 Choose File > Export > Using Compressor.

Final Cut Pro
File
Edit
View
Mark
Modify
Sequence
Effects
Tools
Window
Help
New
New Project
Open...
Open Recent
Close Window
Close Tab
Close Project
Save Project
Save Project As...
Save All
Revert Project
Restore Project...
Import
Export
Send To
Batch Export
Batch Capture...
Log and Capture...
Media Manager...
Reconnect Media...
Set Logging Bin
Print to Video...
Edit to Tape...
QuickTime Movie...
Using Compressor...
Using QuickTime Conversion...
For Soundtrack
For LiveType
Audio to AIFF(s)...
Audio to OMF...
Batch List...
Cinema Tools Audio EDL...
Cinema Tools Change List...
Cinema Tools Film Lists...
EDL...
XML...

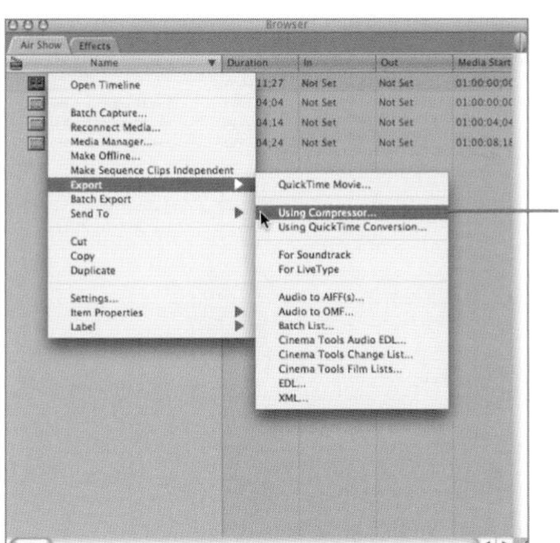
Browser
Air Show
Effects
Name
Duration
In
Out
Media Start
Open Timeline
Batch Capture...
Reconnect Media...
Media Manager...
Make Offline...
Make Sequence Clips Independent
Export
Batch Export
Send To
Cut
Copy
Duplicate
Settings...
Item Properties
Label
QuickTime Movie...
Using Compressor...
Using QuickTime Conversion...
For Soundtrack
For LiveType
Audio to AIFF(s)...
Audio to OMF...
Batch List...
Cinema Tools Audio EDL...
Cinema Tools Change List...
Cinema Tools Film Lists...
EDL...
XML...

You can also Control-click the sequence in the Browser and, from the shortcut menu, choose Export > Using Compressor.

Final Cut Pro Browser window

NOTE ▸ In addition to exporting sequences directly from the Browser window, you can also export individual clips.

Final Cut Pro sends the sequence to Compressor's Batch window. If Compressor is not currently running, it will launch automatically.

Compressor creates a new untitled Batch window and imports the sequence as a new job.

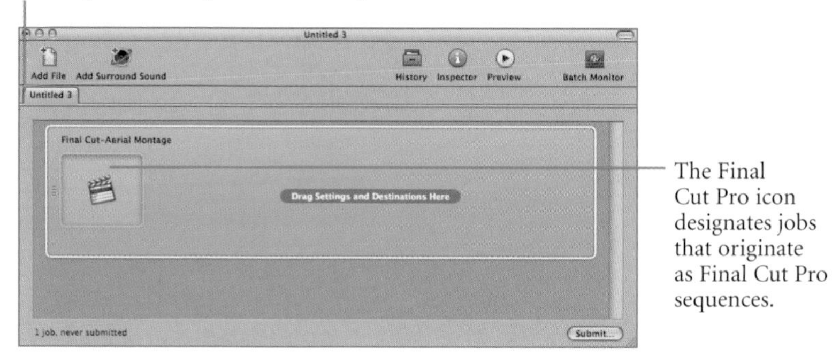
Untitled 3
Add File
Add Surround Sound
History
Inspector
Preview
Batch Monitor
Untitled 3
Final Cut-Aerial Montage
Drag Settings and Destinations Here
1 job, never submitted
Submit...

The Final Cut Pro icon designates jobs that originate as Final Cut Pro sequences.

NOTE ▶ If a job originates as a Final Cut Pro sequence, you cannot scrub the media in Compressor's Batch window.

If Compressor is currently running and you already have an active batch, then a new Batch window will be created and docked as a tab. A new Batch window is also created if you export subsequent sequences from Final Cut Pro during the same Compressor session.

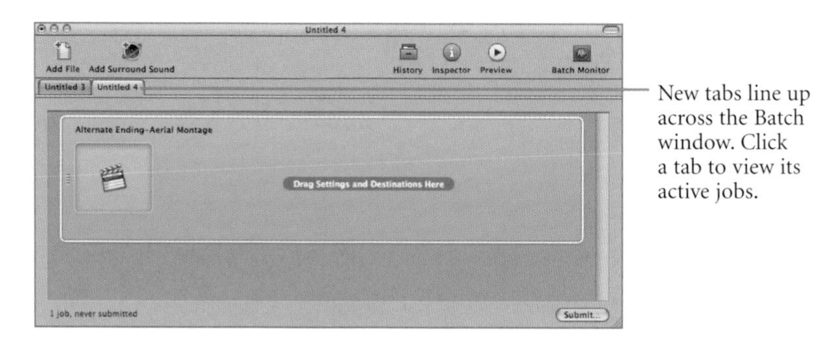
Untitled 4
Add File
Add Surround Sound
History
Inspector
Preview
Batch Monitor
Untitled 3
Untitled 4
Alternate Ending-Aerial Montage
Drag Settings and Destinations Here
1 job, never submitted
Submit...

New tabs line up across the Batch window. Click a tab to view its active jobs.

When exporting directly from Final Cut Pro, there are some pros and cons to consider:

Final Cut Pro Exporting

PRO	CON
Final Cut Pro exports every individual frame from elements such as titles, Motion project files, complex composites, and animations. Compressor receives that raw data regardless of the current sequence settings. As a result, you always send the highest quality media to the encoder. This is unlike sequences exported as QuickTime self-contained or reference movies in which all the elements that require rendering are first rendered in the sequence codec and *then* sent to the encoder via Compressor. So, if your sequence is in DV NTSC format, your Motion project files will first be rendered in DV and then sent to Compressor.	Final Cut Pro cannot be used as an edit station while Compressor encodes the exported media because each frame of the exported sequence passes individually from Final Cut Pro to Compressor.
Real-time workflows inside Final Cut Pro do not have to be rendered before being sent to Compressor. On effects-heavy sequences, this can save both time and space.	Any media loaded into the Preview window will require that Final Cut Pro furnish the frames for playback. You will have to close the Preview window to regain control of Final Cut Pro.

This window displays the frames being passed from Final Cut Pro to Compressor.

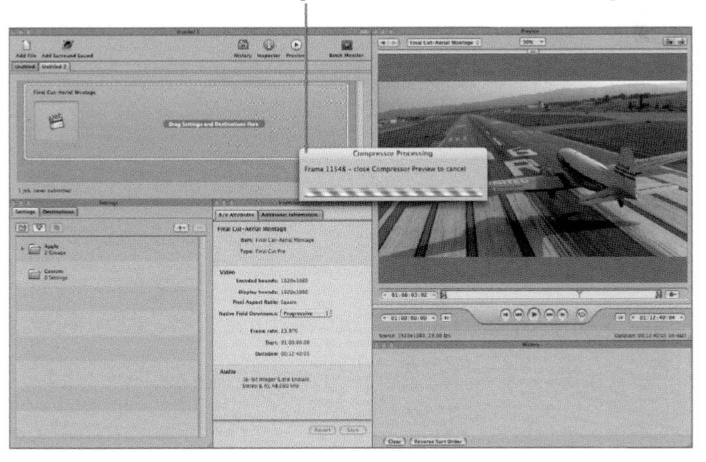
Compressor Processing
Frame 11548 - close Compressor Preview to cancel

Exporting from Motion

Exporting projects directly from Motion is as easy as the Final Cut Pro workflow and adds some time-saving advantages.

With the desired export project active in Motion, choose File > Export using Compressor.

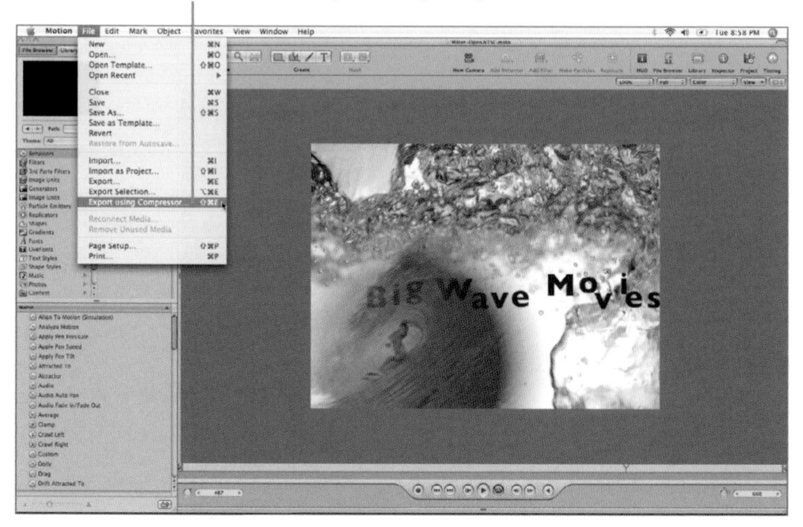
Motion
File
Edit
Mark
Object
View
Window
Help
New
Open...
Open Template...
Open Recent
Close
Save
Save As...
Save as Template...
Revert
Restore from Autosave...
Import...
Import as Project...
Export...
Export Selection...
Export using Compressor...
Reconnect Media...
Remove Unused Media
Page Setup...
Print...
Big Wave Movies

Motion interface

The Compressor Export Options window opens in Motion before final export.

In the Include pop-up menu, you can choose to send the video and audio content together, or to send them individually.

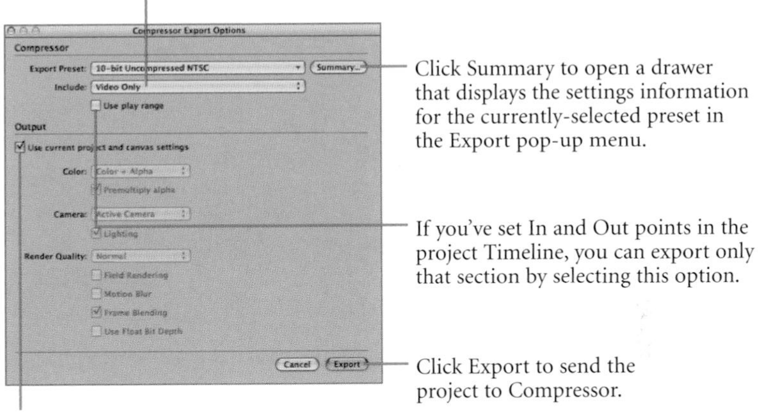
Compressor Export Options
Compressor
Export Preset:
10-bit Uncompressed NTSC
Summary...
Include:
Video Only
Use play range
Output
Use current project and canvas settings
Color:
Camera:
Render Quality:
Cancel
Export

Click Summary to open a drawer that displays the settings information for the currently-selected preset in the Export pop-up menu.

If you've set In and Out points in the project Timeline, you can export only that section by selecting this option.

Click Export to send the project to Compressor.

Override the project's output settings by deselecting this option and manually adjusting the settings below.

Compressor creates a new batch and imports the project as a job.

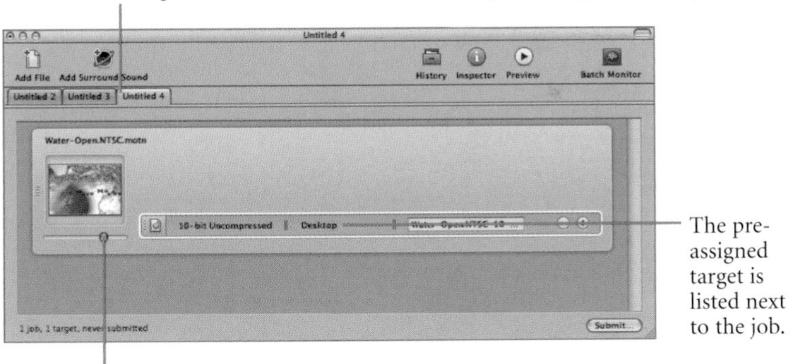
Untitled 4
Add File
Add Surround Sound
History
Inspector
Preview
Batch Monitor
Untitled 2
Untitled 3
Untitled 4
Water-Open.NTSC.motn
10-bit Uncompressed
Desktop
1 job, 1 target, never submitted
Submit...

The pre-assigned target is listed next to the job.

Notice that you can scrub through the thumbnail of an exported Motion project.

TIP You can also import Motion project files directly into Compressor. Because Compressor treats Motion projects like QuickTime movies, use the following steps for importing QuickTime media.

Importing QuickTime Movies

Compressor can import any media file for which QuickTime has the appropriate playback codec. If QuickTime Player can open a file, then Compressor can import it.

Follow these steps to import source media contained on a local or remote storage device into Compressor:

1 Launch Compressor, if it is not already running.

2 Choose Job > New Job With File, or press Command-I.

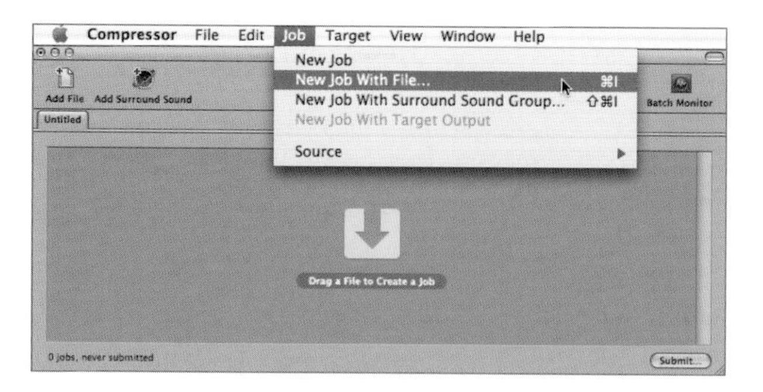
Compressor File Edit Job Target View Window Help
New Job
New Job With File... ⌘I
New Job With Surround Sound Group... ⇧⌘I
New Job With Target Output
Source
Add File
Add Surround Sound
Untitled
Batch Monitor
Drag a File to Create a Job
0 jobs, never submitted
Submit...

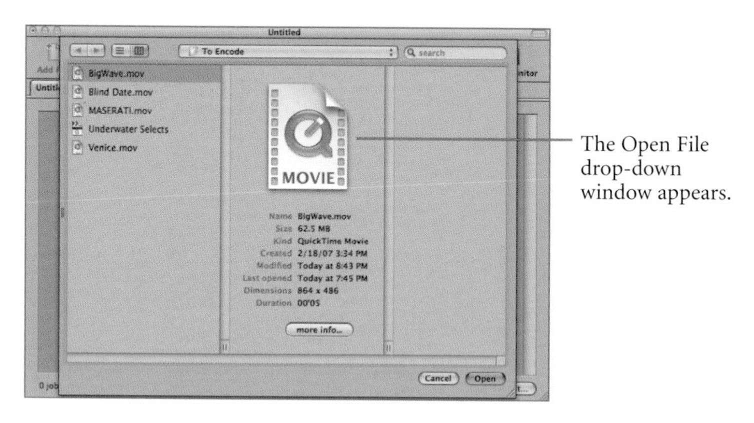
Untitled
To Encode
search
BigWave.mov
Blind Date.mov
MASERATI.mov
Underwater Selects
Venice.mov
MOVIE
Name BigWave.mov
Size 62.5 MB
Kind QuickTime Movie
Created 2/18/07 3:34 PM
Modified Today at 8:43 PM
Last opened Today at 7:45 PM
Dimensions 864 x 486
Duration 00'05
more info...
Cancel
Open

The Open File drop-down window appears.

3 Navigate to the desired file and click Open.

Just like the Final Cut Pro or Motion direct export workflows, imported QuickTime source media files enter the active Batch window as jobs.

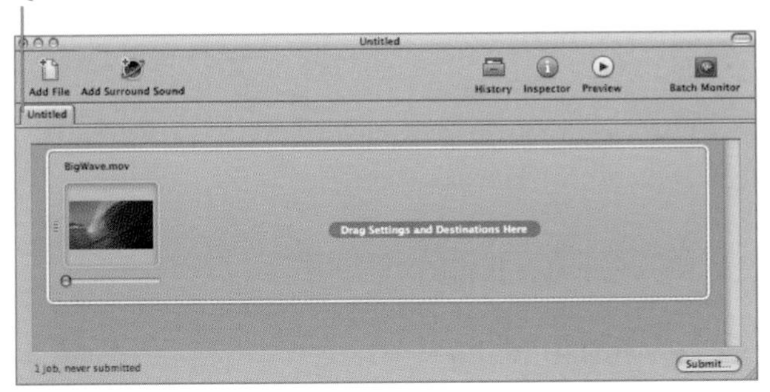
Untitled
Add File
Add Surround Sound
History
Inspector
Preview
Batch Monitor
Untitled
BigWave.mov
Drag Settings and Destinations Here
1 job, never submitted
Submit...

TIP If you have multiple Batch windows docked as tabs, make sure you select the desired Batch tab before importing source media. You can also create a new Batch window for the imported QuickTime media by choosing File > New Batch.

Alternate Import Methods

Compressor offers multiple ways to import QuickTime media into the Batch window.

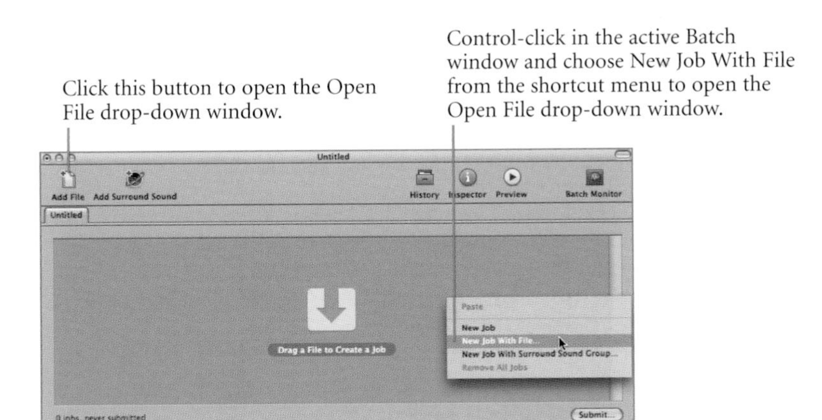
Click this button to open the Open File drop-down window.
Control-click in the active Batch window and choose New Job With File from the shortcut menu to open the Open File drop-down window.
Untitled
Add File
Add Surround Sound
History
Inspector
Preview
Batch Monitor
Untitled
Drag a File to Create a Job
Paste
New Job
New Job With File...
New Job With Surround Sound Group...
Remove All Jobs
0 jobs, never submitted
Submit...

In the Open File drop-down window, navigate to the source media and click Open.

You can also drag and drop source media files directly from the Finder into the Batch window.

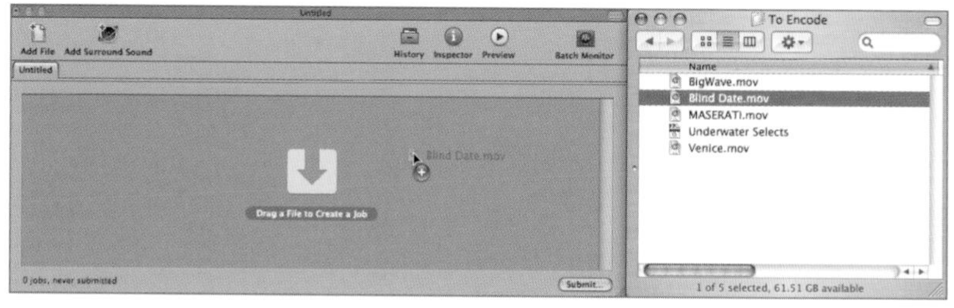
Add File
Add Surround Sound
History
Inspector
Preview
Batch Monitor
Drag a File to Create a Job
To Encode
Name
BigWave.mov
Blind Date.mov
MASERATI.mov
Underwater Selects
Venice.mov
1 of 5 selected, 61.51 GB available

Shift-drag or Command-drag multiple source media files from the Finder to import them as a group.

Exporting from Soundtrack Pro

All of the Compressor encoding options available to Soundtrack Pro are contained within the Soundtrack Pro export function.

Starting with a completed multi-track project in Soundtrack Pro, choose File > Export.

Name the file.

From the Where pop-up menu, choose a location to save the exported media.

From the Exported Items pop-up menu, choose the project elements you want to encode.

From the File Type pop-up menu, choose the desired encoder. In this example, Dolby Digital Professional is selected for a surround-sound project bound for DVD.

This pane displays the encoder settings based on the setting chosen in the File Type pop-up menu. The example displays all of the Dolby encoding settings you would find in the Inspector window.

Click Export to start encoding.

Soundtrack Pro export window

Neither Compressor nor Batch monitor will launch upon export; the processing occurs within Soundtrack Pro.

Exporting...
Time Remaining: About 5 seconds
Cancel

This Soundtrack Pro window displays during encoding.

> **TIP** If you've been working with video in Soundtrack Pro, choose Using Compressor from the File Type pop-up menu to either pass the video through the export process or to choose one of the Compressor settings to transcode the video.

Resolving Source Media Conflicts

Source media listed in the Batch window is just a reference pointing to the actual media on the local or remote drive; Compressor does not actually copy the individual files into the Batch windows. Therefore, avoid changing the name or location of the original source media; otherwise, the job that references that media may become unusable.

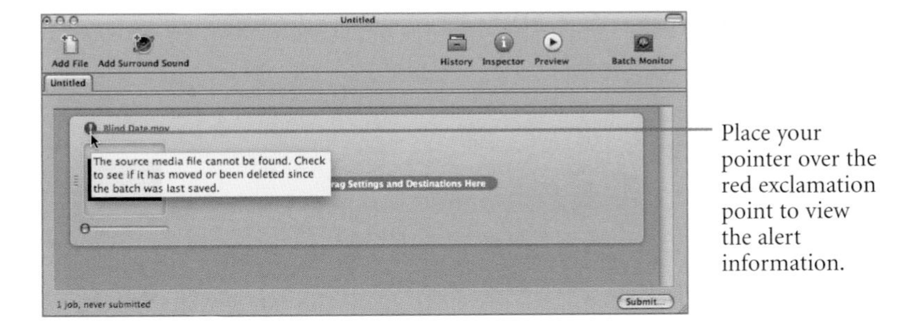
Untitled
Add File
Add Surround Sound
History
Inspector
Preview
Batch Monitor
Untitled
Blind Date.mov
The source media file cannot be found. Check to see if it has moved or been deleted since the batch was last saved.
1 job, never submitted
Submit...

Place your pointer over the red exclamation point to view the alert information.

Import Recommendations

Use the following table to decide which import method is best for your compression workflow.

Import Task:	Best Import/Export Procedure:
Edit using Final Cut Pro while Compressor encodes in the background	Import a QuickTime movie
Save time and storage space by not rendering real-time effects in Final Cut Pro before encoding	Export to Compressor directly from Final Cut Pro
Move a final edit to another computer for encoding	Export a self-contained QuickTime movie from Final Cut Pro, and import that movie into Compressor
Pass high-quality frames directly to the encoder from Motion project files, animations, or text without first rendering them in the Final Cut Pro sequence settings	Export to Compressor directly from Final Cut Pro
Encode using a cluster that does not have access to the Final Cut Pro project and associated files	Export a self-contained QuickTime movie from Final Cut Pro, import it into Compressor, and send that movie to the cluster for encoding
Pass filters (such as Color Correction) directly to Compressor with the source frame, and render them in the output codec instead of in the sequence codec	Export to Compressor directly from Final Cut Pro

3

Working with Presets

Compressor installs with a series of presets that control both encoder settings and output file destinations. You can also create your own settings and destinations presets by modifying the Apple stock presets or by creating new presets from the ground up.

By default, the Presets window is a container for both the Settings and Destinations tabs. This default configuration keeps both of these preset groups in one convenient place.

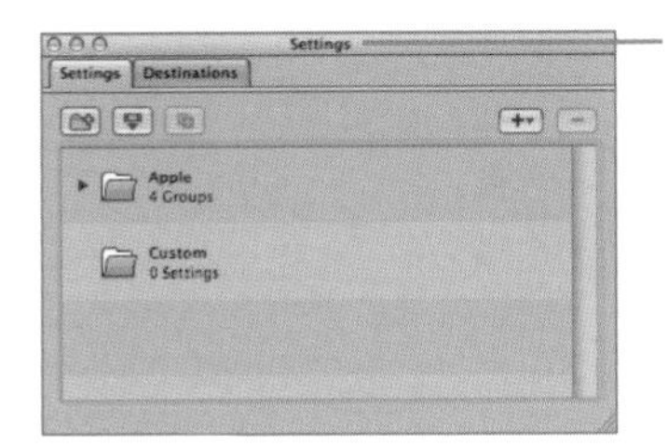
Settings
Settings
Destinations
Apple
4 Groups
Custom
0 Settings

The Preset window label reflects the currently active tab. In this example, the Settings tab is selected and therefore its name is displayed in the label.

Using Settings

Compressor encodes source media according to a collection of parameters and options, known as a *setting*. Compressor installs a library of Apple settings for the most common digital media distribution platforms. These settings are divided into four groups: Apple Devices, DVD, Formats, and Other Workflows.

Use the settings in the Apple Devices group when you encode to Apple TV or iPods with video.

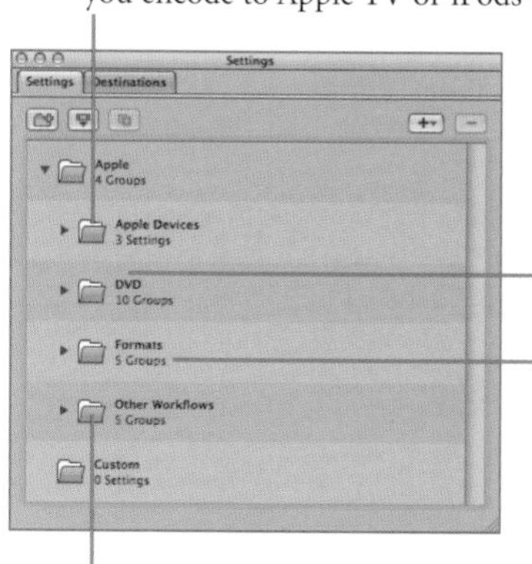
Settings
Settings
Destinations
Apple
4 Groups
Apple Devices
3 Settings
DVD
10 Groups
Formats
5 Groups
Other Workflows
5 Groups
Custom
0 Settings

The DVD group contains settings for both standard and high-definition DVD output.

Use the settings in the Formats group when you encode to a specific file type or media format: MPEG-2 Transport stream or 10-bit Uncompressed, for example.

Use the settings in the Other Workflows group to encode for the Web, motion graphics, mobile devices, or format conversions.

Within each group, a hierarchy of folders becomes increasingly platform specific as you navigate through the path to the individual settings.

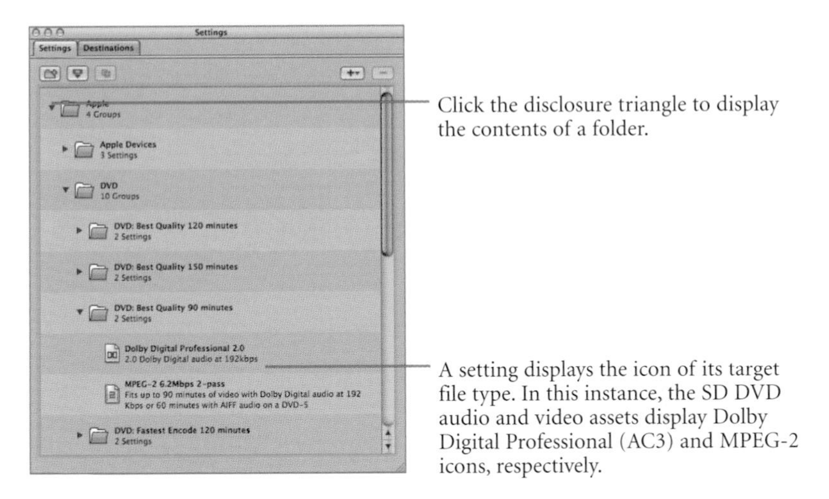
Settings
Settings
Destinations
Apple
4 Groups
Apple Devices
3 Settings
DVD
10 Groups
DVD: Best Quality 120 minutes
2 Settings
DVD: Best Quality 150 minutes
2 Settings
DVD: Best Quality 90 minutes
2 Settings
Dolby Digital Professional 2.0
2.0 Dolby Digital audio at 192kbps
MPEG-2 6.2Mbps 2-pass
Fits up to 90 minutes of video with Dolby Digital audio at 192 Kbps or 60 minutes with AIFF audio on a DVD-5
DVD: Fastest Encode 120 minutes
2 Settings

Click the disclosure triangle to display the contents of a folder.

A setting displays the icon of its target file type. In this instance, the SD DVD audio and video assets display Dolby Digital Professional (AC3) and MPEG-2 icons, respectively.

Select a setting in the list to open it in the Inspector window.

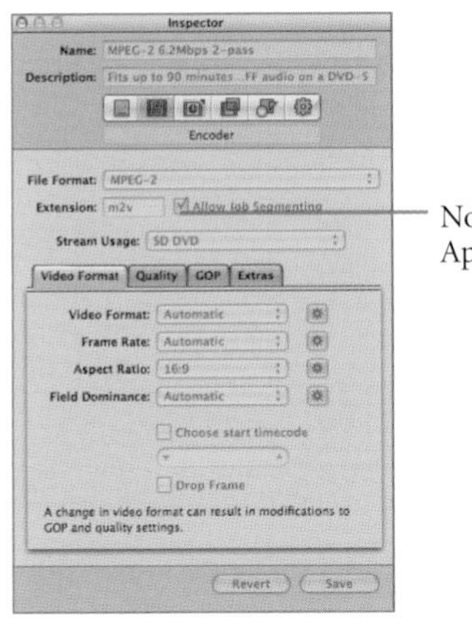
Inspector
Name:
Description:
Encoder
File Format:
Extension:
Stream Usage:
Video Format
Quality
GOP
Extras
Video Format:
Frame Rate:
Aspect Ratio:
Field Dominance:
A change in video format can result in modifications to GOP and quality settings.
Revert
Save

Notice that all options are dimmed because Apple settings cannot be modified or deleted.

Applying Settings to Jobs

When settings are applied to jobs in the Batch window, they create *targets*. A target comprises a setting, a destination, and an output filename. Jobs in the Batch window can have a single target or multiple targets applied to them.

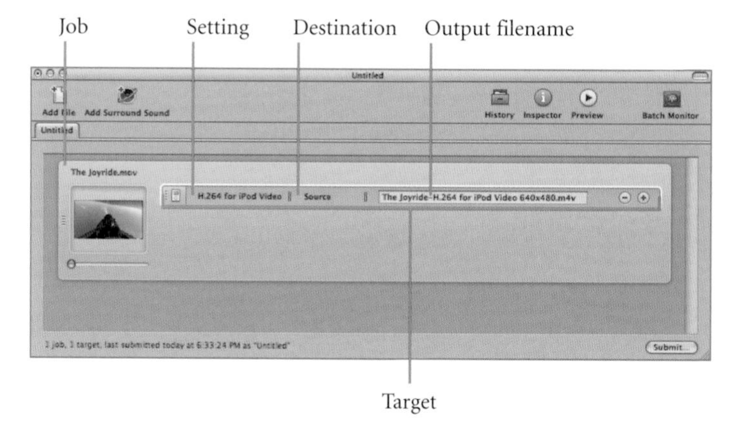
Job
Setting
Destination
Output filename
Target

In the Batch windows, you can apply settings to jobs in one of the following three ways:

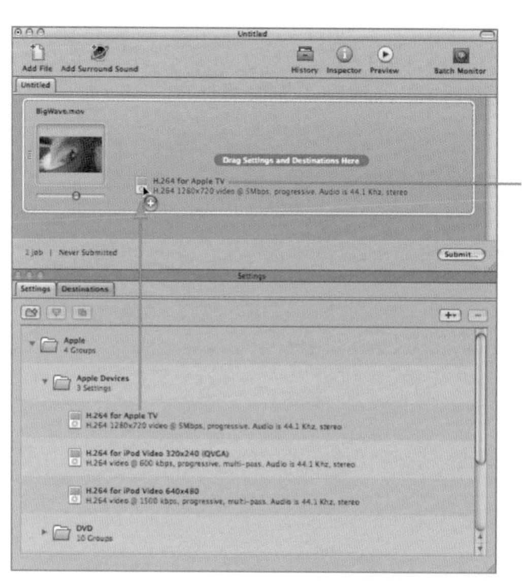

The simplest way to apply a setting to a job in the Batch window is to drag the desired setting or setting group from the Presets window onto a job.

When you add a preset group, all of the settings in the group are applied as targets.

Select a job in the Batch window and choose Target > New Target With Setting. In this drop-down window, navigate to the desired setting, choose it, and click Add.

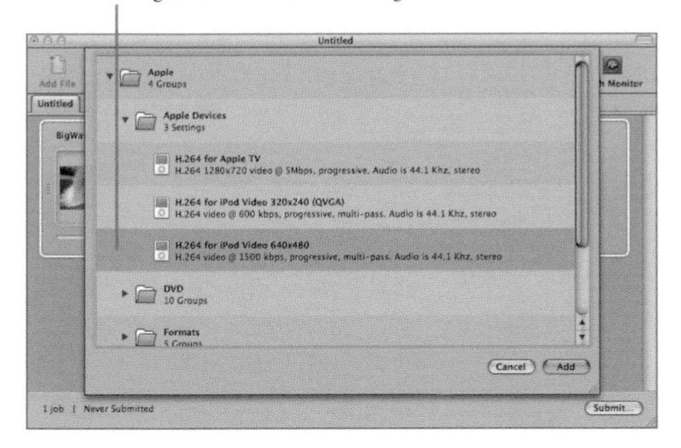
Untitled
Add File
Untitled
Monitor
Apple
4 Groups
Apple Devices
3 Settings
H.264 for Apple TV
H.264 1280x720 video @ 5Mbps, progressive. Audio is 44.1 Khz, stereo
H.264 for iPod Video 320x240 (QVGA)
H.264 video @ 600 kbps, progressive, multi-pass. Audio is 44.1 Khz, stereo
H.264 for iPod Video 640x480
H.264 video @ 1500 kbps, progressive, multi-pass. Audio is 44.1 Khz, stereo
DVD
10 Groups
Formats
Cancel
Add
1 job | Never Submitted
Submit...

Control-click a job in the Batch window and, from the shortcut menu, choose New Target With Setting. Navigate through the submenus and choose the desired setting.

Drag Settings and Destinations Here
Clear
Reverse Sort Order

Modifying the Apple Settings

The most convenient way to create a custom setting is to modify an Apple setting and save the modified setting as a unique preset.

If, for example, your movie is intended to be bonus material on an SD DVD, you could apply an Apple SD DVD setting creating an MPEG-2 target, and then lower the target's bit rate to meet your custom output specifications.

When a setting displays "Selected Target" in the Name field and remains dimmed, it indicates that the setting you are working on is a target from the Batch window.

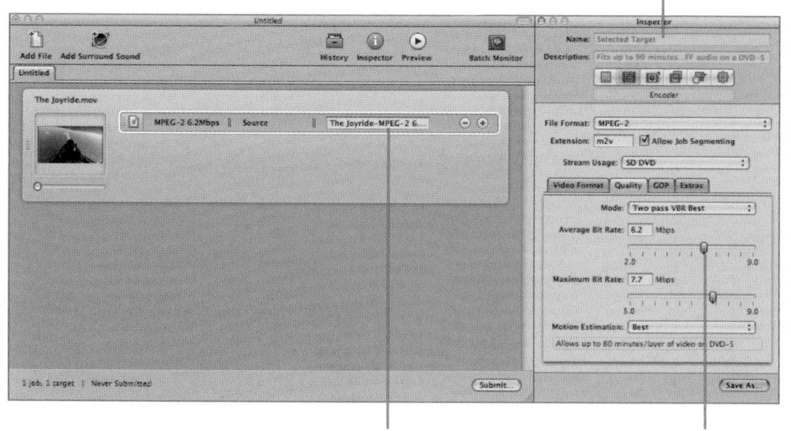
Add File
Add Surround Sound
History
Inspector
Preview
Batch Monitor
Untitled
The Joyride.mov
MPEG-2 6.2Mbps
Source
Inspector
Name:
Selected Target
Description:
Encoder
File Format:
MPEG-2
Extension:
m2v
Allow Job Segmenting
Stream Usage:
SD DVD
Video Format
Quality
GOP
Extras
Mode:
Two pass VBR Best
Average Bit Rate:
6.2
Mbps
Maximum Bit Rate:
7.7
Mbps
Motion Estimation:
Best
Submit...
Save As...

Select a target in the Batch window to load its settings into the Inspector.

You can adjust the target's settings as needed.

NOTE ▶ When you add a setting to a job in the Batch window and create a target, Compressor uses a copy of the setting, not the setting itself. Therefore, any changes you make to settings applied to jobs in the Batch window will not alter the original settings in the Presets window.

Saving Temporary Modifications to Settings

After you submit a batch for encoding, any settings modifications will be lost because the preset reverts to its original parameters in the Presets window. Compressor lets you save your modifications by creating a custom preset that you can apply to subsequent jobs just like the Apple settings.

After you complete a temporary modification to an Apple (or Custom) target setting, click the Save As button in the lower right of the Inspector.

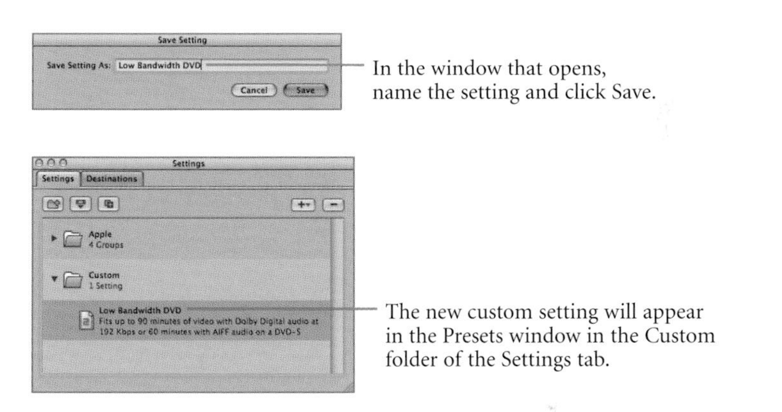
Save Setting
Save Setting As:
Low Bandwidth DVD
Cancel
Save
Settings
Settings
Destinations
Apple
4 Groups
Custom
1 Setting
Low Bandwidth DVD
Fits up to 90 minutes of video with Dolby Digital audio at 192 Kbps or 60 minutes with AIFF audio on a DVD-5

In the window that opens, name the setting and click Save.

The new custom setting will appear in the Presets window in the Custom folder of the Settings tab.

The new custom setting will also appear in the Custom Folder of the target drop-down window and in the New Target With Setting submenu of the shortcut menu in the Batch window.

> **NOTE** ▶ The target from which the new custom setting was derived can be further modified without changing the settings of the new custom preset.

Duplicating Apple Settings

As mentioned previously, Apple settings cannot be modified in the Presets window, but Compressor allows you to duplicate presets with a single click. After a preset is duplicated, you can modify the duplicate and save it as a new preset.

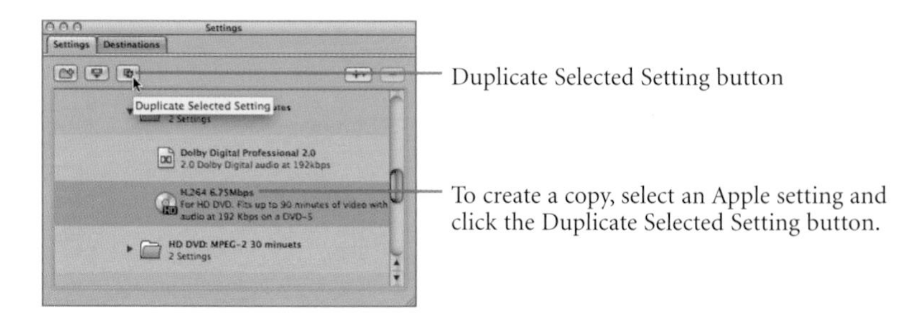
Duplicate Selected Setting button
To create a copy, select an Apple setting and click the Duplicate Selected Setting button.

Compressor automatically appends "copy" to the filename.
Notice that the name and description fields can be edited.

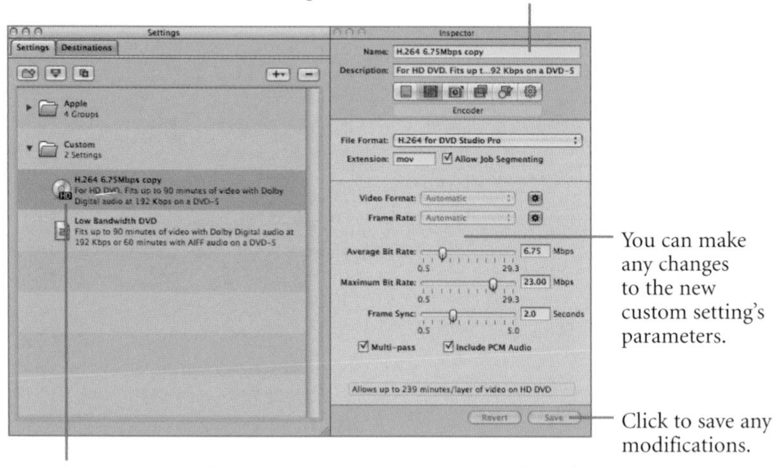
You can make any changes to the new custom setting's parameters.
Click to save any modifications.

Compressor duplicates the selected preset, appends "copy" to the filename, and places the copy in the Custom folder.

Creating Custom Settings Presets

Creating custom presets requires just a few additional steps and a little planning.

First, decide what type of encoding process the preset should address. Compressor offers the following options for custom settings:

Export Option	Primary Use
AIFF	Uncompressed PCM audio for DVD or Audio CD
DV Stream	Encoding for use in iMovie
Dolby Digital Professional	Compressed audio for DVDs. Compressor can produce both 2.0- and 5.1-format files
H.264 for Apple Devices	High-quality media for iPods with video playback and Apple TV
H.264 for DVD Studio Pro	High-definition video assets for high-definition disc delivery
Image Sequence	Creates a sequence of still images from the source media; used primarily for CGI work
MP3	Compressed audio for internet delivery and podcasting
MPEG-1	Lower-quality/lower-bandwidth codec often used for DVD bonus material and cross-platform web delivery
MPEG-2	Standard video encoder for SD DVD and HD discs
MPEG-4	Produces high-quality web media at relatively fast encoding times; requires QuickTime 6 or later for playback (Mac or PC)
QuickTime Export Components	Suitable for cell-phone (3G) delivery or any third-party plug-in that is Compressor compatible
QuickTime Movie	Creates QuickTime container files with any of the available audio or video codecs

You create custom settings directly in the Presets window.

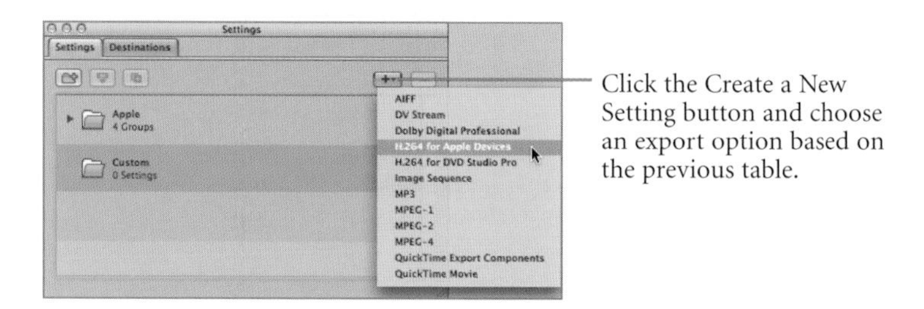
Settings
Settings
Destinations
Apple
4 Groups
Custom
0 Settings
AIFF
DV Stream
Dolby Digital Professional
H.264 for Apple Devices
H.264 for DVD Studio Pro
Image Sequence
MP3
MPEG-1
MPEG-2
MPEG-4
QuickTime Export Components
QuickTime Movie
Click the Create a New Setting button and choose an export option based on the previous table.

Custom settings appear in the Custom folder.

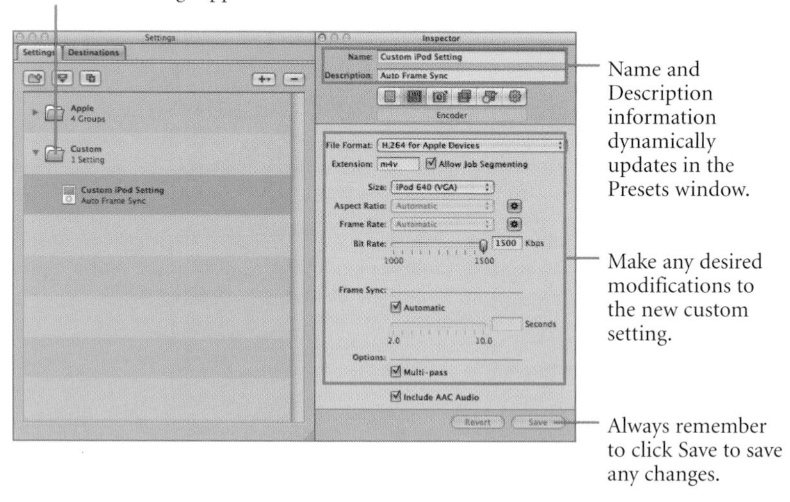
Settings
Destinations
Apple
4 Groups
Custom
1 Setting
Custom iPod Setting
Auto Frame Sync
Inspector
Name: Custom iPod Setting
Description: Auto Frame Sync
Encoder
File Format: H.264 for Apple Devices
Extension: m4v
Allow Job Segmenting
Size: iPod 640 (VGA)
Aspect Ratio: Automatic
Frame Rate: Automatic
Bit Rate:
1500 Kbps
1000
1500
Frame Sync:
Automatic
Seconds
2.0
10.0
Options:
Multi-pass
Include AAC Audio
Revert
Save
Name and Description information dynamically updates in the Presets window.
Make any desired modifications to the new custom setting.
Always remember to click Save to save any changes.

NOTE ► Unlike the Apple settings, custom settings are fully editable in the Presets window. Select any preset in the Custom folder, make the desired changes in the Inspector window, and click Save.

Organizing Custom Settings

Custom settings can be organized into specialized folders and applied to a job as a group, just like Apple settings.

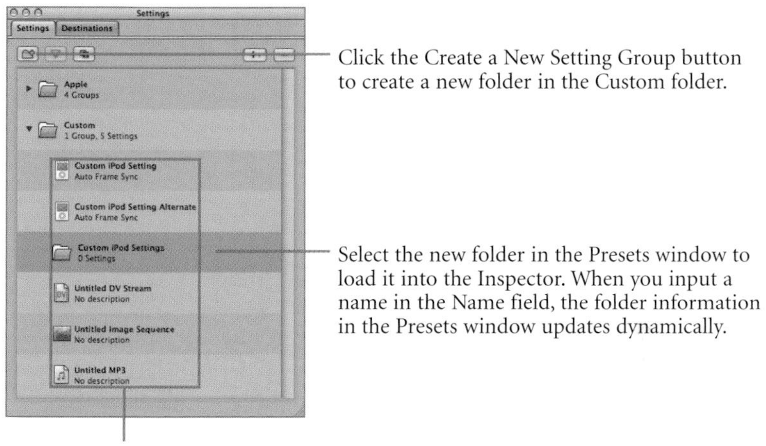
Click the Create a New Setting Group button to create a new folder in the Custom folder.
Select the new folder in the Presets window to load it into the Inspector. When you input a name in the Name field, the folder information in the Presets window updates dynamically.
Custom presets

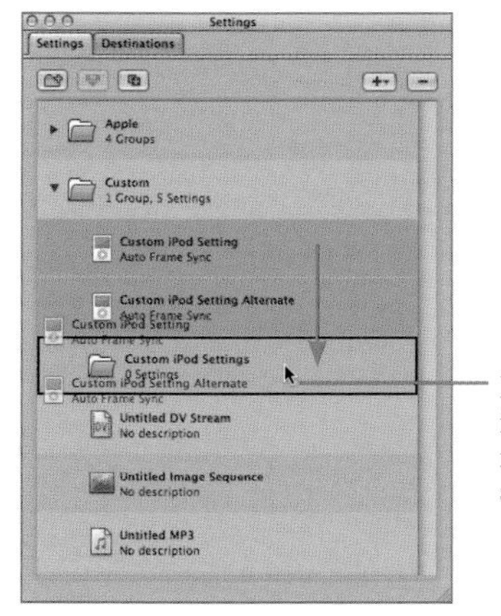

Drag the settings you want to organize together into the Custom folder. Shift-click to select multiple settings or Command-click to select multiple noncontiguous settings.

The settings you've organized together can all be applied to a job by dragging the group folder from the Presets window onto the job in the Batch window.

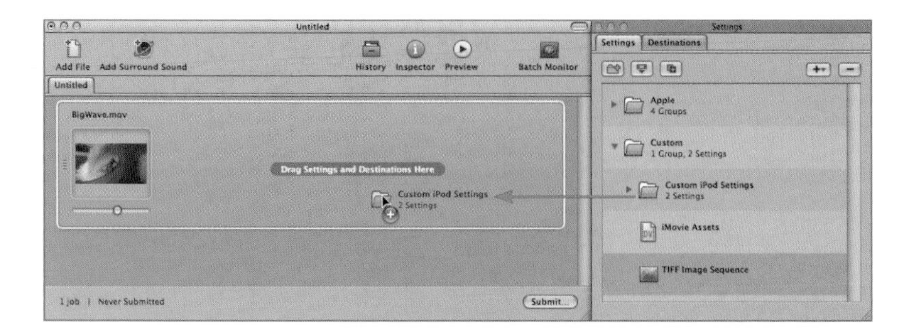
Untitled
Add File
Add Surround Sound
History
Inspector
Preview
Batch Monitor
Untitled
BigWave.mov
Drag Settings and Destinations Here
Custom iPod Settings
2 Settings
1 job | Never Submitted
Submit...
Settings
Settings
Destinations
Apple
4 Groups
Custom
1 Group, 2 Settings
Custom iPod Settings
2 Settings
iMovie Assets
TIFF Image Sequence

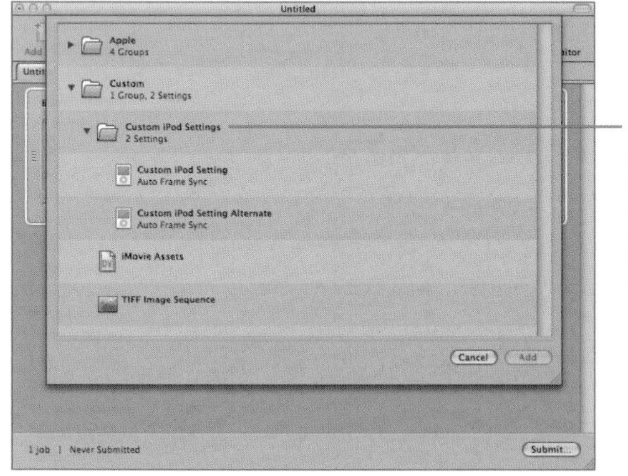
Untitled
Apple
4 Groups
Custom
1 Group, 2 Settings
Custom iPod Settings
2 Settings
Custom iPod Setting
Auto Frame Sync
Custom iPod Setting Alternate
Auto Frame Sync
iMovie Assets
TIFF Image Sequence
Cancel
Add
1 job | Never Submitted
Submit...

Custom settings and groups are also available in the drop-down window after choosing Target > New Target With Setting.

Custom settings and groups are also available in the shortcut menu in the Batch window.

Selecting All inside a setting group will apply every setting in the group to the currently selected job in the Batch window.

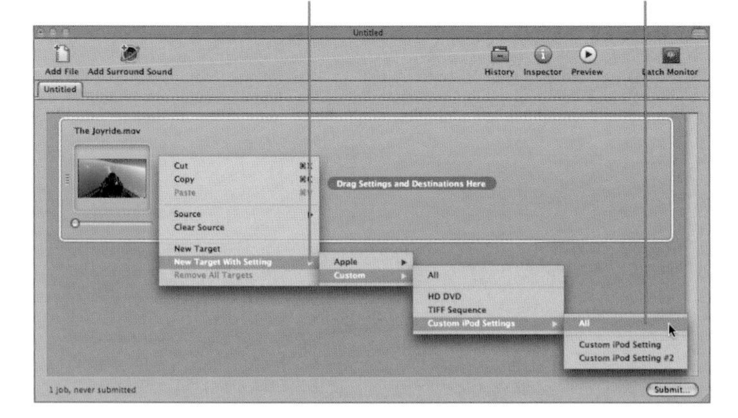
Untitled
Add File
Add Surround Sound
History
Inspector
Preview
Batch Monitor
Untitled
The Joyride.mov
Cut
Copy
Paste
Source
Clear Source
New Target
New Target With Setting
Remove All Targets
Drag Settings and Destinations Here
Apple
Custom
All
HD DVD
TIFF Sequence
Custom iPod Settings
All
Custom iPod Setting
Custom iPod Setting #2
1 job, never submitted
Submit...

Using Destinations

Destinations are a second, very important part of a target, because they tell Compressor where to output the encoded media.

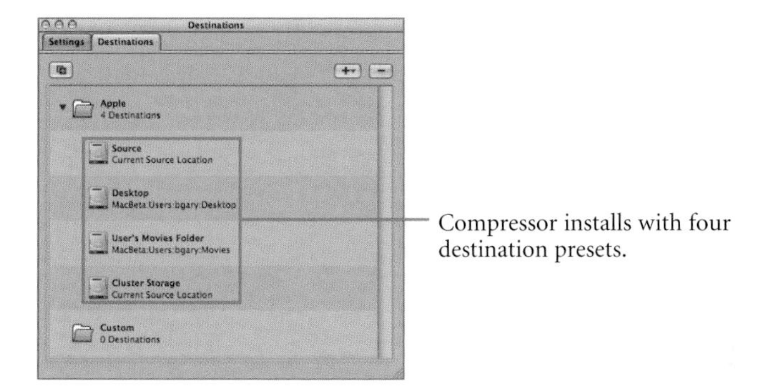
Destinations
Settings
Destinations
Apple
4 Destinations
Source
Current Source Location
Desktop
MacBeta:Users:bgary:Desktop
User's Movies Folder
MacBeta:Users:bgary:Movies
Cluster Storage
Current Source Location
Custom
0 Destinations

Compressor installs with four destination presets.

Applying Destinations

When you create a target in a job in the Batch window, Compressor automatically applies the default destination, Source, which defines the output location as the same folder where the source media originated.

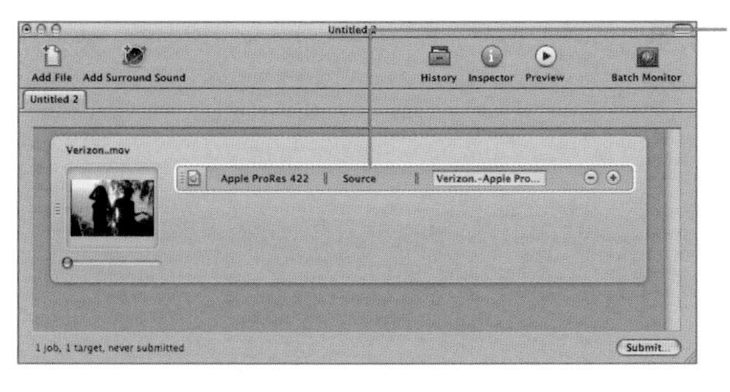
Untitled 2
Add File
Add Surround Sound
History
Inspector
Preview
Batch Monitor
Untitled 2
Verizon.mov
Apple ProRes 422
Source
1 job, 1 target, never submitted
Submit...

The middle entry of the target displays the Destination. In this example, the output file will be saved to the same folder as the source media.

You can change the default destination by changing the Default Destination setting in Compressor preferences.

Modifying a Target's Destination

Compressor offers three ways to change a target's destination from the default destination.

Drag a destination directly onto a target from the Presets window.

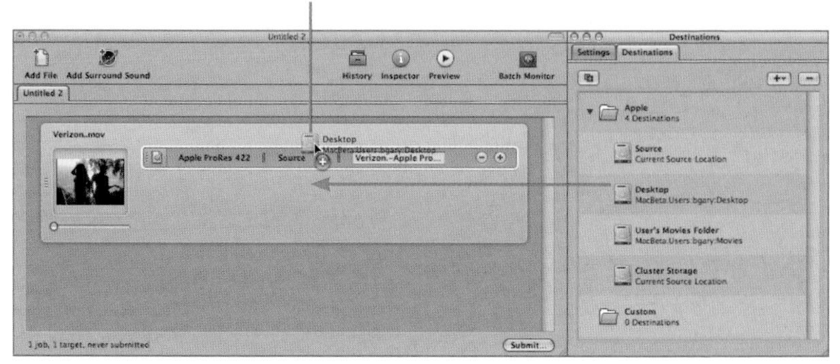
Add File
Add Surround Sound
History
Inspector
Preview
Batch Monitor
Untitled 2
Verizon.mov
Apple ProRes 422
Source
Verizon.-Apple Pro...
Desktop
Settings
Destinations
Apple
4 Destinations
Source
Current Source Location
Desktop
MacBeta:Users:bgary:Desktop
User's Movies Folder
MacBeta:Users:bgary:Movies
Cluster Storage
Current Source Location
Custom
0 Destinations
1 job, 1 target, never submitted
Submit...

Choose Target > Destination and choose a location from the submenu.

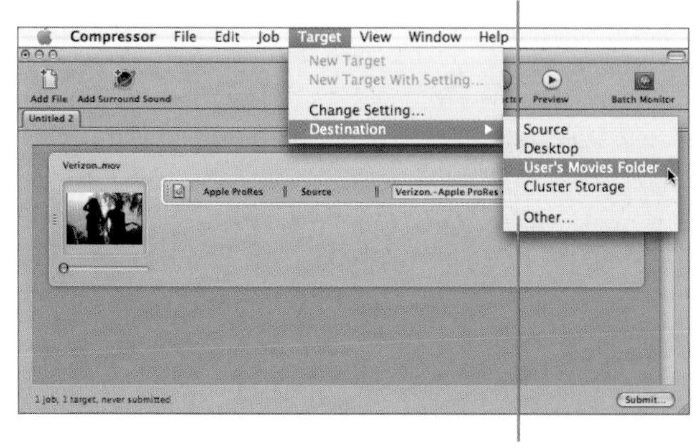
Compressor
File
Edit
Job
Target
View
Window
Help
New Target
New Target With Setting...
Change Setting...
Destination
Source
Desktop
User's Movies Folder
Cluster Storage
Other...
Add File
Add Surround Sound
Preview
Batch Monitor
Untitled 2
Verizon.mov
Apple ProRes
Source
Verizon.-Apple ProRes
1 job, 1 target, never submitted
Submit...

Choose Other to display the Open drop-down window where you can navigate to a temporary destination just for this target.

Control-click the target and, from the shortcut menu, choose Destination. Then, choose a location from the submenu.

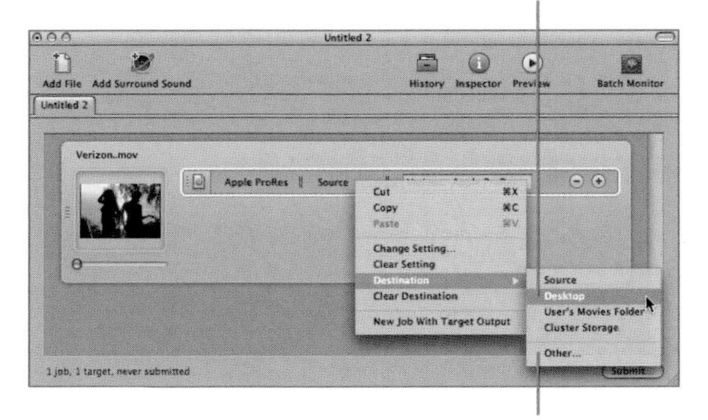
Untitled 2
Add File
Add Surround Sound
History
Inspector
Preview
Batch Monitor
Untitled 2
Verizon.mov
Apple ProRes
Source
Cut
Copy
Paste
Change Setting...
Clear Setting
Destination
Clear Destination
New Job With Target Output
Source
Desktop
User's Movies Folder
Cluster Storage
Other...
1 job, 1 target, never submitted
Submit

Choose Other to display the Open drop-down window where you can navigate to a temporary destination just for this target.

Creating Custom Destinations

You can create permanent custom destinations in the Destinations tab of the Presets window by modifying existing destinations or creating new destinations based on a local or remote output location. Local destinations are storage devices connected to your computer, whereas remote locations are devices that you connected via a network (file server) or the internet (ftp site or .Mac account).

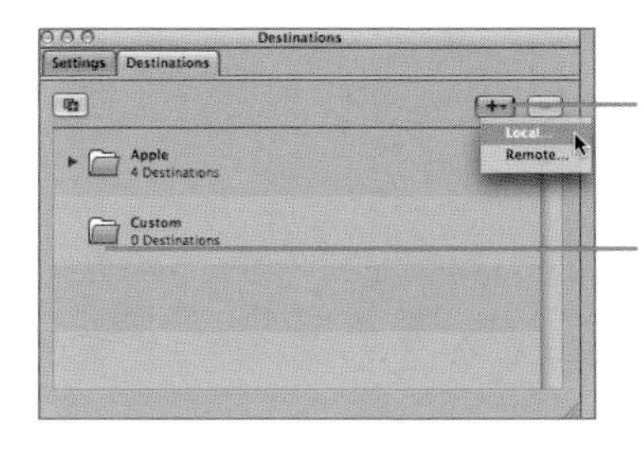
Destinations
Settings
Destinations
Local...
Remote...
Apple
4 Destinations
Custom
0 Destinations

Click the Create a New Destination pop-up menu and choose Local or Remote to create a custom destination.

As with settings, custom destinations you create appear in the Custom folder. You can apply custom destinations to jobs just as you apply Apple destinations.

Choosing Local Destinations

When you choose Local, an Open drop-down window appears in which you can choose the output location on a drive or device directly connected to your computer.

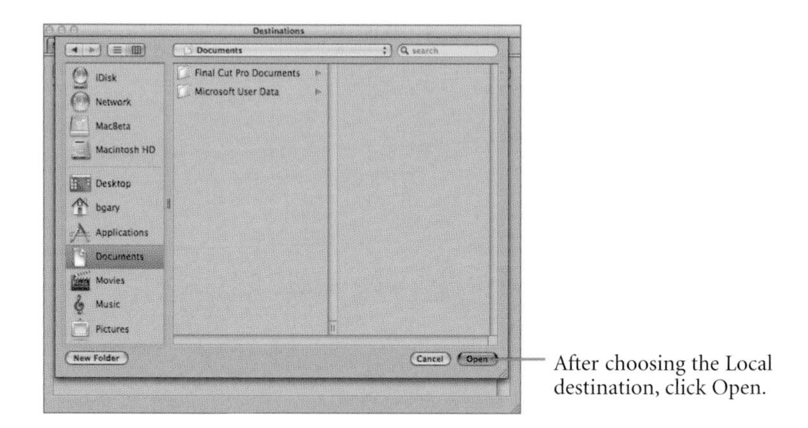
Destinations
Documents
search
iDisk
Network
MacBeta
Macintosh HD
Desktop
bgary
Applications
Documents
Movies
Music
Pictures
Final Cut Pro Documents
Microsoft User Data
New Folder
Cancel
Open

After choosing the Local destination, click Open.

The new custom destination will appear in the Custom folder. Use the Inspector window to name the destination and modify its properties.

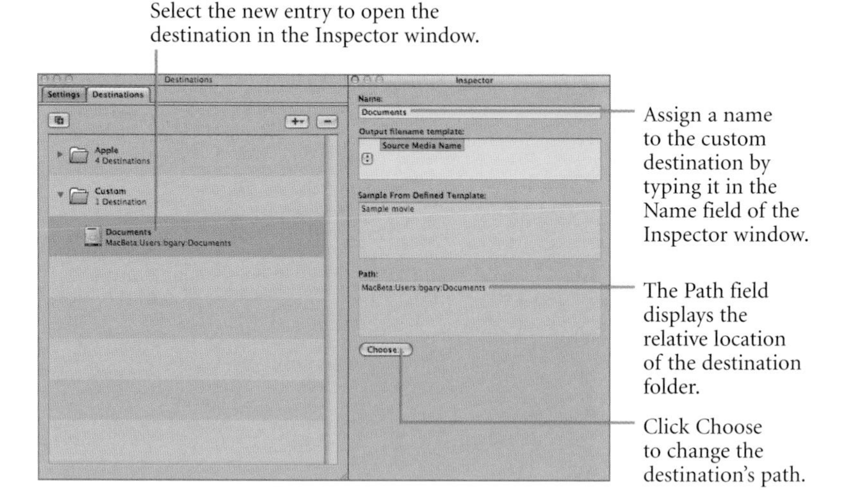
Destinations
Settings
Destinations
Apple
4 Destinations
Custom
1 Destination
Documents
MacBeta:Users:bgary:Documents
Inspector
Name:
Documents
Output filename template:
Source Media Name
Sample From Defined Template:
Sample movie
Path:
MacBeta:Users:bgary:Documents
Choose

Select the new entry to open the destination in the Inspector window.

Assign a name to the custom destination by typing it in the Name field of the Inspector window.

The Path field displays the relative location of the destination folder.

Click Choose to change the destination's path.

You can use the Output filename template field to modify which suffixes Compressor appends to the output filename. The default export option is to use only the source media's name and the target file extension. For example, if your source media is a DV NTSC clip with "My Movie.mov" as the filename, and you apply an Apple TV target, the output filename would be "My Movie.m4v."

You may find that placing more information in the filename is useful when outputting to custom destinations. For example, you can append the current date to the filename to aid the organization of multiple encoding jobs.

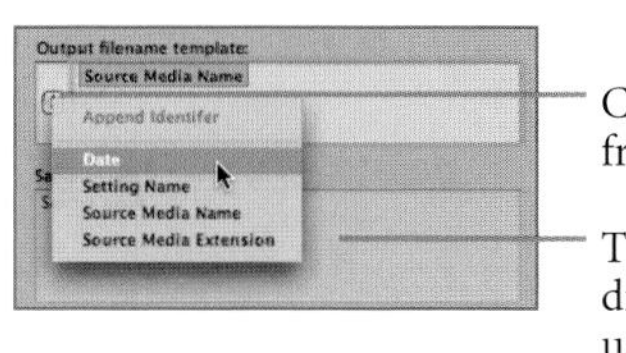
Output filename template:
Source Media Name
Append Identifier
Date
Setting Name
Source Media Name
Source Media Extension

Click the pop-up menu and choose a suffix from the list to append it to the filename.

The Sample From Defined Template field displays a sample of an output filename using your current settings.

TIP When creating files for use in DVD Studio Pro, you should avoid using any identifier other than the source media name. DVD Studio Pro will combine similarly-named audio and video elementary streams as a single unit inside the application—for example, Video.m2v and Audio.ac3 will be paired by DVD Studio Pro even though they are separate assets. Creating a custom destination just for this purpose is a handy, time-saving trick because it avoids manually assigning paired assets during authoring.

Choosing Remote Destinations

When you choose Remote, a drop-down window appears for you to input all of the server connection information.

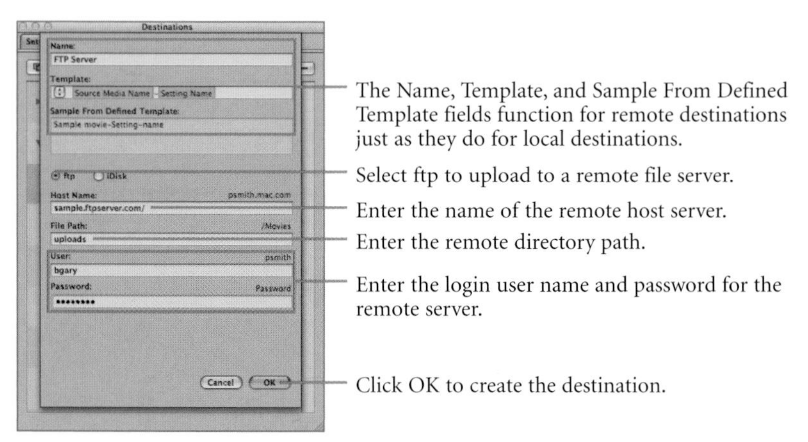
Destinations
Name:
FTP Server
Template:
Source Media Name - Setting Name
Sample From Defined Template:
Sample movie-Setting-name
ftp
iDisk
Host Name:
psmith.mac.com
sample.ftpserver.com/
File Path:
/Movies
uploads
User:
psmith
bgary
Password:
Password
Cancel
OK
The Name, Template, and Sample From Defined Template fields function for remote destinations just as they do for local destinations.
Select ftp to upload to a remote file server.
Enter the name of the remote host server.
Enter the remote directory path.
Enter the login user name and password for the remote server.
Click OK to create the destination.

Consult your network or site administrator for login information.

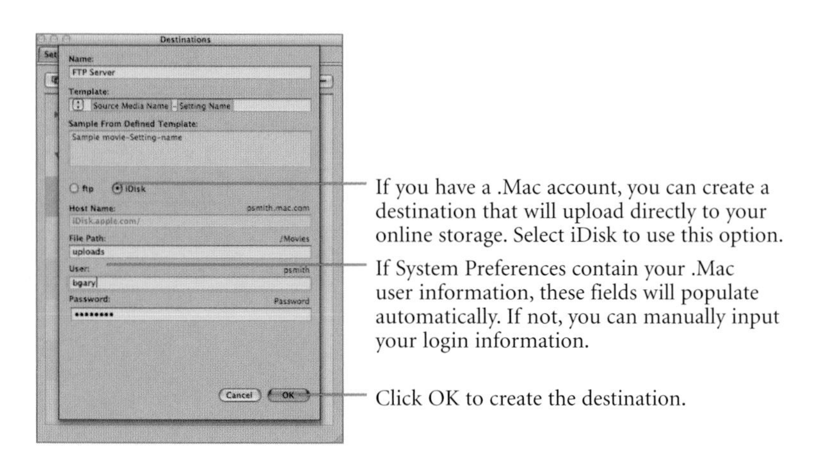
Destinations
Name:
FTP Server
Template:
Source Media Name - Setting Name
Sample From Defined Template:
Sample movie-Setting-name
ftp
iDisk
Host Name:
psmith.mac.com
iDisk.apple.com/
File Path:
/Movies
uploads
User:
psmith
bgary
Password:
Password
Cancel
OK
If you have a .Mac account, you can create a destination that will upload directly to your online storage. Select iDisk to use this option.
If System Preferences contain your .Mac user information, these fields will populate automatically. If not, you can manually input your login information.
Click OK to create the destination.

Working with Droplets

When settings grow up and graduate, they become droplets. Compressor uses droplets to pack settings into an application suitcase so they can stand alone in the Finder and run entirely outside Compressor.

You can create droplets from any Apple or custom setting in the Presets window. Droplets can be quite handy, especially for repetitive encoding tasks in which settings do not change from job to job.

Creating a Single-Setting Droplet

The following example creates a droplet that produces a 16-bit, 48 kHz audio file. It is common in Final Cut Pro sequences to encounter audio files sampled at rates other than 48 kHz, such as 44.1 kHz audio copied from CDs. Using a droplet to quickly convert the files using drag-and-drop is much more efficient than repeating multiple conversion steps inside Compressor.

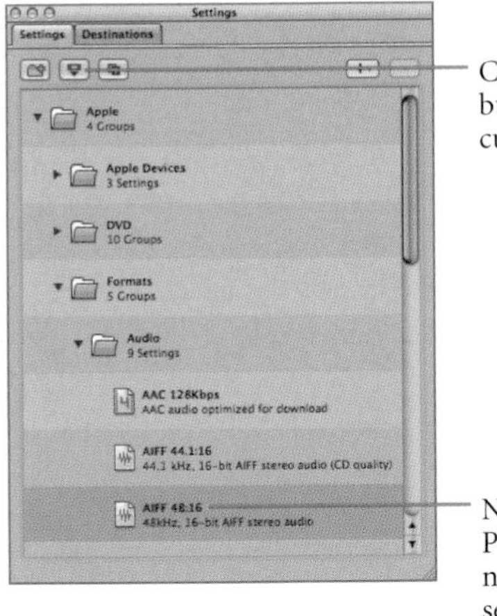
Settings
Settings
Destinations
Apple
4 Groups
Apple Devices
3 Settings
DVD
10 Groups
Formats
5 Groups
Audio
9 Settings
AAC 128Kbps
AAC audio optimized for download
AIFF 44.1:16
44.1 kHz, 16-bit AIFF stereo audio (CD quality)
AIFF 48:16
48kHz, 16-bit AIFF stereo audio

Click the Save Selection as Droplet button to create a droplet from the currently selected setting.

Navigate to the desired setting in the Presets window. For this example, navigate to Apple > Formats > Audio and select the AIFF 48:16 setting.

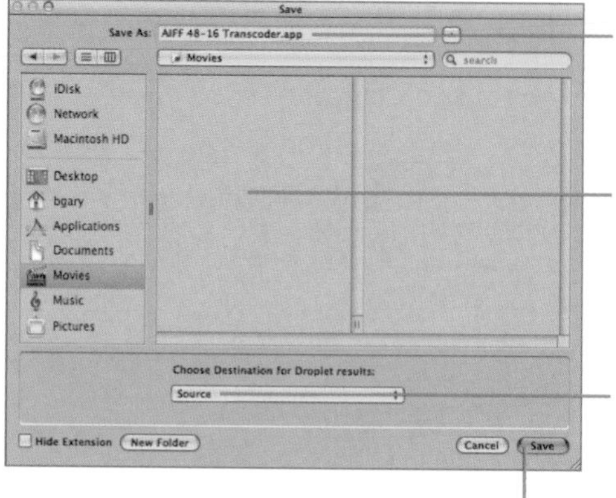
Save
Save As: AIFF 48-16 Transcoder.app
Movies
iDisk
Network
Macintosh HD
Desktop
bgary
Applications
Documents
Movies
Music
Pictures
Choose Destination for Droplet results:
Source
Hide Extension
New Folder
Cancel
Save

In the Save As field, type a custom name for the droplet.

Navigate to the folder where Compressor should save the droplet.

The destination pop-up menu specifies where the droplet will save the output files that it encodes. This location differs from where you saved the droplet. This option is similar to the destination choice you made when applying targets to jobs in the Batch window.

Click the Save button to create the droplet.

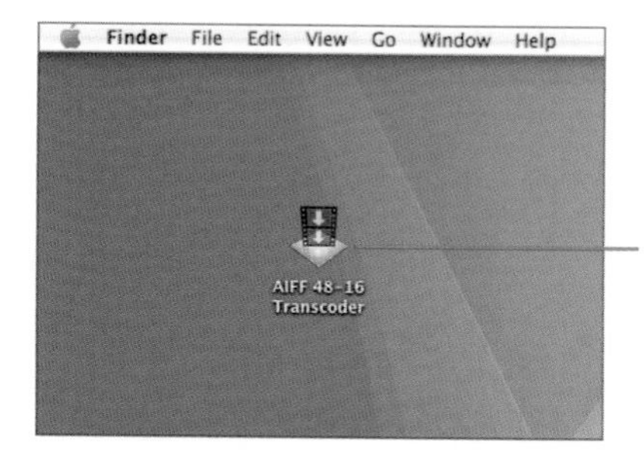
Finder File Edit View Go Window Help
AIFF 48-16
Transcoder

Compressor saves the preset's settings to the directed location as a stand-alone application. Compressor creates the droplet with this icon and names it based on your input in the Save dialog box.

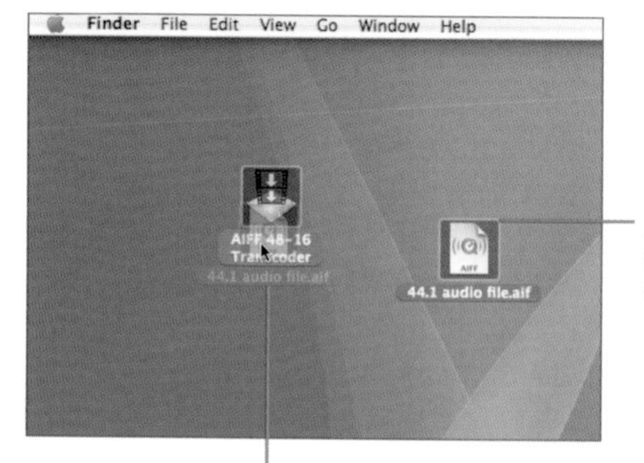
Finder File Edit View Go Window Help
AIFF 48-16
Transcoder
44.1 audio file.aif

Any Compressor-compatible file or files can be dragged onto a droplet to launch the encoding process.

A semitransparent box surrounds the droplet when you have successfully dragged a file or files onto it. Releasing the mouse button will launch the droplet.

The droplet connects to the encoder services and opens the Droplet window, which details the upcoming process.

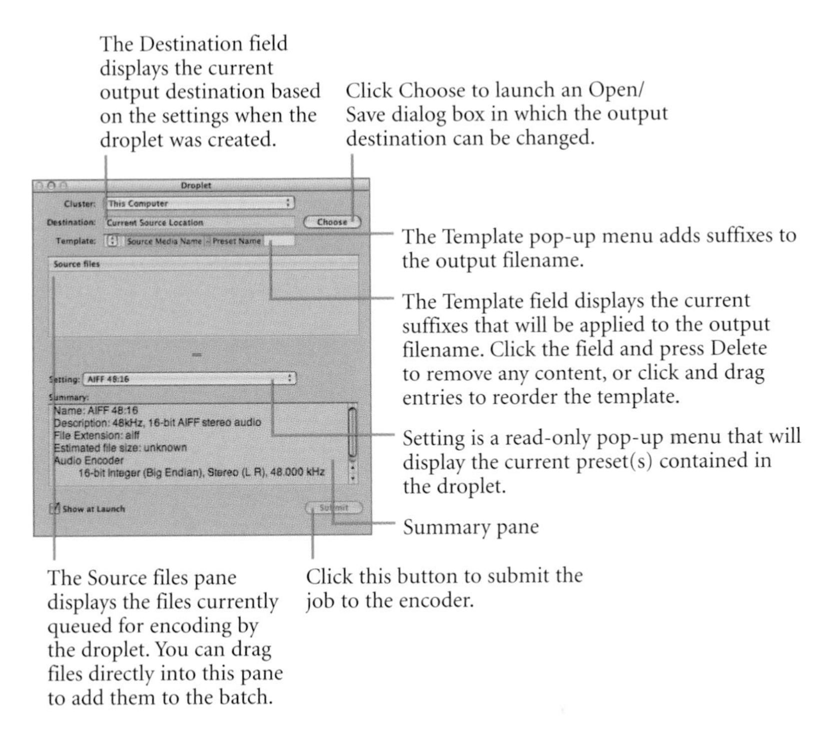
The Destination field displays the current output destination based on the settings when the droplet was created.
Click Choose to launch an Open/Save dialog box in which the output destination can be changed.
The Template pop-up menu adds suffixes to the output filename.
The Template field displays the current suffixes that will be applied to the output filename. Click the field and press Delete to remove any content, or click and drag entries to reorder the template.
Setting is a read-only pop-up menu that will display the current preset(s) contained in the droplet.
Summary pane
The Source files pane displays the files currently queued for encoding by the droplet. You can drag files directly into this pane to add them to the batch.
Click this button to submit the job to the encoder.
Droplet
Cluster: This Computer
Destination: Current Source Location
Choose
Template: Source Media Name - Preset Name
Source files
Setting: AIFF 48:16
Summary:
Name: AIFF 48:16
Description: 48kHz, 16-bit AIFF stereo audio
File Extension: aiff
Estimated file size: unknown
Audio Encoder
16-bit Integer (Big Endian), Stereo (L R), 48.000 kHz
Show at Launch
Submit

Although running Compressor is not a requirement for launching a droplet, the version of Compressor that originally created the droplet must be installed on any computer on which you plan to run the droplet.

Creating a Multiple-Setting Droplet

In the preceding example, one preset was used to create the droplet. Compressor also allows the creation of droplets from preset groups. Instead of selecting a single setting in the Presets window, select a settings group and click the Save Selection as Droplet button.

In the Save dialog box that opens, follow the same steps as you did when creating a single-setting droplet.

Any file dropped onto a multiple-setting droplet will have all the presets in the group applied to it. If you have MPEG-2 and Dolby Digital audio settings in a droplet, for example, any file encoded by the droplet will produce two output files: one MPEG-2 video and one Dolby audio.

Modifying Droplets

To edit a droplet's settings, double-click its icon. The Droplet window will appear. Make changes to the droplet as desired; then choose Droplet > Quit Droplet to save the changes.

4

Batch Encoding

The power of Compressor is unleashed when you manage the flow of multiple jobs through its Batch window.

While importing source media and applying targets to jobs in the Batch table are among the core concepts of the Compressor workflow, the ability to queue up a series of disparate encoding jobs, called a *batch,* and monitor its progress during processing is what makes Compressor the centerpiece of your entire digital distribution pipeline.

A batch comprises individual pieces of source media (a job), and any given batch can contain as many jobs as you require. Targets control the encoding process and are comprised of a setting, a destination and an output filename. Each job can include multiple targets.

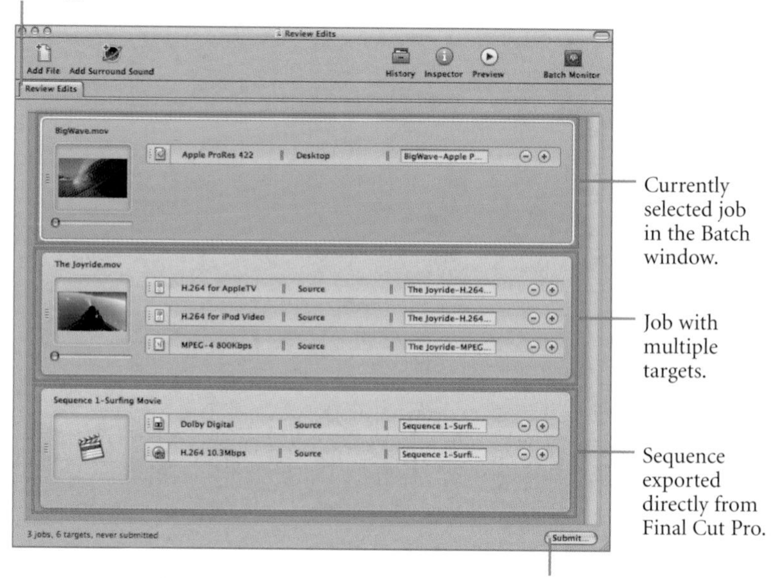
Once a Batch is saved, its name will appear in the Batch tab.
Review Edits
Add File
Add Surround Sound
History
Inspector
Preview
Batch Monitor
BigWave.mov
Apple ProRes 422
Desktop
The Joyride.mov
H.264 for AppleTV
H.264 for iPod Video
MPEG-4 800Kbps
Source
Sequence 1-Surfing Movie
Dolby Digital
H.264 10.3Mbps
3 jobs, 6 targets, never submitted
Submit...
Currently selected job in the Batch window.
Job with multiple targets.
Sequence exported directly from Final Cut Pro.
When a batch is ready for processing, click the Submit button to send the jobs to the encoder.

The Batch window

Managing and Maximizing Batches

Almost limitless scenarios exist for creating Compressor batches that address your encoding needs. Compressor's versatility is especially useful when the overall estimated encoding time for a series of jobs spans several hours (or days). Instead of submitting and monitoring each job individually, you can batch-organize the sessions and let Compressor perform the laborious task of monitoring each job in the series. Furthermore, a series of jobs and targets in a batch is, in essence, a template for your encoding work. That is, you can save a batch and reuse it by replacing the source media.

Jobs and targets are the building blocks of batches. You can combine and manipulate them in the Batch window to create more efficient encoding workflows.

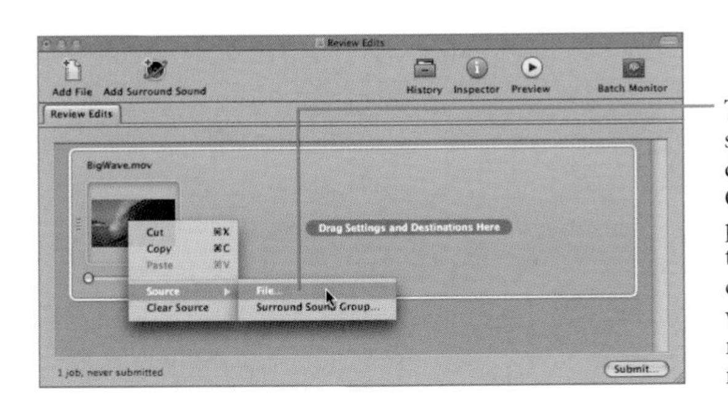
Review Edits
Add File
Add Surround Sound
History
Inspector
Preview
Batch Monitor
Review Edits
BigWave.mov
Drag Settings and Destinations Here
Cut
Copy
Paste
Source
Clear Source
File...
Surround Sound Group...
1 job, never submitted
Submit...

To replace one job's source media with different media, Control-click the job's poster frame and, from the shortcut menu, choose File. In the window that opens, navigate to the new media and click Open.

Click the Minus button to remove a target.

Click the Plus button to add an empty target.

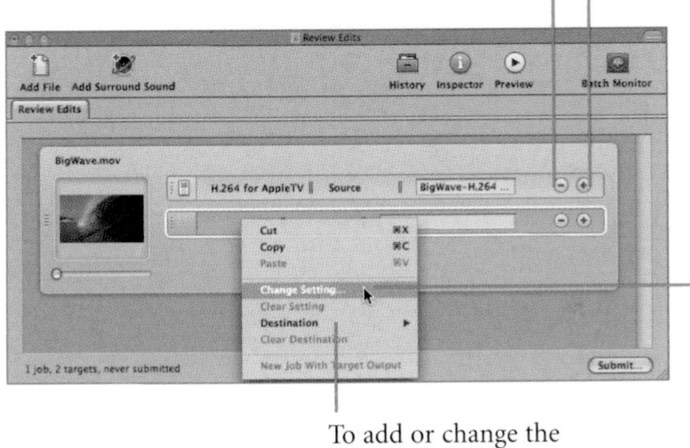
Review Edits
Add File
Add Surround Sound
History
Inspector
Preview
Batch Monitor
Review Edits
BigWave.mov
H.264 for AppleTV
Source
BigWave-H.264 ...
Cut
Copy
Paste
Change Setting...
Clear Setting
Destination
Clear Destination
New Job With Target Output
1 job, 2 targets, never submitted
Submit...

Control-click an empty target and choose Change Setting. From the drop-down window, choose the desired setting and then click Add.

To add or change the target's destination, choose one from the list in the submenu.

Compressor lets you work on jobs and targets individually or as groups. For example, with the Batch window active you could choose Edit > Select All and then choose Target > New Target with Setting. From the drop-down window, choose a setting and then click Add. The same target will be applied to every job in the batch—a real timesaver if, for example, you have 50 jobs you want to encode as podcasts.

To apply all of a group's settings as separate targets, drag a group from the Presets window to a job in the Batch window.

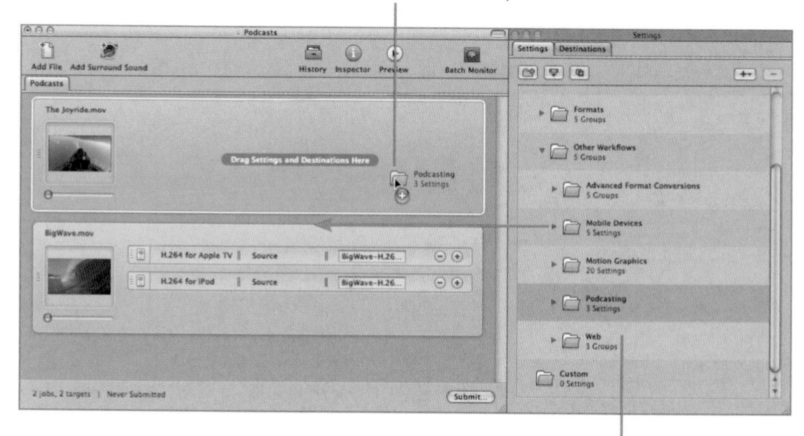
Podcasts
Add File
Add Surround Sound
History
Inspector
Preview
Batch Monitor
Podcasts
The Joyride.mov
Drag Settings and Destinations Here
Podcasting
3 Settings
BigWave.mov
H.264 for Apple TV
Source
H.264 for iPod
Source
2 jobs, 2 targets | Never Submitted
Submit...
Settings
Settings
Destinations
Formats
5 Groups
Other Workflows
5 Groups
Advanced Format Conversions
5 Groups
Mobile Devices
5 Settings
Motion Graphics
20 Settings
Podcasting
3 Settings
Web
3 Groups
Custom
0 Settings

You are not limited to just groups that contain settings; you can drag and drop groups that contain other groups. For example, you can drop the Web group on a test clip and Compressor will add targets for every setting of all three groups inside.

TIP You can create a custom folder that contains all the settings for a particular project or an individual client. Then, you only have to drag and drop the group onto a job to apply all the targets at once, including all the required custom settings.

Copying and Pasting Jobs and Targets

In Compressor, you can manage and recycle your work using convenient cut and paste methods. Encoding can encompass many repetitive tasks, so copying a target from one job to another within the Batch window is a great timesaving trick.

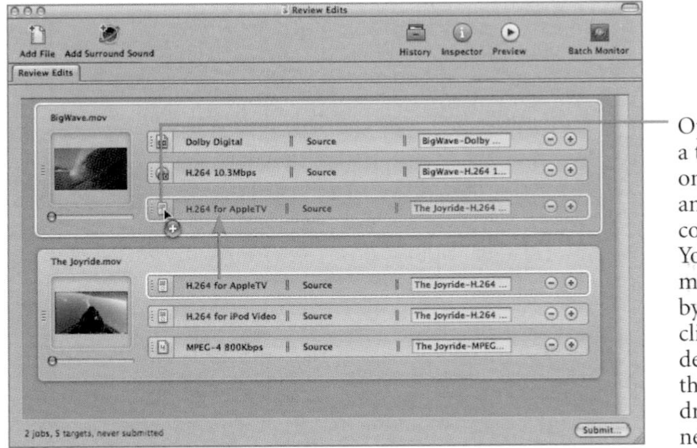
Review Edits
Add File
Add Surround Sound
History
Inspector
Preview
Batch Monitor
Review Edits
BigWave.mov
Dolby Digital
Source
H.264 10.3Mbps
Source
H.264 for AppleTV
Source
The Joyride.mov
H.264 for AppleTV
Source
H.264 for iPod Video
Source
MPEG-4 800Kbps
Source
2 jobs, 5 targets, never submitted
Submit...

Option-drag a target from one job to another to copy the target. You can copy multiple targets by Command-clicking the desired targets, then Option-dragging to the new job.

To move multiple items, as in this example, Command-click the targets in the bottom job to select them, then drag them to the top job.

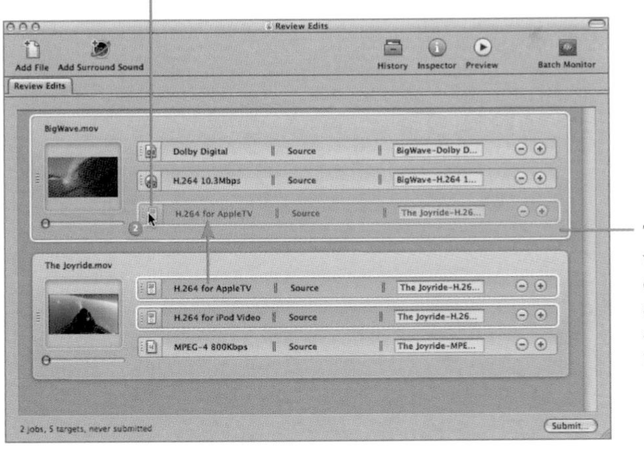
Review Edits
Add File
Add Surround Sound
History
Inspector
Preview
Batch Monitor
Review Edits
BigWave.mov
Dolby Digital
Source
H.264 10.3Mbps
Source
H.264 for AppleTV
Source
The Joyride.mov
H.264 for AppleTV
Source
H.264 for iPod Video
Source
MPEG-4 800Kbps
Source
2 jobs, 5 targets, never submitted
Submit...

The job window resizes dynamically to accommodate additional targets.

The standard cut, copy, and paste commands in the Edit menu (along with their keyboard shortcuts) work both with jobs and targets, meaning that you can cut or copy a target from one job and paste it onto another.

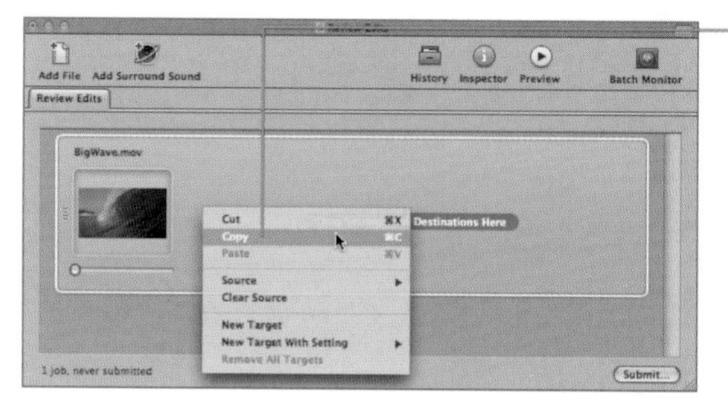
Add File
Add Surround Sound
History
Inspector
Preview
Batch Monitor
Review Edits
BigWave.mov
Cut
Copy
Paste
Source
Clear Source
New Target
New Target With Setting
Remove All Targets
Destinations Here
1 job, never submitted
Submit...

Control-click a job or a specific target and, from the shortcut menu, choose Copy. Continuing with this example, you could paste multiple instances of the same job in the batch (from the shortcut menu, choose Paste, or press Command-V). This technique can be useful when lining up test encodes. (See Chapter 8 for more information on test encodes.)

Creating and Saving Batches

Although Compressor launches with a single empty batch in the Batch window, you can create as many batches as you need by opening new batches as tabs in the current Batch window. To create a new batch, choose File > New Batch.

Compressor also lets you save batches for use with later encoding jobs, or to more efficiently organize current jobs. To save a batch, make sure the Batch window is active, then choose File > Save. In the drop-down window, name the batch, navigate to the desired save location, and click Save. The batch name will appear in the current tab in the Batch window.

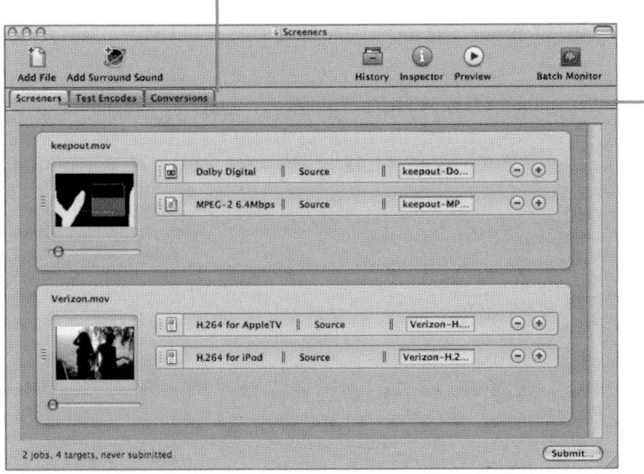
Each batch has its own tab in the Batch window. Click a tab to display the jobs contained in that batch.
Reorder the tabs by dragging a tab left or right to a new location.
Screeners
Add File
Add Surround Sound
History
Inspector
Preview
Batch Monitor
Screeners
Test Encodes
Conversions
keepout.mov
Dolby Digital
Source
keepout-Do...
MPEG-2 6.4Mbps
Source
keepout-MP...
Verizon.mov
H.264 for AppleTV
Source
Verizon-H...
H.264 for iPod
Source
Verizon-H.2...
2 jobs, 4 targets, never submitted
Submit...

To close a batch tab, select it and choose File > Close Tab.

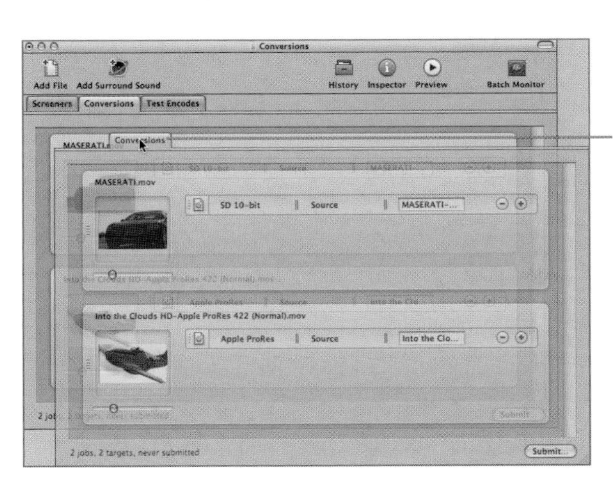
Tear off a tab by dragging it from its original Batch window. This creates a new Batch window that contains the jobs from the torn-off tab. You can also Control-click a tab and, from the shortcut menu, choose Tear Off Tab.
Conversions
Add File
Add Surround Sound
History
Inspector
Preview
Batch Monitor
Screeners
Conversions
Test Encodes
MASERATI.mov
SD 10-bit
Source
MASERATI-...
Into the Clouds HD-Apple ProRes 422 (Normal).mov
Apple ProRes
Source
Into the Clo...
2 jobs, 2 targets, never submitted
Submit...

TIP In Compressor, you can copy, cut, and paste both jobs and targets between all open batches. So, you can cut a job and its targets from one batch, click the tab of another batch, and paste the job and all its targets into that batch. This is useful, for example, when three of the four jobs in a batch are ready for encoding. You can cut and paste the job that is not yet ready into another batch and then submit the three batches that are ready for encoding.

Troubleshooting Batches

When at least one target is applied to all jobs in a batch, you can submit the batch for processing by clicking the Submit button. If no targets have been applied, Compressor displays this error message when you click Submit:

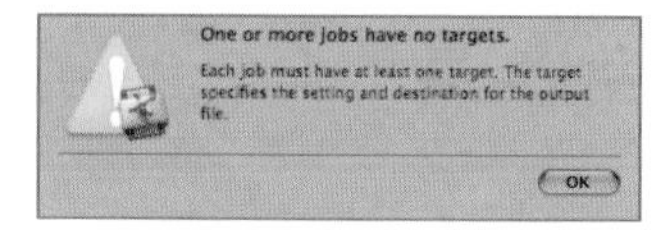
One or more jobs have no targets.
Each job must have at least one target. The target specifies the setting and destination for the output file.
OK

To correct the error, add at least one target to every job in the batch and click Submit.

Batches rely on relative paths to the source media and to the Final Cut Pro sequences or Motion projects that they contain. Therefore, if any source media is moved from the location it occupied when the batch was created, Compressor will no longer be able to locate the file and will display an alert.

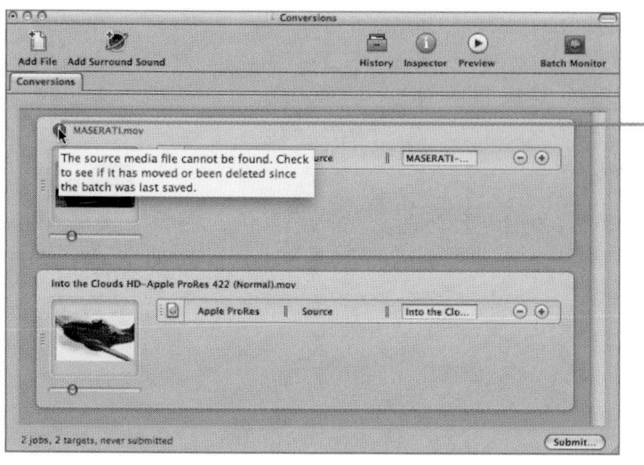
Conversions
Add File
Add Surround Sound
History
Inspector
Preview
Batch Monitor
Conversions
MASERATI.mov
The source media file cannot be found. Check to see if it has moved or been deleted since the batch was last saved.
MASERATI-...
Into the Clouds HD-Apple ProRes 422 (Normal).mov
Apple ProRes
Source
Into the Clo...
2 jobs, 2 targets, never submitted
Submit...

A red alert will appear above the source media poster frame if there is a problem locating source media. Place your pointer over the alert to view the alert details.

To correct a missing media error, Control-click the job's poster frame and, from the shortcut menu, choose Source > File. In the Open window, navigate to the media's new location and then click Open. You can also drag the media directly from the Finder onto the job's poster frame, and Compressor will automatically update the location.

NOTE ► Missing or relocated media can be especially problematic when a saved batch is reopened because you will receive an alert message and the job with the missing source media will be empty if the job's source media is not in the exact location.

Compressor will also alert you when it encounters a job with the same output filename as a file currently in the target destination.

Fix the error by selecting a new destination. Control-click the target and choose a new location from the Destination menu.

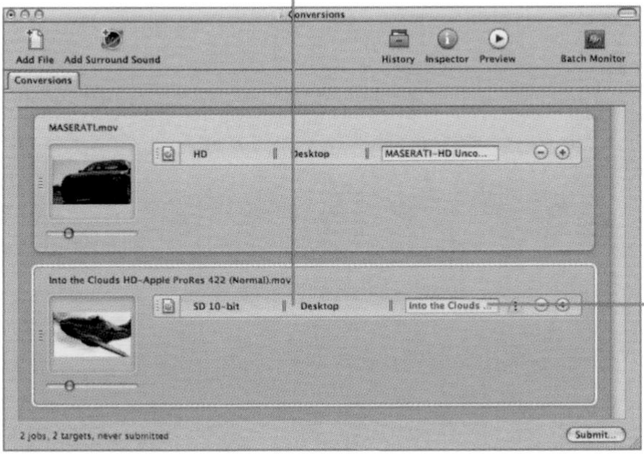

You can also fix the error by directly modifying the output filename in the Filename field.

NOTE ► It's important to understand that this warning will not stop Compressor from encoding the job. If you click Submit without changing the output filename or destination, Compressor will output the file and overwrite the existing file to eliminate the conflict.

Compressor will also display a similar alert message if two targets within the batch could export files with identical filenames.

Creating Batch Templates

Droplets (described in Chapter 3) reduce repetitive workflows by encapsulating settings into standalone applications. You can similarly streamline routine encoding sessions by creating a template from common encoding scenarios. For example, if you consistently encode the same types of media during the early phases of postproduction—such as when creating iPod- and DVD-based screeners—you can, instead, create a template and save the time you would spend configuring those jobs manually.

When you create a new batch, it will open with an empty job by default. Saving the job will display its name in the Batch tab.

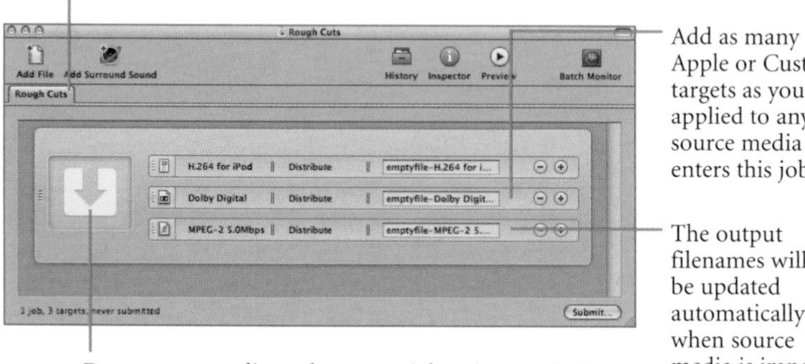
Rough Cuts
Add File
Add Surround Sound
History
Inspector
Preview
Batch Monitor
Rough Cuts
H.264 for iPod
Distribute
emptyfile-H.264 for i...
Dolby Digital
Distribute
emptyfile-Dolby Digit...
MPEG-2 5.0Mbps
Distribute
emptyfile-MPEG-2 5...
1 job, 3 targets, never submitted
Submit...

Add as many Apple or Custom targets as you want applied to any source media that enters this job.

The output filenames will be updated automatically when source media is imported.

Drag source media to the empty job to import it. You can also Control-click the empty poster frame and choose File from the shortcut menu. Navigate to the source media in the drop-down window and click Open.

You can define as many empty jobs with targets as you need to fulfill your encoding workflow.

When the template is populated with source media, it is ready to encode. Batch templates can be modified and adjusted like any batch in Compressor, and you can reuse templates whenever a similar encoding opportunity presents itself. To reuse a template, double-click the saved batch in the Finder or choose File > Open in Compressor.

TIP Any batch that you've created in Compressor can be reused as a template. Save the batch, reopen it at a later date, and replace the source media with new content.

Chaining Jobs

Compressor lets you control and refine the encoding process by setting up a series of two or more jobs that use the output from a preceding job as their source media. This is known as *job chaining*.

For example, an H.264 encoding job with multi-pass engaged could require three or four passes over the media. If any frame controls (see Chapter 10) are enabled, they will process along with each pass. Depending on the settings, this situation can lengthen the encoding time considerably. So, instead of encoding the frame controls during each pass, you can use a job chain to encode them once and then pass the output of that job to the H.264 job.

TIP The Apple ProRes 422 high quality settings are very good for encoding the intermediate movies that pass between jobs in the chain because they retain the base attributes of the source (frame size, rate, and so on). It also employs a high quality, 10-bit encoder in a 4:2:2 colorspace. (See chapter 9 for more information on Apple ProRes 422.)

To create a job chain, import source media, apply a target, and make any necessary changes to the settings. In the following example, an HD clip is being downconverted to a 640 x 360 resolution using frame controls. An Apple ProRes 422 high quality setting was used as the intermediate codec. You'll find it in the Settings tab of the Presets window by following this path: Apple > Other Workflows > Advanced Format Conversions > Apple Codecs.

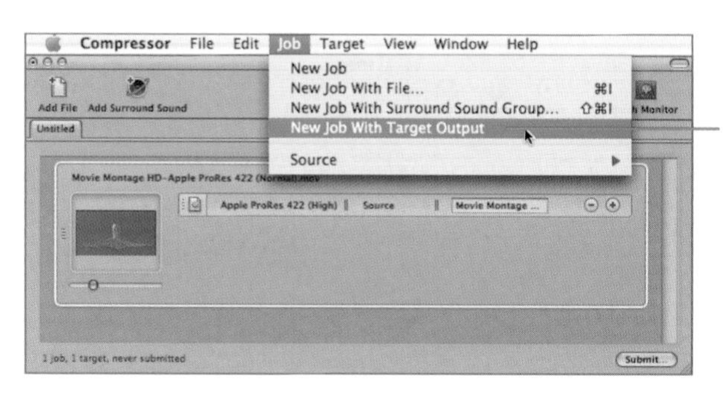
Compressor
File
Edit
Job
Target
View
Window
Help
New Job
New Job With File...
New Job With Surround Sound Group...
New Job With Target Output
Source
Add File
Add Surround Sound
Untitled
Movie Montage HD-Apple ProRes 422 (Normal).mov
Apple ProRes 422 (High)
Source
Movie Montage ...
1 job, 1 target, never submitted
Submit...

Select the job to which you want to chain the output, and choose Job > New Job With Target Output.

Compressor adds a new job to the batch and displays the chain symbol as the poster frame to indicate that the job requires source media to be produced by a previous job in the chain. The input filename at the top of the job window also reflects the incoming media.

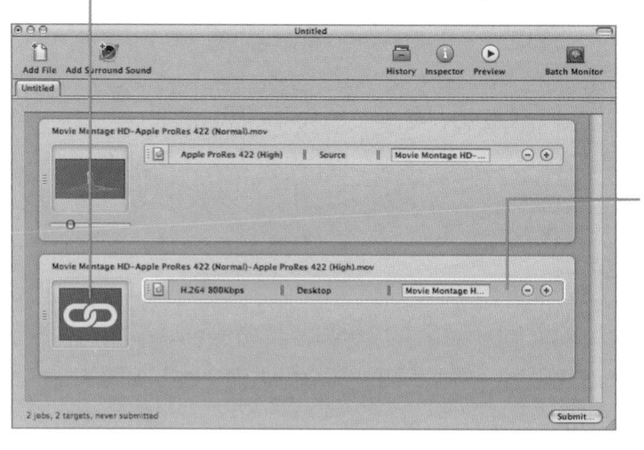
Untitled
Add File
Add Surround Sound
History
Inspector
Preview
Batch Monitor
Untitled
Movie Montage HD-Apple ProRes 422 (Normal).mov
Apple ProRes 422 (High)
Source
Movie Montage HD-...
Movie Montage HD-Apple ProRes 422 (Normal)-Apple ProRes 422 (High).mov
H.264 300Kbps
Desktop
Movie Montage H...
2 jobs, 2 targets, never submitted
Submit...

You can add as many targets as necessary to a job. The job will start processing once the previous job passes the new source media to it.

In the above example, the 640 x 360 Apple ProRes 422 movie output from the first job passes to the next job in the chain where an H.264 encoder is applied. Since the previous job already set the output frame size using frame controls, the Geometry parameters (Chapter 11) can be set to 100% of the source. This process retains all of the image quality but realizes a benefit in efficiency because the time-consuming frame controls processes are encoded only once.

Think of job chaining as a form of assembly-line encoding that lets you control the stacking order of encoding tasks based on necessity or personal preference. For example, you may want to encode all frame rate conversions before processing any frame size conversions. Using job chaining, you can establish the task order by controlling the encoding order within each of the steps. In essence, each job in the chain becomes a part of the larger job of outputting the final movie.

Using Batch Monitor

Batch Monitor is a separate application that can open when Compressor submits a batch for encoding. It provides real-time feedback on the status of the current encoding job and lists the jobs pending in the batch.

By default, Compressor does not open Batch Monitor automatically because the History window provides a basic view of the currently-encoding batches and any batches that have been processed (see Chapter 1). Batch Monitor will open automatically if you choose Compressor > Preferences and select the Auto Launch Batch Monitor checkbox.

When you first submit a job from the Batch window, a drop-down window opens to permit some last-minute adjustments before the job goes to processing.

You can input a name so that each processing job in Batch Monitor is easier to identify.

By default, jobs will encode on This Computer, meaning your local machine. If you have Distributed Processing enabled (see Chapter 12), you can choose an alternative cluster from the pop-up menu.

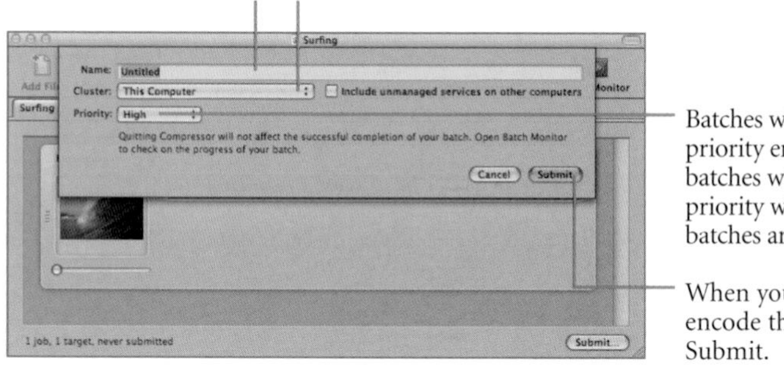
Surfing
Name: Untitled
Cluster: This Computer
Include unmanaged services on other computers
Priority: High
Quitting Compressor will not affect the successful completion of your batch. Open Batch Monitor to check on the progress of your batch.
Cancel
Submit
1 job, 1 target, never submitted
Submit...

Batches with higher priority encode before batches with lower priority when mulitple batches are in the queue.

When you are ready to encode the batch, click Submit.

Batch Monitor is divided into three sections: the Toolbar, the Status window, and the Cluster window. Each of these sections provides two functions: monitoring and management.

Toolbar

The Status window provides real-time monitoring and managing of the encoding process.

The Cluster window displays all available clusters that you can monitor. Selecting a cluster in the list will display its batches in the Status window. This Computer is the default cluster that Batch Monitor oversees.

The Toolbar controls how batches display in the Status window. You can modify which icons appear in the Toolbar by choosing View > Customize Toolbar, or you can Control-click the Toolbar and, from the shortcut menu, choose Customize Toolbar. From the drop-down window, drag desired items to the Toolbar.

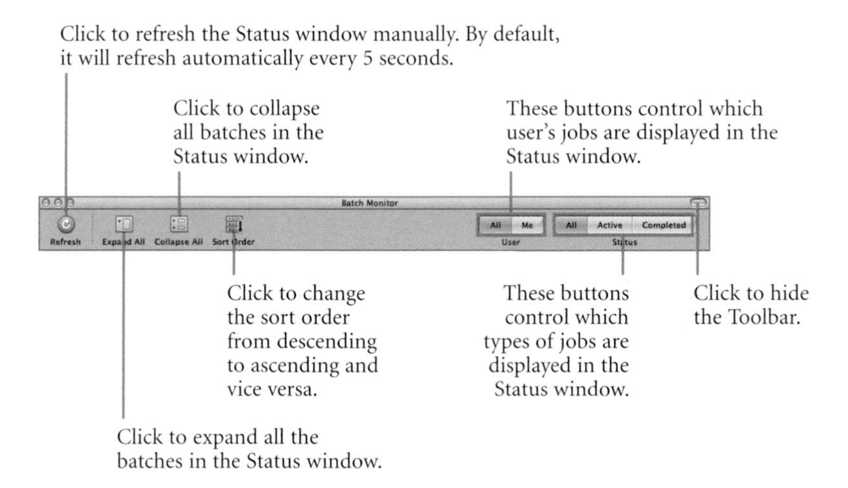
Click to refresh the Status window manually. By default, it will refresh automatically every 5 seconds.
Click to collapse all batches in the Status window.
These buttons control which user's jobs are displayed in the Status window.
Batch Monitor
Refresh
Expand All
Collapse All
Sort Order
All
Me
User
All
Active
Completed
Status
Click to change the sort order from descending to ascending and vice versa.
These buttons control which types of jobs are displayed in the Status window.
Click to hide the Toolbar.
Click to expand all the batches in the Status window.

TIP To change the automatic refresh duration, choose Batch Monitor > Preferences and enter a new value in the Update Every field.

In addition to displaying information on currently-encoding batches and jobs, the Status window lets you manage that encoding process. The three buttons to the right of each batch and each job provide information as well as the ability to pause and delete processes.

Control an entire batch using these buttons (see following figure).

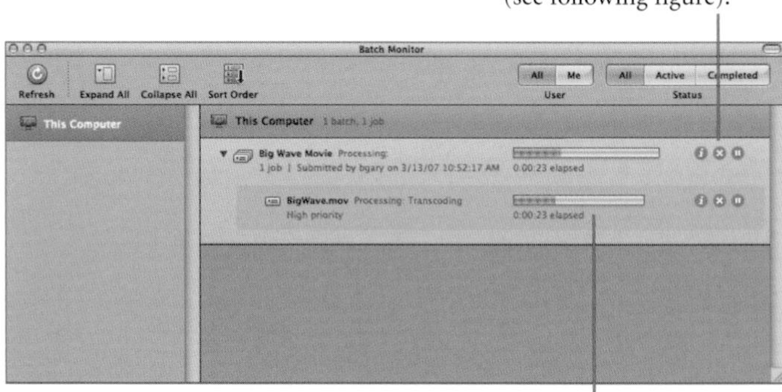
Batch Monitor
Refresh
Expand All
Collapse All
Sort Order
All
Me
User
All
Active
Completed
Status
This Computer
This Computer 1 batch, 1 job
Big Wave Movie Processing
1 job | Submitted by bgary on 3/13/07 10:52:17 AM
0:00:23 elapsed
BigWave.mov Processing: Transcoding
High priority
0:00:23 elapsed

To display an estimation of the remaining job time, instead of the time elapsed, choose View > Time Remaining.

Each individual job has its own set of buttons that control the encoding process.

Click this button to delete the currently encoding job or batch.

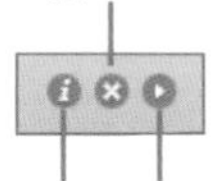

Click to open an information window containing status information for the corresponding job or batch. (See the following section, "Viewing Job and Batch Status.")

If a job or batch is currently stopped, the Status window displays a Play button. Click the Play button to start or resume encoding. If a job or batch is currently encoding, the Status window displays a Pause button. Click the Pause button to stop encoding.

Some restrictions apply to starting and stopping encoding jobs and batches in the Batch Monitor. Some codecs, such as MPEG-2, allow you to pause and then resume processing from the point at which the encoding stopped. Other codecs, such as H.264, only let you stop processing and then force the encoder to restart the job from the beginning when encoding resumes.

If the job or batch you are attempting to stop will be affected by a total loss of currently-encoded material, you will receive this message from Batch Monitor after clicking the Pause button:

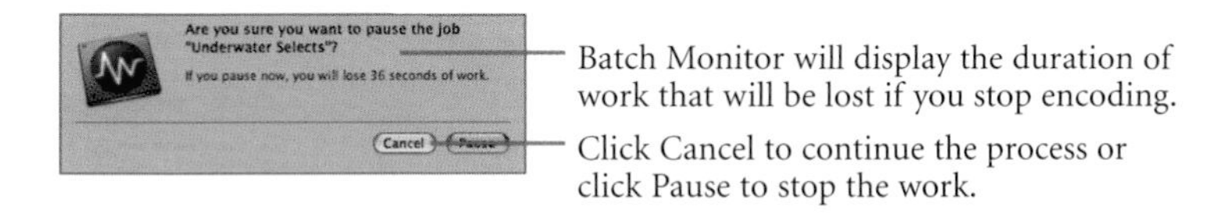
Are you sure you want to pause the job "Underwater Selects"?
If you pause now, you will lose 36 seconds of work.
Cancel
Pause
Batch Monitor will display the duration of work that will be lost if you stop encoding.
Click Cancel to continue the process or click Pause to stop the work.

Viewing Job and Batch Status

When you click the Information button, it opens an Information window for that job.

Click the Log tab to see the process log of the currently selected job or batch. This can be helpful when troubleshooting encoding issues.

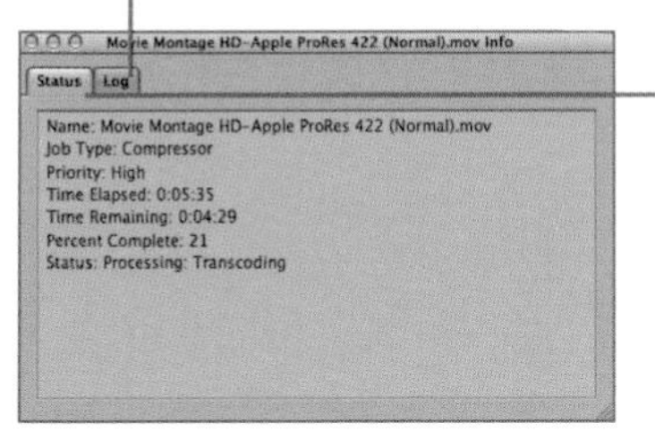
Movie Montage HD-Apple ProRes 422 (Normal).mov Info
Status
Log
Name: Movie Montage HD-Apple ProRes 422 (Normal).mov
Job Type: Compressor
Priority: High
Time Elapsed: 0:05:35
Time Remaining: 0:04:29
Percent Complete: 21
Status: Processing: Transcoding

Click the Status tab to view the real-time status of the selected job or batch.

5

Encoding for DVD

Compressor can encode content for digital video discs in standard definition (SD DVD) and high definition (HD DVD).

SD and HD DVD Parameters

Parameter	SD DVD	HD DVD
Video encoder	MPEG-2, MPEG-1	H.264, MPEG-2
Audio encoder	Linear PCM, Dolby Digital Professional	Linear PCM, Dolby Digital Professional
Frame size (in pixels)	720 x 480 NTSC, 720 x 576 PAL	Up to 1920 x 1080 for MPEG-2 and H.264
Frame rate (per second)	23.98 progressive or 29.97 interlaced for NTSC, 25 progressive for PAL	23.98 progressive up to 59.94 interlaced
Optical media	DVD-5 (4.7 GB), DVD-9 (9.4 GB)	DVD-5, DVD-9, HD-DVD (30 GB)

Understanding Disc Capacity

Only 4.3 GB of data fits on a 4.7 GB DVD. The discrepancy arises because DVD manufacturers use decimals to calculate 1 GB as 1 billion bytes (1000 x 1000 x 1000). Computer data storage, on the other hand, is calculated using a binary byte system (in which 1 KB is actually 1024 bytes) when written to DVD media. That roughly equals a 7 percent difference when the two systems are compared: 4.7 GB media will hold only 4.37 GB of data.

The same applies to dual-layer media, in which a 9.4 GB disc will actually hold only 8.54 GB of data.

DVD Studio Pro displays disc space usage based on the stated capacity of the disc (4.7 or 9.4 GB).

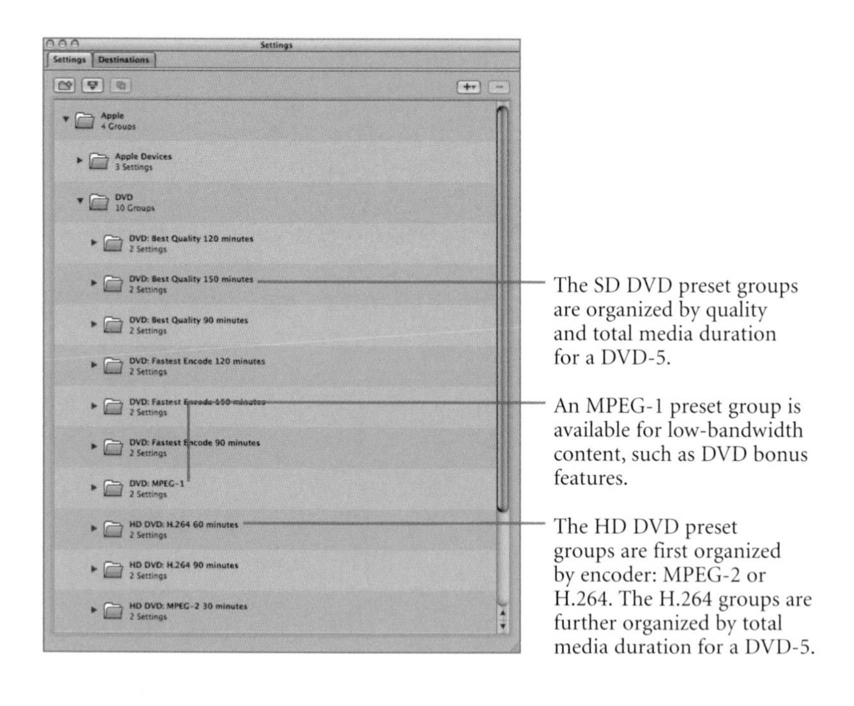
Settings
Settings
Destinations
Apple
4 Groups
Apple Devices
3 Settings
DVD
10 Groups
DVD: Best Quality 120 minutes
2 Settings
DVD: Best Quality 150 minutes
2 Settings
DVD: Best Quality 90 minutes
2 Settings
DVD: Fastest Encode 120 minutes
2 Settings
DVD: Fastest
2 Settings
DVD: Fastest
code 90 minutes
2 Settings
DVD: MPEG-1
2 Settings
HD DVD: H.264 60 minutes
2 Settings
HD DVD: H.264 90 minutes
2 Settings
HD DVD: MPEG-2 30 minutes
2 Settings

The SD DVD preset groups are organized by quality and total media duration for a DVD-5.

An MPEG-1 preset group is available for low-bandwidth content, such as DVD bonus features.

The HD DVD preset groups are first organized by encoder: MPEG-2 or H.264. The H.264 groups are further organized by total media duration for a DVD-5.

SD DVD Encoding

All encoding in Compressor is based on a balance among encoding speed, file size, and image quality. Each asset type created in Compressor calculates that balance differently, based largely on the source media and distribution platform. The following table organizes that balance according to the general components required for encoding SD video assets:

Choosing SD Video Encoding Options

MPEG-2 Setting	Smaller File Size	Faster Encoding	Best Quality
Encoding mode	Two pass VBR	One pass	Two pass VBR Best
Average bit rate	3.7 Mbps	Any	7 Mbps
Max bit rate	7 Mbps	N/A	8 Mbps
Motion estimation	Best	Good	Best
Frame size	Automatic	Automatic	Automatic
Frame rate	Automatic	Automatic	Automatic
Frame controls	Automatic	Off	Automatic
Compressor preset group	DVD: Best Quality 150 minutes	DVD: Fastest Encode (150, 120, or 90 minutes, based on total source media)	DVD: Best Quality 90 minutes

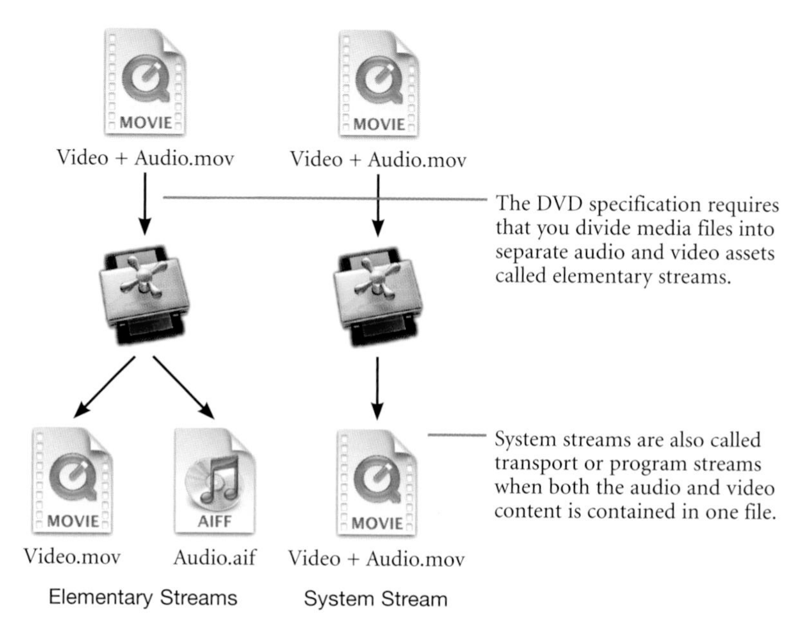
MOVIE
Video + Audio.mov
MOVIE
Video + Audio.mov
The DVD specification requires that you divide media files into separate audio and video assets called elementary streams.
MOVIE
AIFF
MOVIE
System streams are also called transport or program streams when both the audio and video content is contained in one file.
Video.mov
Audio.aif
Video + Audio.mov
Elementary Streams
System Stream

Each of the Apple MPEG-2 preset groups in Compressor contains a video setting and an audio setting.

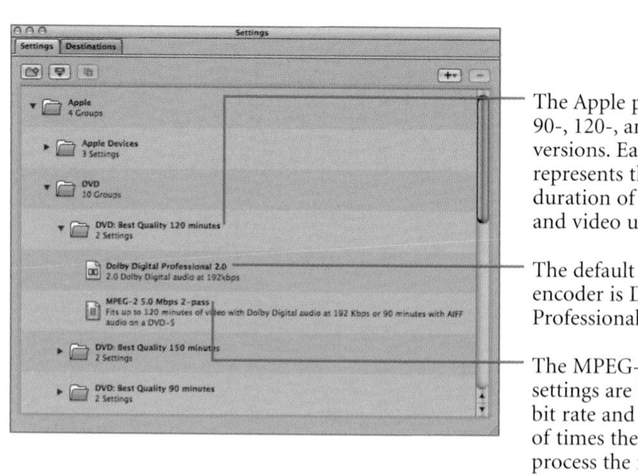
Settings
Settings
Destinations
Apple
4 Groups
Apple Devices
3 Settings
DVD
10 Groups
DVD: Best Quality 120 minutes
2 Settings
Dolby Digital Professional 2.0
2.0 Dolby Digital audio at 192kbps
MPEG-2 5.0 Mbps 2-pass
Fits up to 120 minutes of video with Dolby Digital audio at 192 Kbps or 90 minutes with AIFF audio on a DVD-5
DVD: Best Quality 150 minutes
2 Settings
DVD: Best Quality 90 minutes
2 Settings

The Apple presets include 90-, 120-, and 150-minute versions. Each designation represents the maximum duration of encoded audio and video using that preset.

The default DVD audio encoder is Dolby Digital Professional 2.0.

The MPEG-2 video settings are identified by bit rate and the number of times the encoder will process the media.

Based on a quick calculation known as *bit budgeting*, whereby you determine the total amount of media that will fit on a disc at a given data rate, you may find that the Apple presets offer exactly the settings you need to realize your desired encoding results. If, for example, you have a 60-minute movie that you want to include on a DVD-5, first try applying the DVD: Best Quality 90 minutes preset group.

Basic SD DVD Media Creation

Compressor installs several preset groups dedicated to creating standard-definition DVDs. The preset groups are organized by total media duration, encoding speed, and picture quality.

In the following example, a trailer for the movie *One Six Right* (www.onesixright.com) is prepared for inclusion on an SD DVD.

Import the movie directly from Final Cut Pro into Compressor, or choose Job > New Job with File (Command-I) to import QuickTime-compatible source media.

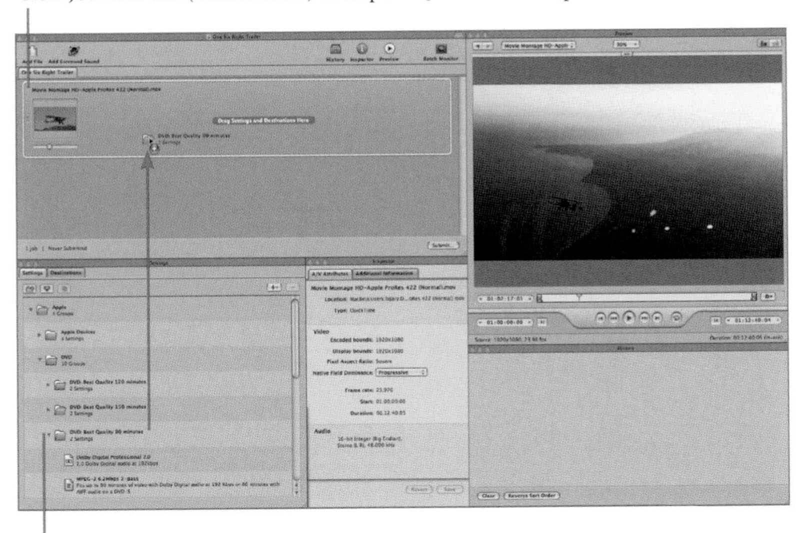

From the Settings tab of the Presets window, drag a SD DVD preset group onto the job in the Batch window. In this example, the trailer is 3 minutes long, so the "DVD: Best Quality 90 minutes" group was used.

Choose a destination for the target by Control-clicking the target and choosing an Apple or custom preset from the Destinations shortcut menu.

If you are authoring with DVD Studio Pro, make sure that output filenames are identical, except for the extensions.

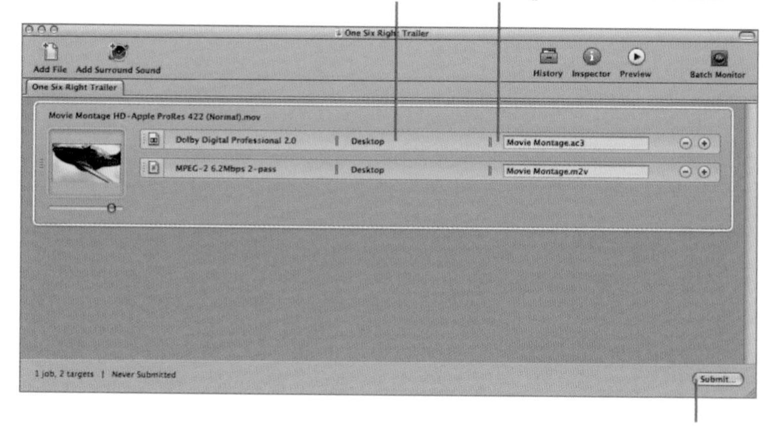
One Six Right Trailer
Add File
Add Surround Sound
History
Inspector
Preview
Batch Monitor
One Six Right Trailer
Movie Montage HD-Apple ProRes 422 (Normal).mov
Dolby Digital Professional 2.0
Desktop
Movie Montage.ac3
MPEG-2 6.2Mbps 2-pass
Desktop
Movie Montage.m2v
1 job, 2 targets | Never Submitted
Submit...

Click to submit the batch to the encoder.

Compressor encodes the source media into separate audio and video files and saves those files in the selected output destination. You can import the files into a DVD-authoring application such as DVD Studio Pro, where they will appear as individual assets.

> **NOTE ▶** The DVD specification allows the use of PCM audio streams for audio content. See Chapter 6 for information on how to create an AIFF audio asset using 16-bit 48 kHz PCM audio.

Custom Encoding for SD DVDs

Even if you choose not to use the default settings of Apple presets, it is advisable to employ Apple presets as starting points for your encoding settings.

To begin encoding for SD DVD, apply an Apple MPEG-2 setting from one of the SD DVD preset groups to your imported media; then click the target in the Batch window to open it in the Inspector window.

When a target is loaded from the Batch window, the Name field displays "Batch selection."

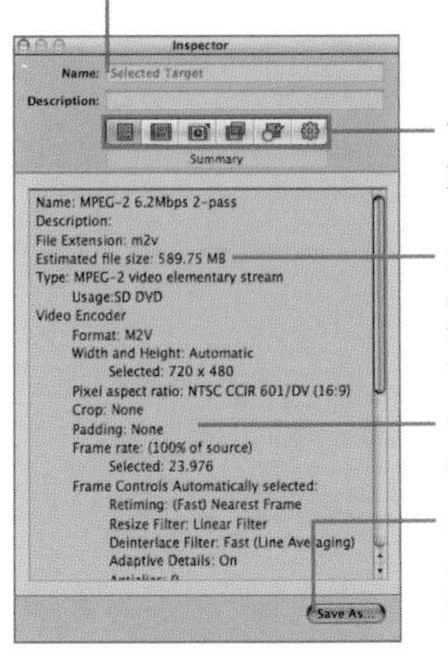
Inspector
Name: Selected Target
Description:
Summary
Name: MPEG-2 6.2Mbps 2-pass
Description:
File Extension: m2v
Estimated file size: 589.75 MB
Type: MPEG-2 video elementary stream
Usage:SD DVD
Video Encoder
Format: M2V
Width and Height: Automatic
Selected: 720 x 480
Pixel aspect ratio: NTSC CCIR 601/DV (16:9)
Crop: None
Padding: None
Frame rate: (100% of source)
Selected: 23.976
Frame Controls Automatically selected:
Retiming: (Fast) Nearest Frame
Resize Filter: Linear Filter
Deinterlace Filter: Fast (Line Averaging)
Adaptive Details: On
Save As...

Use the pane selection buttons to navigate among the panes of the Inspector window (see figure below).

In the Summary pane, Compressor displays an estimated file size that helps determine whether the output media will fit into your bit budget when using the applied preset.

The Summary pane displays all the preset's information in one place.

Click Save As to create a custom preset using the existing preset as the base template. Compressor saves the new preset in the Custom folder of the Presets window.

The Frame Controls button opens the Frame Controls pane, where the Optical Flow settings for frame size and rate conversion can be accessed. This pane is not available for every Apple or custom preset.

The Summary button opens the Summary pane, where all the preset parameters are listed in a table.

The Geometry button opens the Geometry pane, where you can adjust the ouptut frame size and aspect ratio. This pane is not available for all Apple or custom presets.

Summary

The field below the button bar displays the name of the active pane.

The Encoder button opens the Encoder pane, where you can modify the individual codec settings.

The Actions button opens the Actions pane, where you can schedule email notification and AppleScripts that will run after a job is processed.

The Filters button opens the Filters pane, where the 12 available filters can be applied with the preset.

When working with MPEG-2 settings and targets in Compressor, you will frequently access the Encoder pane. The lower half of the Encoder pane is divided into four tabs: Video Format, Quality, GOP, and Extras.

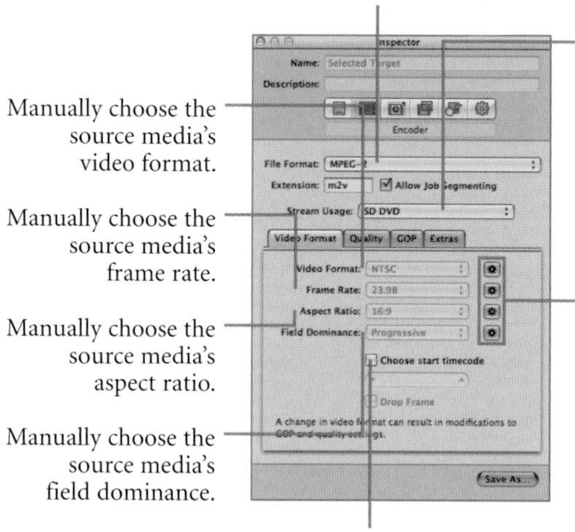
The File Format pop-up menu reflects the selected destination format—in this case, MPEG-2 for SD DVD. The Extension field displays the corresponding file extension—in this case, m2v.
In the Stream Usage pop-up menu, you can choose the target delivery format for the video asset: SD DVD, Generic, Blu-ray, and HD DVD.
Manually choose the source media's video format.
Manually choose the source media's frame rate.
Manually choose the source media's aspect ratio.
Manually choose the source media's field dominance.
The automatic settings buttons are enabled by default, and therefore the corresponding pop-up menus are dimmed. To manually adjust a setting, deselect the automatic settings button and change the option in the corresponding pop-up menu.
To override the source media's timecode, select the "Choose start timecode" checkbox, and enter a custom start time manually or by clicking the triangles to the right and left of the field. If you want to enable drop-frame custom timecode, select the Drop Frame checkbox.
Name:
Description:
Encoder
File Format:
Extension: m2v
Stream Usage:
SD DVD
Quality
GOP
Extras
Video Format:
NTSC
Frame Rate:
23.98
Aspect Ratio:
16:9
Field Dominance:
Progressive
Choose start timecode
Drop Frame
Save As...

Working with Encoding Modes

The options in the Quality tab control the MPEG-2 encoding bandwidth. You can set constant or variable bit rates and set the data rate in terms of megabits per second.

Choose the encoding method Compressor will use to process the source media (see the following table).

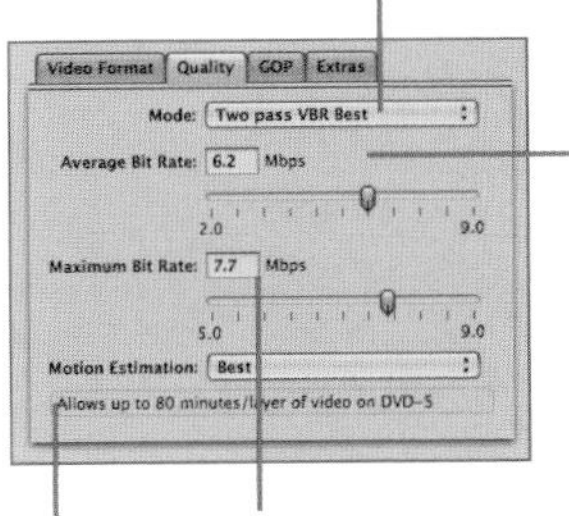
Video Format
Quality
GOP
Extras
Mode:
Two pass VBR Best
Average Bit Rate:
6.2
Mbps
2.0
9.0
Maximum Bit Rate:
7.7
Mbps
5.0
9.0
Motion Estimation:
Best

The bit rate sliders directly address the balance between output file size and quality (see the next section, "Working with Bit Rates"). The lower the average and maximum bit rate settings, the smaller the output file will be, but at the expense of encoding quality. The higher the bit rate settings are, the better the image quality, but at the expense of a larger file.

If either of the CBR modes are chosen, the Maximum Bit Rate setting will be unavailable.

This information display updates dynamically as you adjust the sliders. The readout assumes a 192 kHz Dolby Digital audio stream and a DVD-5 as the destination medium.

Choosing an Encoding Mode

Encoding Mode	Description
One pass CBR	The fastest encoding. Compressor processes the media in one pass at a constant bit rate. One pass delivers good to very good quality at bit rates over 5 Mbps. At rates under 5 Mbps, the quality in one pass mode is reduced. One pass turns off the Maximum Bit Rate slider, and you set the constant bit rate with the Average Bit Rate slider.
One pass VBR	Adds a fluctuating bit rate (variable bit rate) to a one-pass encoding to produce constant quality instead of a constant bit rate. Compressor uses a higher bit rate in sections that need it—such as content with motion—and a lower bit rate in more static areas of the source media.
Two pass VBR	Starts the encoding process with a first-pass variable bit rate analysis of the entire movie and places higher bit rates where needed. The analysis produces much better results than a one-pass encode. On the second pass, the encoder compresses the media based on the analysis. The two-pass VBR process can require up to twice the encoding time of a one-pass encode.
Two pass VBR Best	This mode uses two-pass VBR encoding at higher quality and produces excellent results at average bit rates down to 3 Mbps. The increased encoding quality also results in the slowest compression speeds of any mode.

Working with Bit Rates

No magic number or setting works to encode all source media. Every job is unique and has individual requirements that you will need to address both objectively (Will a DVD-5 provide enough space?) and subjectively (Does that high-motion section look good enough for prime time?). Encoding is both a science and an art.

Here are some elements to consider when adjusting bit rate:

- 10.08 Mbps is the maximum bit rate allowed by the standard-definition DVD specification. That limit, however, applies to the combined bit rates of all audio and video content. If a movie is playing concurrently with its soundtrack and an additional commentary track, these three streams combined cannot exceed the 10.08 Mbps rate. Use caution when manually adjusting bit rate so that you do not exceed this allowable limit for DVD players.
- Audio bit rates, whether AIFF or Dolby 2.0, are not variable, so they are much easier to calculate. AIFF has a constant bit rate of 1.5 Mbps, and Dolby 2.0 can deliver similar quality at about one-tenth that rate. Therefore, when you're combining a single AIFF stream with a single video stream, the Maximum Bit Rate slider should not exceed 7.8 Mbps. When using Dolby 2.0, you can safely increase the rate to 8.5 Mbps on the Maximum Bit Rate slider.
- Keep a spread of at least 1 Mbps between the average bit rate and maximum bit rate to allow Compressor enough room to implement the variable bit rate modes and deliver consistent quality.
- Bit rates between 3 Mbps and 4.5 Mbps are the most challenging in terms of quality control. The two-pass modes produce better results and are definitely worth the increased encoding times.

TIP Although a constant bit rate of of 2 Mbps will produce movies with reduced quality, it also allows up to 4 hours of media to be stored on a single DVD-5 (with properly encoded Dolby 2.0 audio). You can use this bit rate to create long-duration, low-resolution DVDs (such as screener DVDs). During a project's editorial phase, these discs work well for dailies or rough cuts, where quality is not as significant as the amount of content on the disc.

Working with Motion Estimation

The choices in the Motion Estimation pop-up menu represent a trade-off between better output quality of high-motion content and faster overall encoding times.

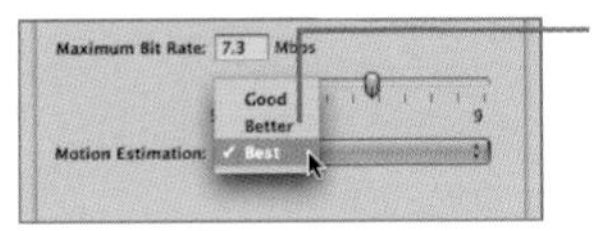
Maximum Bit Rate: 7.3 Mbps
Good
Better
Motion Estimation: ✓ Best

The Motion Estimation pop-up menu works in conjunction with the Mode pop-up menu. It is best to choose the Good setting for "One pass CBR" mode, Better for "One pass VBR" and "Two pass VBR" modes, and Best for "One pass VBR Best" and "Two pass VBR Best" modes. If your source video contains high motion content, use Best regardless of the mode setting.

GOP and Extras Tabs

The GOP tab includes two pop-up menus and a set of radio buttons. Though a description of the GOP (Group of Pictures) structure is beyond the scope of this book, a few items in this pane are worth noting. Most often, you can use the default values even when creating custom MPEG-2 presets.

The three choices in this pop-up menu manage the number of B frames in the structure. The default structure of IBBP works for most media. Reducing the structure to IP increases quality but also increases output file size.

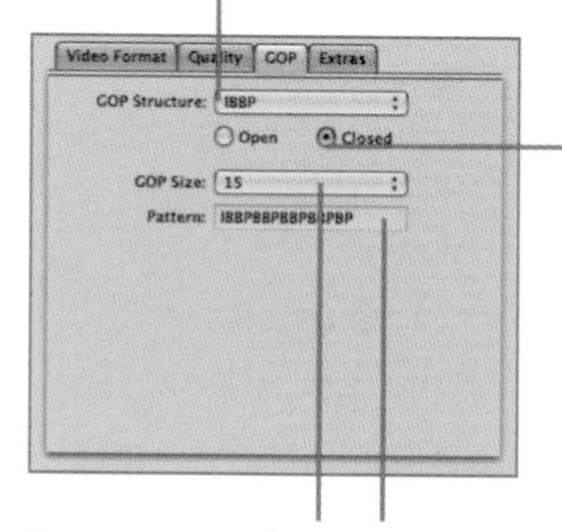
Video Format
Quality
GOP
Extras
GOP Structure:
IBBP
Open
Closed
GOP Size:
15
Pattern:

Select Closed for the overwhelming majority of your jobs. In DVD authoring programs such as DVD Studio Pro, chapter markers can be placed only at the beginning of closed GOPs. Final Cut Pro and Compressor automatically place chapter markers at the beginning of closed GOPs. DVD assets used in multi-angle or mixed-angle streams must have closed GOP structure.

Increase or reduce the GOP size.

The Pattern field displays the combination of the GOP structure and GOP size. In this example, an IBBP structure repeats every 15 frames.

NOTE ▶ MPEG-2 is an interframe codec, meaning that the majority of frame information is discarded. Full frames, called I frames, are separated by interpreted frames called B and P frames. Very simply, the GOP structure is based on the distance between I frames: The farther apart the I frames are, the larger the GOP structure; the larger the GOP is, the more efficient the encoder in terms of file size. However, quality is reduced because the I frames that hold full image data are farther apart and require more interpretation (B and P frames) to connect them in the data stream.

The Extras tab includes three checkboxes; the top checkbox is selected by default.

Metadata permits faster media importation to DVD Studio Pro version 2 and later. Selecting this box makes the encoded files unreadable by versions of DVD Studio Pro before version 2, and to some other DVD authoring systems.

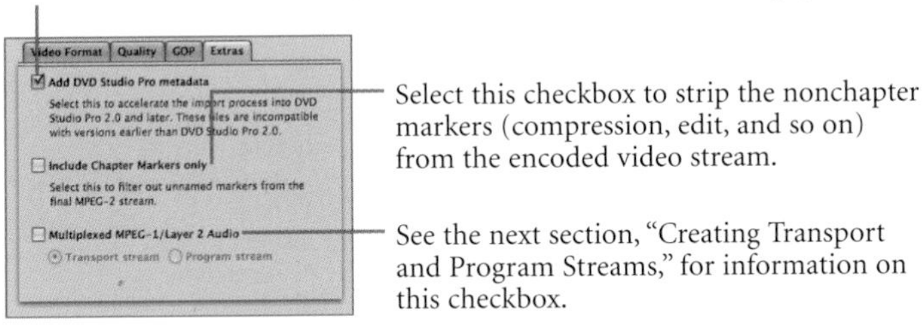
Video Format
Quality
GOP
Extras
Add DVD Studio Pro metadata
Select this to accelerate the import process into DVD Studio Pro 2.0 and later. These files are incompatible with versions earlier than DVD Studio Pro 2.0.
Include Chapter Markers only
Select this to filter out unnamed markers from the final MPEG-2 stream.
Multiplexed MPEG-1/Layer 2 Audio
Transport stream
Program stream
Select this checkbox to strip the nonchapter markers (compression, edit, and so on) from the encoded video stream.
See the next section, "Creating Transport and Program Streams," for information on this checkbox.

NOTE ▸ The DVD specification has strict guidelines for frame size dimensions; therefore, the frame dimension options are dimmed in the Geometry pane of the Inspector window for any of the MPEG-2 settings and targets.

Creating Transport and Program Streams

Transport streams (also called program streams) are multiplexed audio and video contained in the same file. This delivery format is commonly used in broadcast and satellite television, or for delivery over a network. Transport streams and program streams are basically identical, but with one significant difference: program streams can be played by QuickTime player, and transport streams cannot. Additionally, both formats produce files that are unusable in DVD authoring.

Compressor contains settings for both transport and program streams in the Apple > Formats > MPEG 2 group. Transport and program streams are encoded with MPEG-2, so the Encoder pane of the Inspector window displays almost identical settings when compared to SD DVD encoding.

NOTE ▸ Compressor supports the creation of only single-channel transport streams.

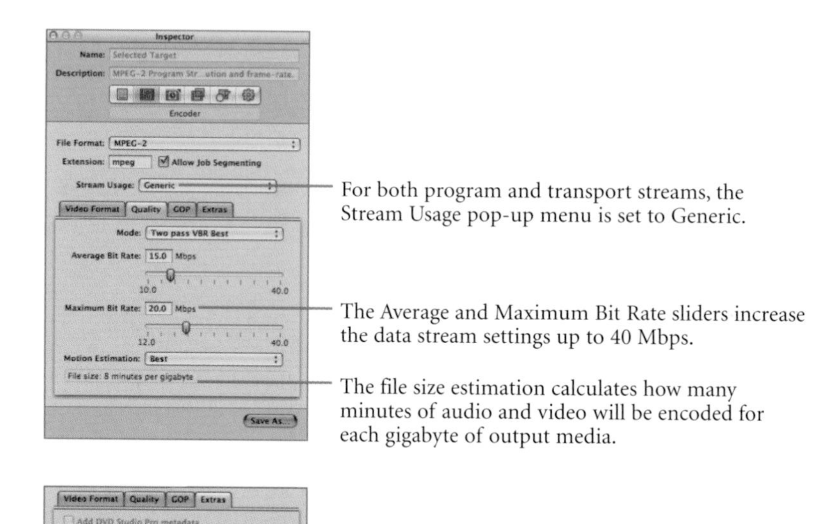
Inspector
Name: Selected Target
Description: MPEG-2 Program Str...ution and frame-rate.
Encoder
File Format: MPEG-2
Extension: mpeg
Allow Job Segmenting
Stream Usage: Generic
Video Format
Quality
GOP
Extras
Mode: Two pass VBR Best
Average Bit Rate: 15.0 Mbps
10.0
40.0
Maximum Bit Rate: 20.0 Mbps
12.0
40.0
Motion Estimation: Best
File size: 8 minutes per gigabyte
Save As...

For both program and transport streams, the Stream Usage pop-up menu is set to Generic.

The Average and Maximum Bit Rate sliders increase the data stream settings up to 40 Mbps.

The file size estimation calculates how many minutes of audio and video will be encoded for each gigabyte of output media.

Video Format | Quality | GOP | Extras

Add DVD Studio Pro metadata

Select this to accelerate the import process into DVD Studio Pro 2.0 and later. These files are incompatible with versions earlier than DVD Studio Pro 2.0.

Include Chapter Markers only

Select this to filter out unnamed markers from the final MPEG-2 stream.

Multiplexed MPEG-1/Layer 2 Audio

Transport stream   Program stream

In the Extras tab, the Add DVD Studio Pro Metadata option is dimmed.

The Multiplexed MPEG-1/Layer 2 Audio option is selected, and the corresponding "Program stream" or "Transport stream" button is selected depending on the target you applied.

TIP You can set the data rates of transport and program streams extremely high (40 Mbps) to increase overall picture quality and file size, but to make sure your delivery environment can handle the settings, create a test clip (see Chapter 8) and send it through your distribution pipeline.

The 24p Workflow

Twenty-four frame progressive video (strictly speaking, 23.98 fps in NTSC) has a more cinematic look than interlaced video running at 29.97 fps. The recent proliferation of progressive displays and disc devices capable of playing progressive frame content allow for a 24p workflow from capture to distribution:

1. Shoot in 24p, using an advanced pulldown cadence of 2:3:3:2.
2. Log and capture the footage in Final Cut Pro, using Advanced Pulldown Removal.
3. Edit in a 23.98 fps sequence.
4. Export directly from Final Cut Pro to Compressor.
5. Apply the appropriate MPEG-2 preset.
6. Using the automatic settings, Compressor will interpret the footage as 23.98 progressive in the Video Format tab of the Inspector window.
7. When imported to DVD Studio Pro, the assets will be flagged properly so that set-top players, depending on their setup, will either add a 3:2 pulldown for interlaced playback or present the movie in progressive mode.

Using the same settings as 29.97 fps interlaced media, 24p video assets have the advantage of taking less time to encode and requiring less disc space at no reduction in quality because, over time, those six fewer frames per second really add up. Conversely, you can apply those savings to an increase in quality while achieving a similar output file size as the same footage running at 29.97 fps.

MPEG-1 Encoding for SD DVDs

The DVD specification allows for the inclusion and mixing of MPEG-1– and MPEG-2–encoded media on SD DVDs.

The MPEG-1 video setting is contained within the "DVD: MPEG-1" group and is accompanied by a Dolby Digital 2.0 setting for the audio asset.

> **NOTE ▸** MPEG-1 files encoded with a "DVD: MPEG-1" preset will create movies with a frame size of 352 x 240 pixels and the native frame rate of the source media. DVD players are programmed to scale up MPEG-1 content to fill the television screen.

When loaded into the Inspector window, the MPEG-1 setting displays an Encoder pane divided into two tabs: Video and Audio.

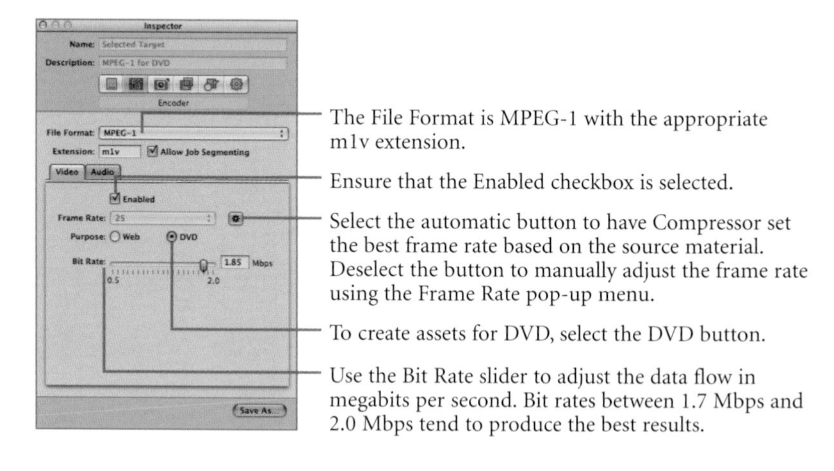
Inspector
Name: Selected Target
Description: MPEG-1 for DVD
Encoder
File Format: MPEG-1
Extension: m1v
Allow Job Segmenting
Video
Audio
Enabled
Frame Rate: 25
Purpose: Web DVD
Bit Rate: 1.85 Mbps
0.5
2.0
Save As...
The File Format is MPEG-1 with the appropriate m1v extension.
Ensure that the Enabled checkbox is selected.
Select the automatic button to have Compressor set the best frame rate based on the source material. Deselect the button to manually adjust the frame rate using the Frame Rate pop-up menu.
To create assets for DVD, select the DVD button.
Use the Bit Rate slider to adjust the data flow in megabits per second. Bit rates between 1.7 Mbps and 2.0 Mbps tend to produce the best results.

> **NOTE ▸** Since MPEG-1 assets must be elementary streams, in the Audio tab the Enabled checkbox must be deselected when creating the video stream.

The quality of MPEG-1 encoding is inferior to MPEG-2, but the reduced file size warrants its use as an encoder for bonus material or for screener discs.

High-Definition Disc Encoding

The high definition disc specification allows MPEG-2 encoding at much higher bit rates—up to three times the bit rate of SD DVDs. Additionally, the Moving Pictures Experts Group (MPEG) created a new MPEG codec called MPEG-4 part 10, more commonly known as H.264. This extremely efficient codec produces very high quality media at about half the bit rates that MPEG-2 would require to produce similar quality. Although new disc formats have significantly increased storage capacity (HD DVDs store up to 30 GB on a dual-layer disc), the same encoding trade-offs of size and quality apply.

Encoding HD DVDs with MPEG-2

Compressor has one preset group for HD DVD encoding with MPEG-2 that contains an MPEG-2 setting capable of encoding a video asset up to 30 minutes in length for a DVD-5 disc, or up to 100 minutes for an HD DVD. The preset group also contains a Dolby Digital 2.0 setting for encoding the audio asset.

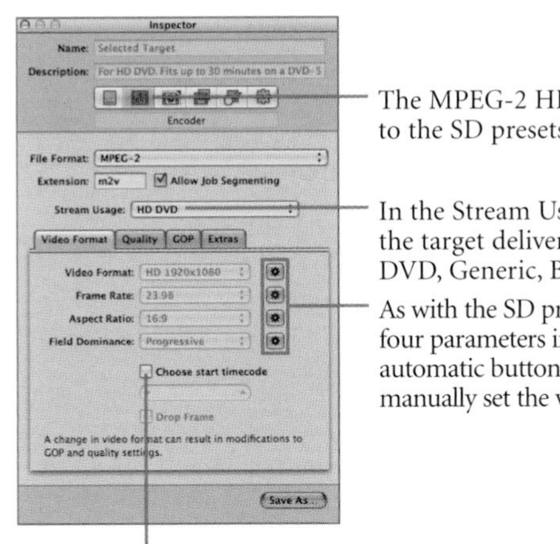
Inspector
Name:
Selected Target
Description:
Encoder
File Format:
MPEG-2
Extension:
m2v
Allow Job Segmenting
Stream Usage:
HD DVD
Video Format
Quality
GOP
Extras
Video Format:
HD 1920x1080
Frame Rate:
23.98
Aspect Ratio:
16:9
Field Dominance:
Progressive
Choose start timecode
Drop Frame
A change in video format can result in modifications to GOP and quality settings.
Save As...

The MPEG-2 HD Encoder pane is almost identical to the SD presets pane.

In the Stream Usage pop-up menu, you can identify the target delivery format for the video asset: SD DVD, Generic, Blu-ray, and HD DVD.

As with the SD presets, you can automatically set the four parameters in the Video Format tab by selecting the automatic buttons, or you can deselect the buttons and manually set the values by using the pop-up menus.

If you want to override the source's timecode, select the "Choose start timecode" checkbox, and enter a custom start time manually or by clicking the triangles to the right and left of the field. If you want to enable drop-frame custom timecode, select the Drop Frame checkbox.

You can adjust the Average Bit Rate and Maximum Bit Rate sliders to customize bit rates for HD encoding, just as you can for SD projects. Because only VBR options are available, you will need to coordinate the two sliders for optimum efficiency, maintaining a minimum buffer of 5 Mbps between the two settings.

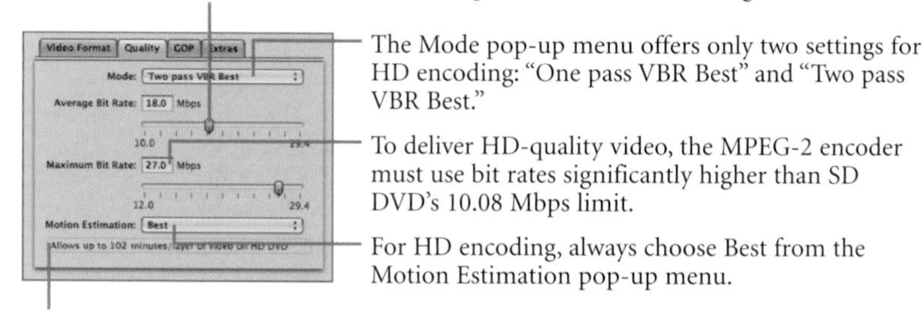
Video Format
Quality
GOP
Extras
Mode:
Two pass VBR Best
Average Bit Rate:
18.0
Mbps
10.0
Maximum Bit Rate:
27.0
Mbps
12.0
29.4
Motion Estimation:
Best

The Mode pop-up menu offers only two settings for HD encoding: “One pass VBR Best” and “Two pass VBR Best.”

To deliver HD-quality video, the MPEG-2 encoder must use bit rates significantly higher than SD DVD’s 10.08 Mbps limit.

For HD encoding, always choose Best from the Motion Estimation pop-up menu.

Based on the bit rate settings, and assuming a PCM audio track, Compressor displays an estimate of the total media duration that will fit on an HD DVD.

All of the options are dimmed in the GOP tab, and the Extras tab contains the identical settings to the SD DVD presets. See “GOP and Extras Tab” earlier in this chapter more information.

High-Definition Disc Encoding with H.264

The high-quality, ultra-efficient H.264 encoder for high definition discs has two stock preset groups in Compressor. The groups differ in only one setting: average bit rate. As with MPEG-2, reducing the bit rate in H.264 produces smaller files at the expense of image quality.

Overall, H.264 produces much better output for HD delivery and should be your first choice when creating an HD disc, unless you have specific technical reasons for using MPEG-2.

Compressor has two HD DVD preset groups that encode using H.264 delineated by output duration: 60 or 90 minutes. Each HD DVD preset group contains a Dolby Digital 2.0 setting for the audio asset.

When you open the H.264 for HD DVD target in the Inspector window and view the Encoder pane, you’ll see a different set of options than those available for MPEG-2 encoding.

Encoder button

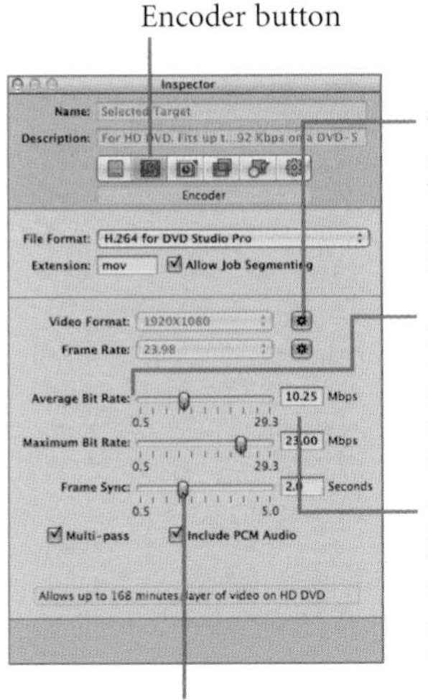
Inspector
Name: Selected Target
Description: For HD DVD. Fits up t...92 Kbps on a DVD-5
Encoder
File Format: H.264 for DVD Studio Pro
Extension: mov
Allow Job Segmenting
Video Format: 1920X1080
Frame Rate: 23.98
Average Bit Rate: 10.25 Mbps
0.5
29.3
Maximum Bit Rate: 23.00 Mbps
0.5
29.3
Frame Sync: 2.0 Seconds
0.5
5.0
Multi-pass
Include PCM Audio
Allows up to 168 minutes/layer of video on HD DVD

The automatic buttons, which are selected by default, control the Video Format and Frame Rate settings. You can manually change the settings by deselecting the automatic buttons and choosing a custom setting from the pop-up menus.

All H.264 encoding is variable bit rate, so the Average Bit Rate and Maximum Bit Rate sliders work as they do for MPEG-2 encoding: Average is the target bit rate, and maximum is the highest data rate available for encoding content that requires increased bandwidth.

H.264 delivers high-quality media at about half the bit rates of MPEG-2. You can start encoding with an average bit rate range of 7 to 15 Mbps. For optimal compatibility with HD DVD players, avoid data rates above 18 Mbps.

The Frame Sync slider controls the frequency of keyframes in the data stream (measured in seconds). The higher the frequency is, the greater the quality, but at the cost of increased file size. A common interval is a keyframe every 2 seconds.

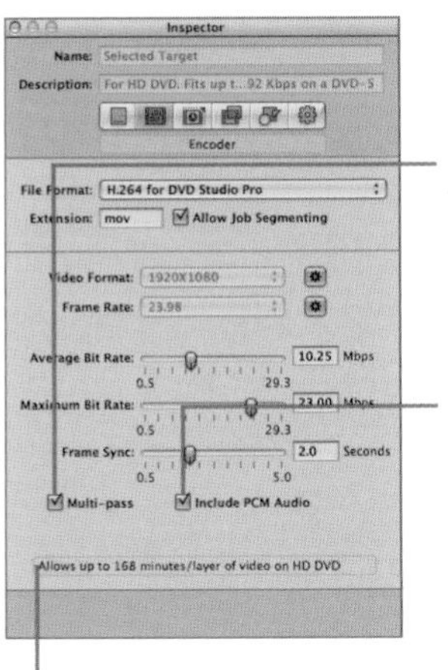
Inspector
Name: Selected Target
Description: For HD DVD. Fits up t...92 Kbps on a DVD-5
Encoder
File Format: H.264 for DVD Studio Pro
Extension: mov
Allow Job Segmenting
Video Format: 1920X1080
Frame Rate: 23.98
Average Bit Rate: 10.25 Mbps
0.5
29.3
Maximum Bit Rate: 23.00 Mbps
0.5
29.3
Frame Sync: 2.0 Seconds
0.5
5.0
Multi-pass
Include PCM Audio
Allows up to 168 minutes/layer of video on HD DVD

The Multi-pass checkbox toggles the encoder between a single-pass (deselected) and a two-pass (selected) compression process. Multiple passes produce greater quality but at approximately double the encoding time. If encoding speed is your main concern, deselect this checkbox.

Selecting this checkbox includes a 16-bit, 48 kHz audio stream within the output file. Compressor flags the output appropriately so that authoring applications such as DVD Studio Pro interpret the single QuickTime movie as two separate elementary streams. If you are encoding your audio with Dolby Digital Professional, deselect this option.

The information display at the bottom of the pane adjusts dynamically with the bit-rate sliders. It calculates according to the disc capacity of an HD DVD and assumes a 192 kHz Dolby Digital audio asset. If your bit-budgeting elements differ, you can use the Summary pane's Estimated File Size entry to aid your calculations.

TIP If your HD movie contains a 5.1 surround-sound audio mix, see Chapter 6 for information on encoding the surround-sound audio asset using the Dolby Digital Professional 5.1 setting. If your soundtrack was mixed in Soundtrack Pro 2, see Chapter 2 for information on encoding your mix into Dolby Digital Surround Sound directly from Soundtrack Pro 2.

Understanding Frame Sync

You'll notice that there are no GOP settings in H.264 encoding, because the Frame Sync setting defines the size of the GOP. Higher frame sync settings produce larger GOPs and vice versa. When using H.264, any frame within a GOP can reference any other frame within the same GOP. (In MPEG-2 encodes, frames can reference only the preceding and subsequent frames.) Although longer frame sync durations do produce more frames within the GOP, they also require the decoder to maintain all the frame information in the buffer, which decreases compression efficiency. The first frame of a new GOP flushes the buffer.

An average frame sync setting of 2 seconds will work well with most content. Increase the frame sync duration when you need to encode extended complex sequences that will benefit if the decoder has access to more frame information at once.

To comply with the HD DVD specification Compressor places a partial sync key frame every half a second.

Creating Chapter and Compression Markers

You can create DVD chapter markers directly in Compressor that will appear in DVD Studio Pro when authoring your DVD.

Open a job in the Preview window and follow these steps to add chapter markers:

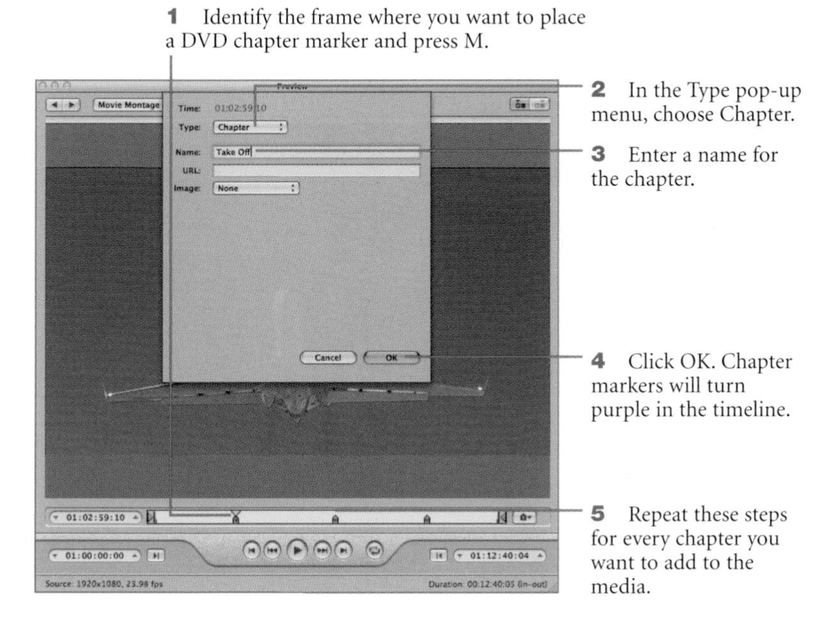
1 Identify the frame where you want to place a DVD chapter marker and press M.
2 In the Type pop-up menu, choose Chapter.
3 Enter a name for the chapter.
4 Click OK. Chapter markers will turn purple in the timeline.
5 Repeat these steps for every chapter you want to add to the media.
Movie Montage
Time:
Type:
Chapter
Name:
Take Off
URL:
Image:
None
Cancel
OK
01:02:59:10
01:00:00:00
01:12:40:04

Placing Compression markers in the Preview window forces an I-Frame at the marker location during encoding. This can be helpful during a quick pan or with fast, onscreen motion because it forces the encoder to add more bits to that section during encoding.

When you add a marker to any frame in Compressor's Preview window, a Compression marker is placed by default. You can view the marker's settings by positioning the playhead directly on the marker and pressing Command E.

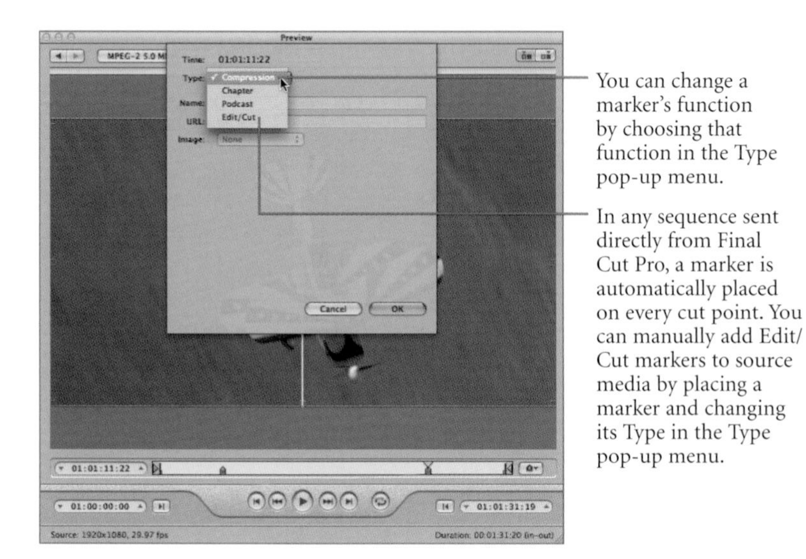
Preview
Time: 01:01:11:22
Type: ✓ Compression
Chapter
Podcast
Edit/Cut
Name:
URL:
Image:
Cancel
OK
01:01:11:22
01:00:00:00
01:01:31:19
Source: 1920x1080, 29.97 fps
Duration: 00:01:31:20 (in-out)
You can change a marker's function by choosing that function in the Type pop-up menu.
In any sequence sent directly from Final Cut Pro, a marker is automatically placed on every cut point. You can manually add Edit/Cut markers to source media by placing a marker and changing its Type in the Type pop-up menu.

TIP Use Compression markers sparingly and place them on only the most challenging parts of your source media. Placing too many Compression markers will clog the encoder with I-Frames and defeat the overall purpose of compression.

6

Encoding Audio

In addition to encoding video, Compressor encodes audio in multiple formats, from standalone CD tracks to audio podcasts to 5.1 Dolby Digital audio streams for DVD.

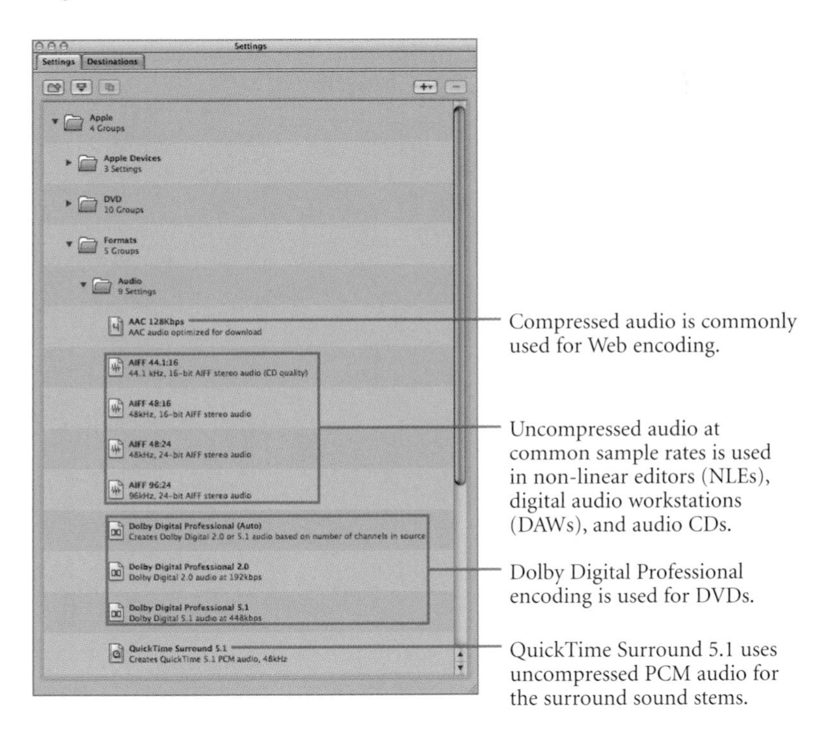
Settings
Settings
Destinations
Apple
4 Groups
Apple Devices
3 Settings
DVD
10 Groups
Formats
5 Groups
Audio
9 Settings
AAC 128Kbps
AAC audio optimized for download
AIFF 44.1:16
44.1 kHz, 16-bit AIFF stereo audio (CD quality)
AIFF 48:16
48kHz, 16-bit AIFF stereo audio
AIFF 48:24
48kHz, 24-bit AIFF stereo audio
AIFF 96:24
96kHz, 24-bit AIFF stereo audio
Dolby Digital Professional (Auto)
Creates Dolby Digital 2.0 or 5.1 audio based on number of channels in source
Dolby Digital Professional 2.0
Dolby Digital 2.0 audio at 192kbps
Dolby Digital Professional 5.1
Dolby Digital 5.1 audio at 448kbps
QuickTime Surround 5.1
Creates QuickTime 5.1 PCM audio, 48kHz
Compressed audio is commonly used for Web encoding.
Uncompressed audio at common sample rates is used in non-linear editors (NLEs), digital audio workstations (DAWs), and audio CDs.
Dolby Digital Professional encoding is used for DVDs.
QuickTime Surround 5.1 uses uncompressed PCM audio for the surround sound stems.

Using AIFF Containers

The easiest way to manage audio in Compressor is to use the Apple Audio Interchange File Format (AIFF) settings. AIFF is not a codec or an encoder; AIFF is a container format that lets computers interact with digital audio data.

Compressor allows AIFF files to include codecs, but the AIFF files are most commonly stored uncompressed as a linear pulse code modulation (PCM) stream. Linear PCM is a digital representation of analog signals. Most audio workstations use linear PCM in WAV, SDII, or AIFF containers. Apple developed AIFF, which is widely used on the Mac for professional, high-quality audio content.

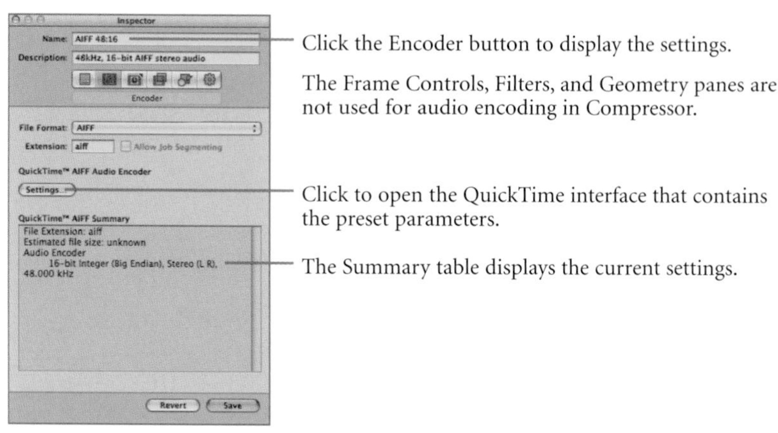
Inspector
Name: AIFF 48:16
Description: 48kHz, 16-bit AIFF stereo audio
Encoder
File Format: AIFF
Extension: aiff
Allow Job Segmenting
QuickTime™ AIFF Audio Encoder
Settings...
QuickTime™ AIFF Summary
File Extension: aiff
Estimated file size: unknown
Audio Encoder
16-bit Integer (Big Endian), Stereo (L R), 48.000 kHz
Revert
Save
Click the Encoder button to display the settings.
The Frame Controls, Filters, and Geometry panes are not used for audio encoding in Compressor.
Click to open the QuickTime interface that contains the preset parameters.
The Summary table displays the current settings.

An AIFF setting loaded in the Inspector window.

TIP You can choose any of the Apple AIFF presets, depending on the desired target sample and bit rate of the output audio. For example, if you have audio that you want to convert for use on an audio CD, choose the Apple AIFF 44.1:16 setting.

In most instances, the AIFF settings will perform a conversion without any customization; but if you need to adjust the parameters, click the Settings button to open the QuickTime interface.

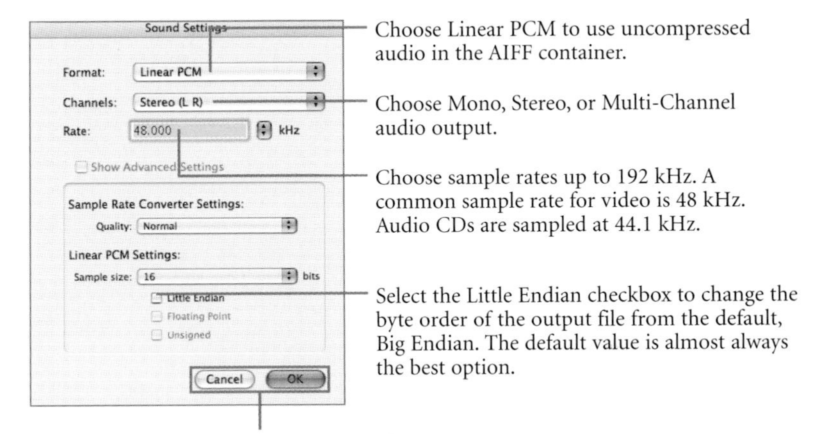
Sound Settings
Format:
Linear PCM
Channels:
Stereo (L R)
Rate:
48.000
kHz
Show Advanced Settings
Sample Rate Converter Settings:
Quality:
Normal
Linear PCM Settings:
Sample size:
16
bits
Little Endian
Floating Point
Unsigned
Cancel
OK
Choose Linear PCM to use uncompressed audio in the AIFF container.
Choose Mono, Stereo, or Multi-Channel audio output.
Choose sample rates up to 192 kHz. A common sample rate for video is 48 kHz. Audio CDs are sampled at 44.1 kHz.
Select the Little Endian checkbox to change the byte order of the output file from the default, Big Endian. The default value is almost always the best option.

Click OK to save changes and return to the Inspector window, or click Cancel to reject changes and close the window.

The Quality pop-up menu sets the speed of encoding. Choosing Faster encodes in the least time, whereas choosing Best offers optimum quality at a longer encoding time. This setting does not affect the output file size.

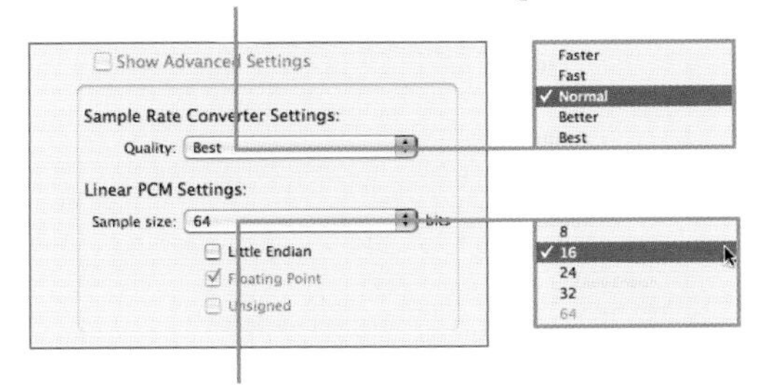
Show Advanced Settings
Sample Rate Converter Settings:
Quality:
Best
Linear PCM Settings:
Sample size:
64
bits
Little Endian
Floating Point
Unsigned
Faster
Fast
Normal
Better
Best
8
16
24
32
64

Compressor can process a maximum 64-bit PCM sample size, but the 64-bit setting may be dimmed when you first click the pop-up menu.

The higher the sample size is, the greater the resulting quality, but at the cost of increased output file size.

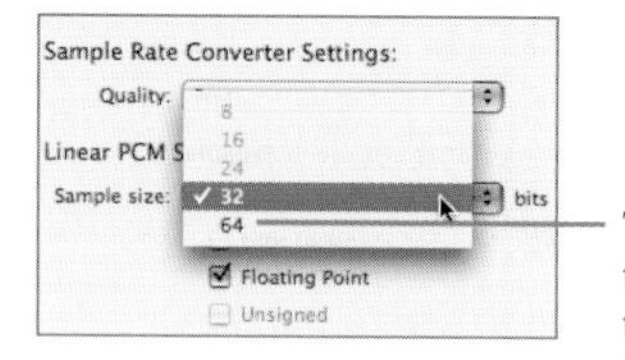
Sample Rate Converter Settings:
Quality:
8
16
24
Linear PCM S
Sample size:
✓ 32
64
bits
Floating Point
Unsigned

To choose a 64-bit size, first choose 32-bit from the "Sample size" pop-up menu, and then select the Floating Point checkbox. Both 32- and 64-bit sizes will now be available. To return to a setting below 32-bit, reverse the steps.

Sample Rate Conversions

Converting from one audio sample rate to another is a common use for the Apple AIFF settings. For example, you may have an audio CD with content that you want to include in a Final Cut Pro Timeline. You could import all the media from the disc into a Compressor batch, apply the AIFF 48:16 setting to all the jobs, and then convert the entire disc as a single encoding session.

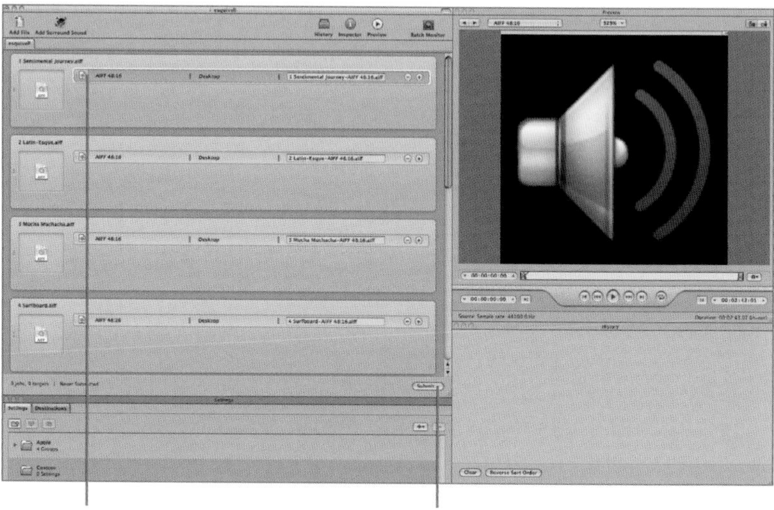

Each track becomes a job with the 48:16 setting as the target.

Click Submit to send the batch to the encoder.

Custom AIFF Settings

Although the most common AIFF encoding uses uncompressed audio, you can create custom settings that include encoders as part of the AIFF container file.

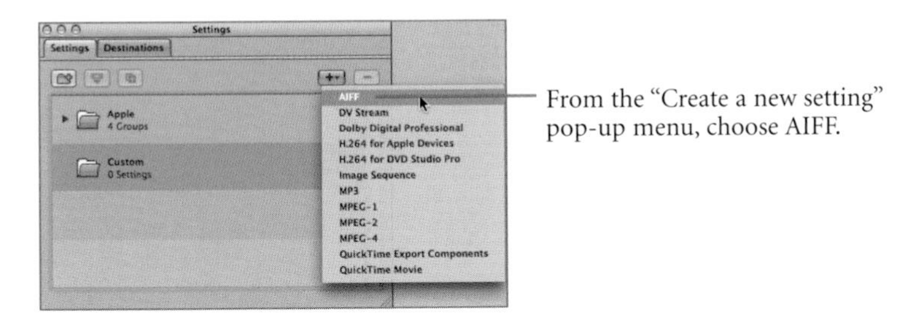
Settings
Settings
Destinations
Apple
4 Groups
Custom
0 Settings
AIFF
DV Stream
Dolby Digital Professional
H.264 for Apple Devices
H.264 for DVD Studio Pro
Image Sequence
MP3
MPEG-1
MPEG-2
MPEG-4
QuickTime Export Components
QuickTime Movie

From the "Create a new setting" pop-up menu, choose AIFF.

Open the new custom setting in the Inspector window, enter a name and description for the setting, and click Save. In the Encoder pane, click the Settings button to access the audio parameters.

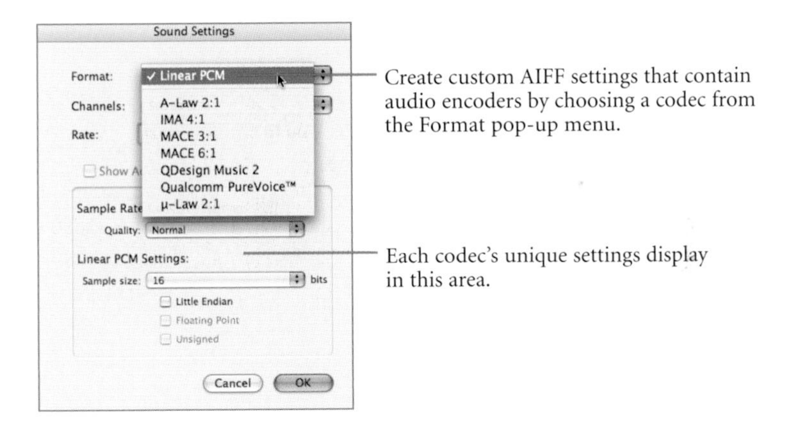
Sound Settings
Format:
✓ Linear PCM
Channels:
Rate:
A-Law 2:1
IMA 4:1
MACE 3:1
MACE 6:1
QDesign Music 2
Qualcomm PureVoice™
μ-Law 2:1
Sample Rate
Quality:
Normal
Linear PCM Settings:
Sample size:
16
bits
Little Endian
Floating Point
Unsigned
Cancel
OK

Create custom AIFF settings that contain audio encoders by choosing a codec from the Format pop-up menu.

Each codec's unique settings display in this area.

Each audio codec is preferable for certain output scenarios, as shown in this table:

Audio Codec	Summary
QDesign Music 2	A very good multipurpose encoder that handles a broad range of source media, not just music. This codec is a good place to start when creating compressed AIFF output.
Qualcomm PureVoice	This codec works especially well with source media containing only speech.
IMA (Interactive Multimedia Association)	This codec is a good choice when the audio stream is secondary to the video stream, especially in bandwidth-challenged scenarios such as dial-up Internet distribution. The audio stream is highly compressed, allowing more data to flow in the video stream.
A-Law 2:1 and µ-Law 2:1	These codecs cut the sample rate in half (hence, the 2:1), most commonly from 16-bit to 8-bit. They differ slightly in how the algorithms approach the task, so experimenting with each one in the source media is your best option.
MACE (Macintosh Audio Compression/Expansion) 3:1 and 6:1	These codecs compress the audio aggressively and are best suited for voice-only content.

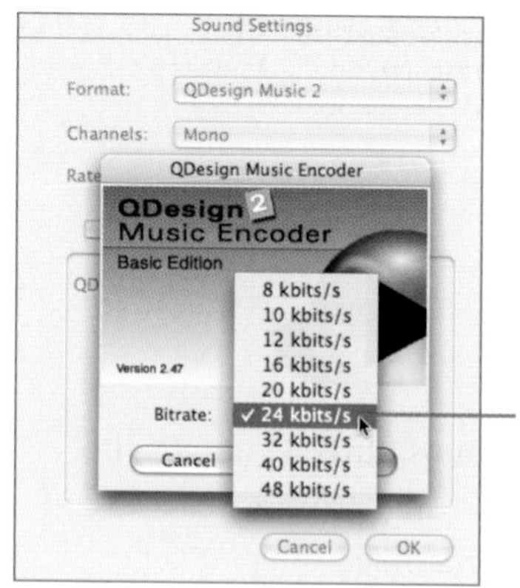
Sound Settings
Format:
QDesign Music 2
Channels:
Mono
QDesign Music Encoder
QDesign 2
Music Encoder
Basic Edition
8 kbits/s
10 kbits/s
12 kbits/s
16 kbits/s
20 kbits/s
✓ 24 kbits/s
32 kbits/s
40 kbits/s
48 kbits/s
Bitrate:
Cancel
Cancel
OK

When chosen, each codec displays extended options in the Format settings field. The Qualcomm and QDesign codecs display an Options button that opens another dialog containing extended settings.

Encoding with Dolby Digital Professional

In all DVD preset groups (SD and HD), a Dolby 2.0 preset is available for encoding stereo (left and right channel) audio into DVD-compliant AC3 elementary streams. Dolby encoding is highly efficient and can save a considerable amount of disc space compared to uncompressed linear PCM streams and with little noticeable loss in quality.

The Target System pop-up menu has three options: DVD Video, DVD Audio, and Generic AC3. Although DVD Audio might be the obvious choice for DVD assets, you should choose the default option—DVD Video—when working with most DVD-authoring applications, such as DVD Studio Pro.

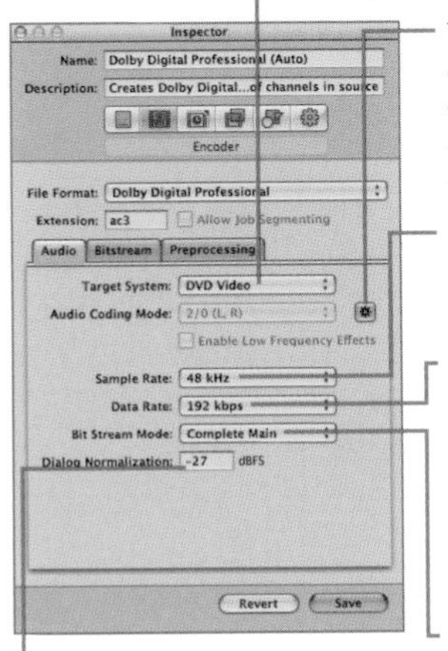
Inspector
Name: Dolby Digital Professional (Auto)
Description: Creates Dolby Digital...of channels in source
Encoder
File Format: Dolby Digital Professional
Extension: ac3
Allow Job Segmenting
Audio
Bitstream
Preprocessing
Target System: DVD Video
Audio Coding Mode: 2/0 (L, R)
Enable Low Frequency Effects
Sample Rate: 48 kHz
Data Rate: 192 kbps
Bit Stream Mode: Complete Main
Dialog Normalization: -27 dBFS
Revert
Save

With the automatic button selected, Compressor determines the coding mode based on the number of channels in the source media. When you deselect the automatic function, the pop-up menu becomes available and you can manually choose the coding mode.

The Sample Rate should be set to 48 kHz when encoding files for DVD. You can manually set the value for different output rates.

The Data Rate pop-up menu is analogous to the Bit Rate sliders in MPEG-2 encoding, in that it controls the balance between quality and output file size: The higher the data rate is, the higher the quality, at the cost of larger output files, and vice versa. For 2.0 audio, the most common data rate is 192 kbps; for 5.1 audio, the most common data rate is 448 kbps.

The choices in the Bit Stream Mode pop-up menu add to the stream metadata that can be read by some DVD players. In most cases, the default option—Complete Main—is the best choice.

Dialog Normalization allows the DVD player to control the relative volume of all audio streams on the disc, regardless of how they were mixed. A setting of –31 turns off any normalization by the encoder. (See the following sidebar, "Understanding Dialog Normalization".)

In addition to the settings in the DVD groups, three Dolby Digital Professional settings are available in the Settings window in Apple > Formats > Audio. The Dolby Digital Professional (Auto) setting requires very little user customization to produce great-sounding, low-bandwidth audio streams in either 2.0 or 5.1 formats, depending on the number of channels in the source media. In the Inspector window, the Dolby Digital Professional (Auto) encoder settings are organized into three tabs: Audio, Bitstream, and Preprocessing.

When you're encoding Dolby 2.0 files, the top two pop-up menus in the Bitstream tab will be dimmed because they are not applicable to left- and right-only encoding.

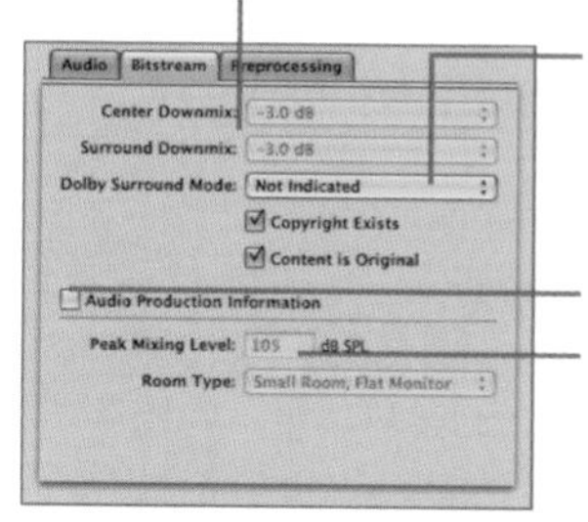
Audio
Bitstream
Preprocessing
Center Downmix:
-3.0 dB
Surround Downmix:
-3.0 dB
Dolby Surround Mode:
Not Indicated
Copyright Exists
Content is Original
Audio Production Information
Peak Mixing Level:
105
dB SPL
Room Type:
Small Room, Flat Monitor

If your source media was created with Dolby Pro Logic Surround, choose Encoded from the Dolby Surround Mode pop-up menu; otherwise, accept the default setting (Not Indicated).

Select this checkbox to enable audio metadata.

Audio Production Information is read by some DVD players and is used to fine-tune audio playback.

Understanding Dialog Normalization

Dialog normalization produces a consistent listening volume across all the audio assets on a DVD disc. (In this context, dialog normalization should not be confused with the audio normalization process that you might apply to tracks in Soundtrack Pro.) For example, if your main movie was edited in Final Cut Pro with audio mixed at –12 decibels (dB), and you have commentary tracks that were mixed in a DAW at –27 dB, you could have the DVD player adjust the volumes of the tracks so that they sound as though they were mixed at the same level. In the Dialog Normalization field, enter the average volume of the source media relative to full modulation. If all your source media files were mixed identically (or you don't know the audio levels), turn off Dialog Normalization by entering a value of –31 dB rather than entering the same value for each stream.

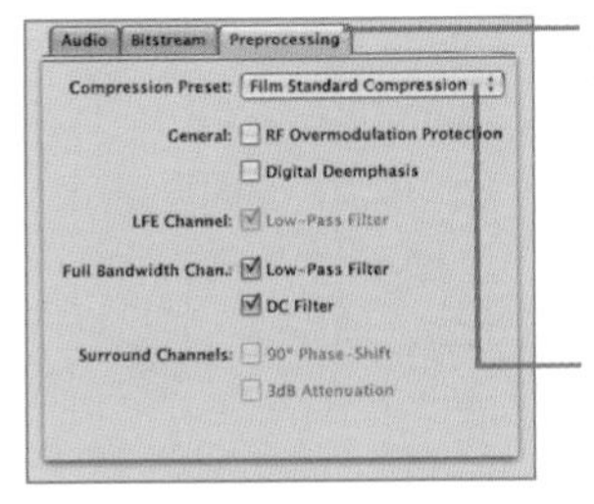
Audio
Bitstream
Preprocessing
Compression Preset: Film Standard Compression
General: RF Overmodulation Protection
Digital Deemphasis
LFE Channel: Low-Pass Filter
Full Bandwidth Chan.: Low-Pass Filter
DC Filter
Surround Channels: 90° Phase-Shift
3dB Attenuation

Most settings in the Preprocessing tab are highly technical and refer to engineering concepts in the Dolby Digital Professional specification; therefore, the default options are the best. Consult a surround-sound technician for help with modifying these settings.

In most instances, choose None, unless one of the available choices specifically pertains to your source audio mix.

Creating Dolby 5.1 Surround-Sound Assets

Creating a surround-sound mix is a five-step process, but Compressor is involved in only the final two steps:

1. Record audio on a sound stage or in a recording studio.
2. Mix down the audio into separate audio channels that locate the sounds in surround space. You can use Soundtrack Pro 2 to create a surround-sound mix.
3. Digitize the audio into 48 kHz audio files (in AIFF, QuickTime, or WAV format).
4. Identify the channel placement for DVD playback in 5.1 surround sound.
5. Encode the source media into a single AC3 file that a DVD player will decode as 5.1 surround sound.

The first three steps require a considerable amount of hardware and software, but after the resulting source media files are created, follow these steps to produce a 5.1 surround-sound AC3 file for your DVD project:

1 Click the Add Surround Sound button.

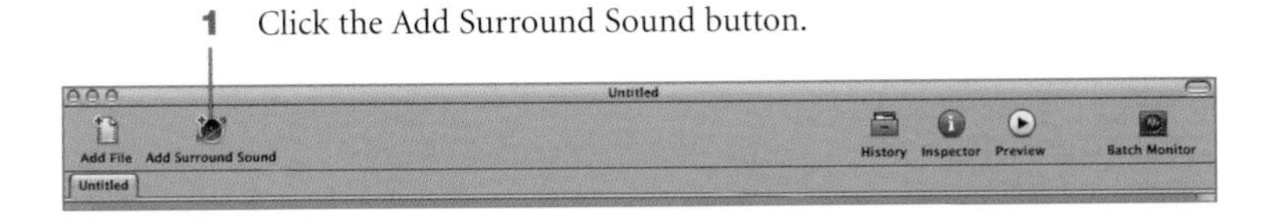
Untitled
Add File
Add Surround Sound
History
Inspector
Preview
Batch Monitor
Untitled

2 When the channel assignment interface opens, drag the source sound files from the Finder to the corresponding channel.

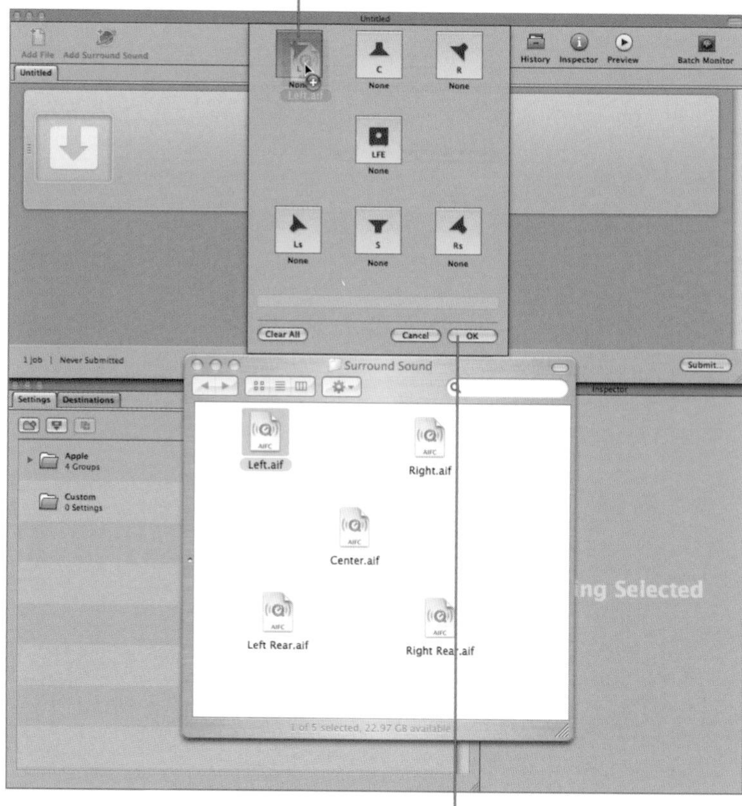
History
Inspector
Preview
Batch Monitor
C
R
None
LFE
Ls
S
Rs
Clear All
Cancel
OK
Submit...
Settings
Destinations
Apple
4 Groups
Custom
0 Settings
Surround Sound
Left.aif
Right.aif
Center.aif
Left Rear.aif
Right Rear.aif

3 When all the channels are assigned, click OK. Compressor will place a single entry in the Batch table comprising all the input channels.

TIP As another method, click the channel icons in the channel assignment interface; then choose the source media from the Open dialog that opens automatically.

If you need to edit the channels, select the surround-sound entry in the Batch table to open the channel assignment interface in the Inspector window. In the Inspector, click Save to save any changes.

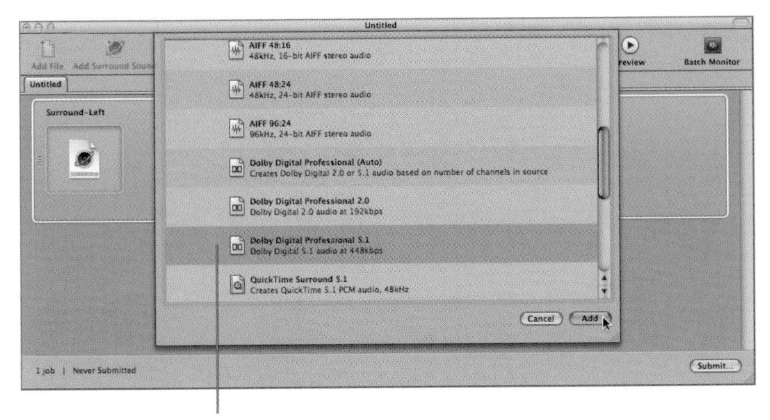
Untitled
AIFF 48:16
48kHz, 16-bit AIFF stereo audio
AIFF 48:24
48kHz, 24-bit AIFF stereo audio
AIFF 96:24
96kHz, 24-bit AIFF stereo audio
Dolby Digital Professional (Auto)
Creates Dolby Digital 2.0 or 5.1 audio based on number of channels in source
Dolby Digital Professional 2.0
Dolby Digital 2.0 audio at 192kbps
Dolby Digital Professional 5.1
Dolby Digital 5.1 audio at 448kbps
QuickTime Surround 5.1
Creates QuickTime 5.1 PCM audio, 48kHz
Cancel
Add
Surround-Left
Batch Monitor
1 job | Never Submitted
Submit...

4 From the Audio Formats preset group, apply the Dolby 5.1 stock preset.

5 In the Inspector window, make any necessary adjustments in the Audio, Bitstream, or Preprocessing tabs.

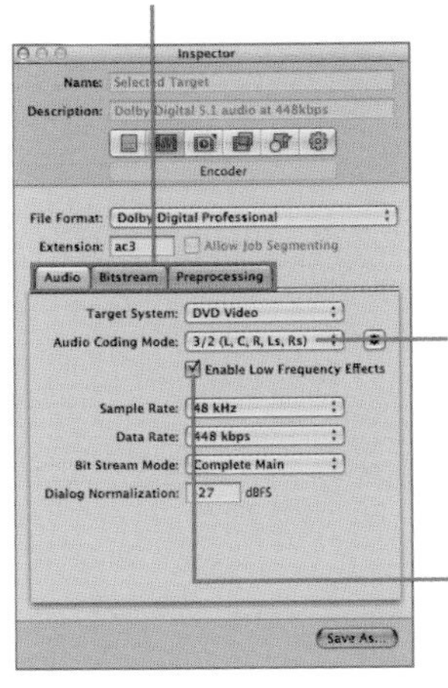
Inspector
Name:
Description:
Encoder
File Format: Dolby Digital Professional
Extension: ac3
Allow Job Segmenting
Audio
Bitstream
Preprocessing
Target System: DVD Video
Audio Coding Mode: 3/2 (L, C, R, Ls, Rs)
Enable Low Frequency Effects
Sample Rate: 48 kHz
Data Rate: 448 kbps
Bit Stream Mode: Complete Main
Dialog Normalization: 27 dBFS
Save As...

Your choice in the Audio Coding Mode pop-up menu should coincide with the assignments you made while importing the surround-sound elements into the channel assignment interface. You can also click the automatic button to instruct Compressor to determine the best audio coding setting.

If you added a low frequency effects channel (LFE) in your assignments, be sure to select the Enable Low Frequency Effects checkbox.

After all of the assignments and modifications are complete, click the Submit button in the Batch window.

NOTE ▶ You can submit Dolby Digital Professional 2.0 jobs by following the same steps outlined in this section, but assign the left and right channels manually and then add a Dolby Digital Professional 2.0 target.

Auditioning AC3 Assets

You can preview Dolby Digital Professional encoded files (AC3) within Compressor before you send the assets to a DVD-authoring platform such as DVD Studio Pro.

Import an AC3 file into the Batch window as you would import any source media.

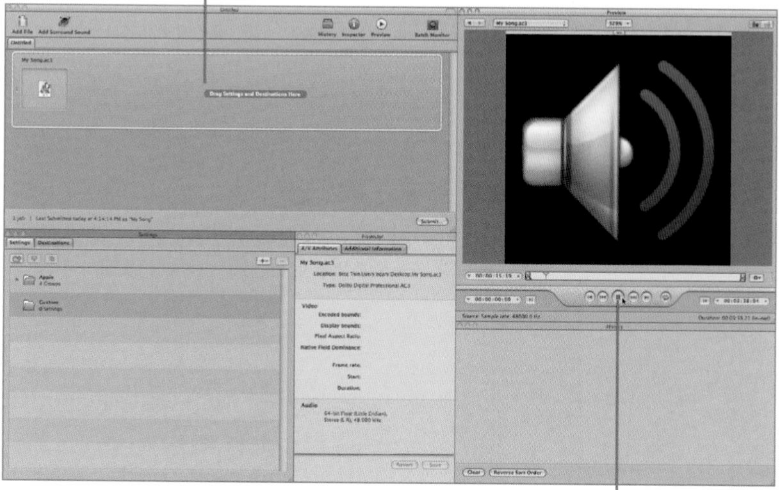

Select the AC3 job, and in the Preview window, click the Play button to audition the audio file.

NOTE ▶ If you do not have a 5.1 sound system connected to your computer, Compressor will down mix the audio to Dolby 2.0 (stereo) during playback.

Encoding QuickTime 5.1 Surround-Sound Audio

The QuickTime architecture combines with Core Audio inside Mac OS X v10.4 and higher to create 5.1 surround-sound files from uncompressed PCM audio. Though QuickTime surround-sound files are not necessarily practical for final distribution output due to overall file size and bandwidth requirements, they can be efficient when testing a mix because you don't need to spend time encoding the media.

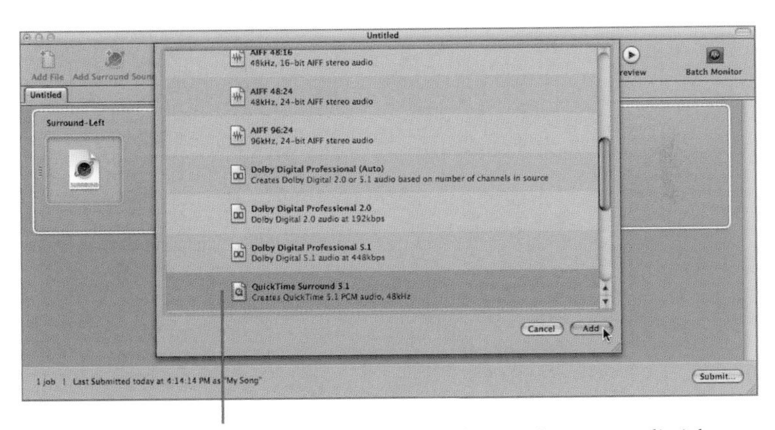
Untitled
Add File
Batch Monitor
Untitled
Surround-Left
48kHz, 16-bit AIFF stereo audio
AIFF 48:24
48kHz, 24-bit AIFF stereo audio
AIFF 96:24
96kHz, 24-bit AIFF stereo audio
Dolby Digital Professional (Auto)
Creates Dolby Digital 2.0 or 5.1 audio based on number of channels in source
Dolby Digital Professional 2.0
Dolby Digital 2.0 audio at 192kbps
Dolby Digital Professional 5.1
Dolby Digital 5.1 audio at 448kbps
QuickTime Surround 5.1
Creates QuickTime 5.1 PCM audio, 48kHz
Cancel
Add
1 job | Last Submitted today at 4:14:14 PM as "My Song"
Submit...

Add a QuickTime Surround 5.1 setting to an audio job in the Batch window. The default settings create PCM audio in each of the channels sampled at 48 kHz.

NOTE ▶ To make any adjustments to the QuickTime Surround 5.1 target, refer to "Using AIFF Containers" earlier in this chapter.

Encoding with MP3

MP3 (MPEG-1 Audio Layer 3) is a very common, highly compatible audio format used for web delivery and portable devices. MP3 is a lossy compression scheme that achieves its low bandwidth by removing sound that is either outside the range of human hearing or less noticeable to human hearing.

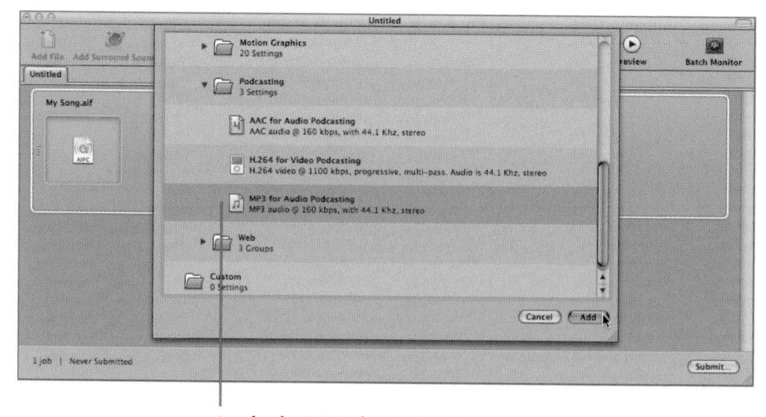
Untitled
Motion Graphics
20 Settings
Podcasting
3 Settings
AAC for Audio Podcasting
AAC audio @ 160 kbps, with 44.1 Khz, stereo
H.264 for Video Podcasting
H.264 video @ 1100 kbps, progressive, multi-pass. Audio is 44.1 Khz, stereo
MP3 for Audio Podcasting
MP3 audio @ 160 kbps, with 44.1 Khz, stereo
Web
3 Groups
Custom
0 Settings
Cancel
Add
Batch Monitor
My Song.aif
1 job | Never Submitted
Submit...

Apply the MP3 for Audio Podcasting setting to an audio job in the Batch window to create an MP3 target.

Select the MP3 target to open its settings into the Inspector window.

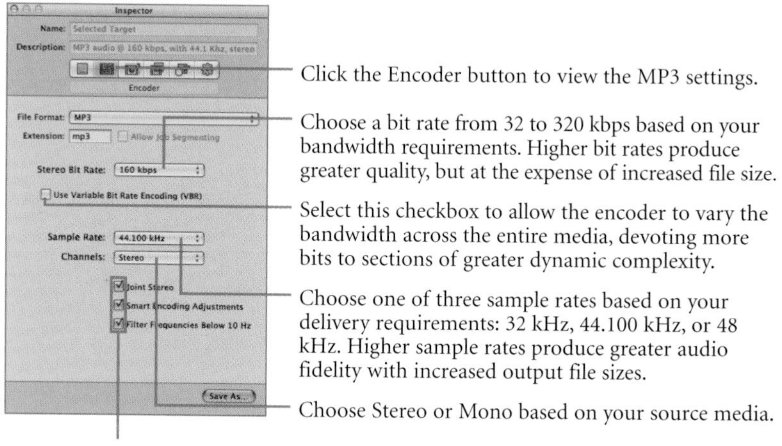
Inspector
Name: Selected Target
Description: MP3 audio @ 160 kbps, with 44.1 Khz, stereo
Encoder
File Format: MP3
Extension: mp3
Allow Job Segmenting
Stereo Bit Rate: 160 kbps
Use Variable Bit Rate Encoding (VBR)
Sample Rate: 44.100 kHz
Channels: Stereo
Joint Stereo
Smart Encoding Adjustments
Filter Frequencies Below 10 Hz
Save As...
Click the Encoder button to view the MP3 settings.
Choose a bit rate from 32 to 320 kbps based on your bandwidth requirements. Higher bit rates produce greater quality, but at the expense of increased file size.
Select this checkbox to allow the encoder to vary the bandwidth across the entire media, devoting more bits to sections of greater dynamic complexity.
Choose one of three sample rates based on your delivery requirements: 32 kHz, 44.100 kHz, or 48 kHz. Higher sample rates produce greater audio fidelity with increased output file sizes.
Choose Stereo or Mono based on your source media.

These three checkboxes are selected by default and allow the MP3 encoder to more efficiently compress the source media.

Encoding Audio Using AAC

AAC (Advanced Audio Coding) is a high-quality codec that achieves audio fidelity comparable to the MP3 codec with smaller output files, or it produces superior quality with similar file sizes. The Apple iTunes media player uses 128 Kbps AAC encoding as the default rate for importing (ripping) audio from CDs. The Apple AAC 128 Kbps preset produces high-quality audio files (similar to the default iTunes quality) suitable for download or transfer to portable devices with no need for customization.

AAC also adds *variable bit rate* (VBR) encoding to its audio compression. AAC is a perceptual codec, meaning that it reduces file size by discarding audio information that it deems less important to perceived quality.

Creating Custom AAC Settings Using MPEG-4

The easiest way to create a custom AAC preset using MPEG-4 as the file format is to duplicate the existing Apple AAC preset. The following example will create a custom AAC preset in the Custom folder:

Select a preset in the Settings window.

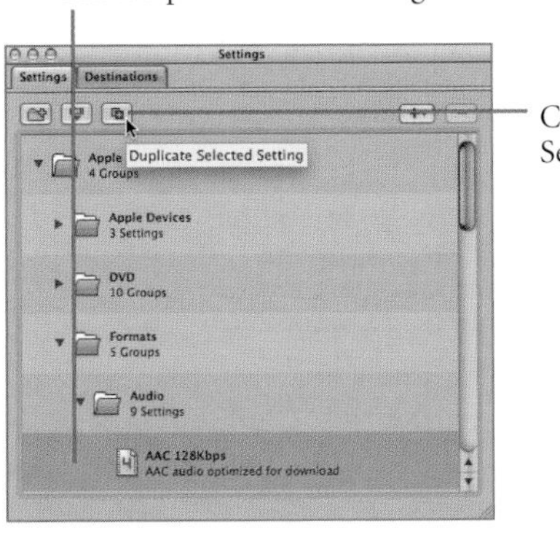
Settings
Settings
Destinations
Duplicate Selected Setting
Apple
4 Groups
Apple Devices
3 Settings
DVD
10 Groups
Formats
5 Groups
Audio
9 Settings
AAC 128Kbps
AAC audio optimized for download

Click the Duplicate Selected Setting button.

In the Audio tab, ensure that Audio Enabled is selected. In the Video tab, you can deselect the Video Enabled checkbox to create an audio-only setting.

If your left and right audio channels contain identical content, consider choosing Mono to reduce the output file size with no loss in quality.

You can often downsample 48 kHz audio to 44.1 kHz with no noticeable degradation in fidelity but with a smaller output file size.

The Quality settings—Low, Medium, and High—reflect audio quality, as well as the encoding time Compressor requires at each level. The setting does not affect the output file size.

To choose a sample rate higher than 44.1 kHz, you must set Bit Rate to 112 Kbps or higher.

Use the slider to increase or decrease the bit rate. The higher the bit rate is, the better the quality, but at the cost of increased output file size.

Select this checkbox if you intend to include podcasting information in the data stream, such as annotations, chapter markers, URLs, or embedded images.

NOTE ▶ See Chapter 7 for information on media streaming.

Custom AAC Settings Using AIFF

You can create AAC presets by defining custom QuickTime movie settings in the Presets window. QuickTime container presets in the Inspector window display a different interface compared to MPEG-4 presets, but the core AAC encoding concepts are similar. One significant advantage to using AIFF over MPEG-4 is that you can employ VBR (Variable Bit Rate) encoding instead of CBR (Constant Bit Rate).

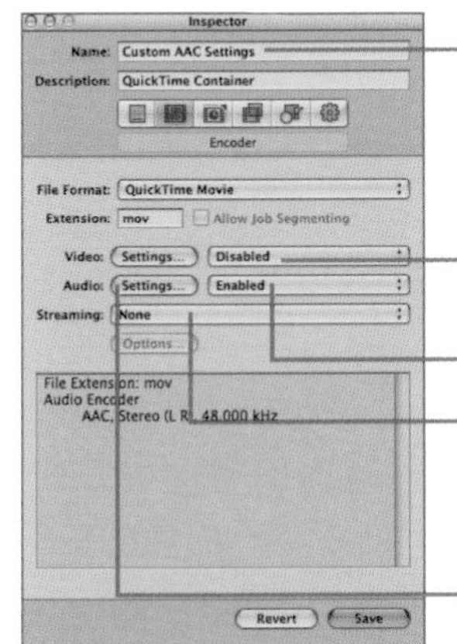
Inspector
Name: Custom AAC Settings
Description: QuickTime Container
Encoder
File Format: QuickTime Movie
Extension: mov
Allow Job Segmenting
Video: Settings... Disabled
Audio: Settings... Enabled
Streaming: None
Options...
File Extension: mov
Audio Encoder
AAC, Stereo (L R), 48.000 kHz
Revert
Save

1 Create a custom QuickTime Movie preset, and load it into the Inspector window. Enter a unique name and description for the preset.

2 Choose Disabled from the Video pop-up menu because audio-only encoding is desired.

3 Choose Enabled from the Audio pop-up menu.

4 Choose any desired streaming settings. The Options button is available only when Hinted Streaming is selected in the Streaming pop-up menu. Click Options to further change the parameters.

5 Click the Audio Settings button to open the Sound Settings dialog.

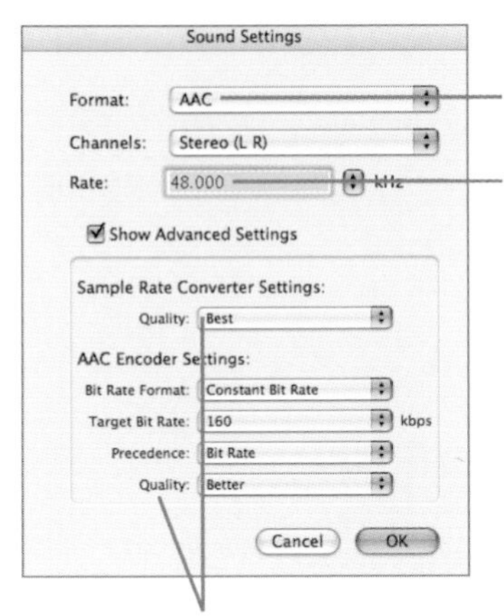
Sound Settings
Format: AAC
Channels: Stereo (L R)
Rate: 48.000 kHz
Show Advanced Settings
Sample Rate Converter Settings:
Quality: Best
AAC Encoder Settings:
Bit Rate Format: Constant Bit Rate
Target Bit Rate: 160 kbps
Precedence: Bit Rate
Quality: Better
Cancel
OK

6 Choose AAC from the Format pop-up menu.

7 Choose the desired settings from the Channels and Rate pop-up menus. Choose Recommended from the Rate pop-up menu if you want Compressor to define the sample rate on output based on the combination of source media and the encoder's advanced settings.

Both of the Quality pop-up menus determine how much time Compressor will spend addressing quality during the encode. The range is from Faster (speed over quality) to Best (quality over speed). These settings will not affect output file size.

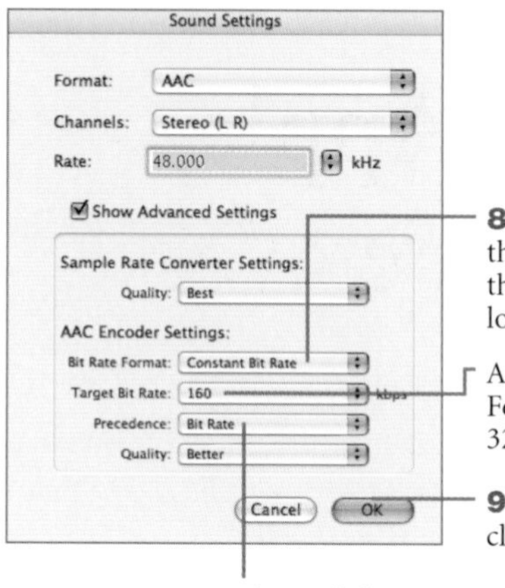
Sound Settings
Format:
AAC
Channels:
Stereo (L R)
Rate:
48.000
kHz
Show Advanced Settings
Sample Rate Converter Settings:
Quality:
Best
AAC Encoder Settings:
Bit Rate Format:
Constant Bit Rate
Target Bit Rate:
160
Precedence:
Bit Rate
Quality:
Better
Cancel
OK

8 Choose a constant or variable bit rate from the Bit Rate Format pop-up menu. VBRs use the available data more efficiently but take longer to encode.

A constant bit rate setting in the Bit Rate Format pop-up menu will list a range of 16 to 320 kbps in the Target Bit Rate pop-up menu.

9 Click OK to save the settings and close the dialog.

The Precedence pop-up menu dictates how the encoder weighs bit rate against sample rate when deciding which information to keep and which to discard. Choosing None forces Compressor to make decisions based on the codec's algorithms and the source media examined.

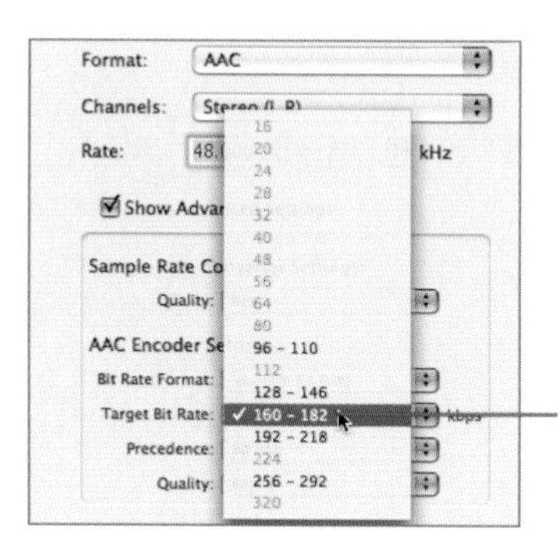
Format:
AAC
Channels:
Rate:
kHz
Show Advan
Sample Rate Co
Quality:
AAC Encoder Se
Bit Rate Format:
Target Bit Rate:
Precedence:
Quality:
16
20
24
28
32
40
48
56
64
80
96 - 110
112
128 - 146
✓ 160 - 182
192 - 218
224
256 - 292
320

Choosing Variable Bit Rate in the Bit Rate Format pop-up menu alters how the values in the Target Bit Rate pop-up menu appear. Instead of a single value, Compressor presents five ranges from which to choose. VBRs are more effective with dynamic audio content because the encoder increases the bit rate during sections that require more data and maintains constant quality across the entire media file.

7

Encoding for Apple Devices and the Web

Compressor includes three H.264 settings for Apple devices: one setting for Apple TV and two settings for iPod players with video (differentiated by output frame size). In addition, Compressor includes many settings aimed at creating content for Internet-based delivery.

> **NOTE** ▶ The MPEG-4 codec in Compressor is provided in two versions: Part 2 and Part 10 (more commonly known as H.264). To distinguish between these two MPEG-4 codecs, this book refers to the MPEG-4 Part 2 codec as MPEG-4, and Part 10 as H.264.

Encoding for Apple TV

Apple TV is a device that connects to a standard-definition or high-definition television and can wirelessly broadcast content from a Mac or Windows-based computer using iTunes. By default, the Apple TV setting encodes for HD output, but you can make a simple adjustment in the Inspector to change an applied target to encode SD content.

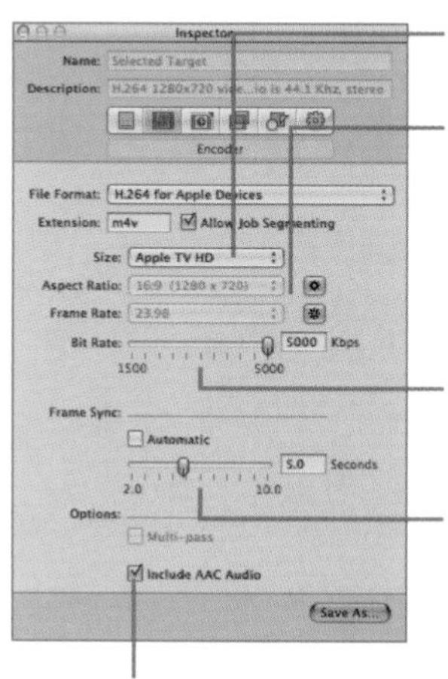
Inspector
Name:
Selected Target
Description:
Encoder
File Format:
H.264 for Apple Devices
Extension:
m4v
Allow Job Segmenting
Size:
Apple TV HD
Aspect Ratio:
16:9 (1280 x 720)
Frame Rate:
23.98
Bit Rate:
5000
Kbps
1500
5000
Frame Sync:
Automatic
5.0
Seconds
2.0
10.0
Options:
Multi-pass
Include AAC Audio
Save As...

In the Size pop-up menu, you can choose HD or SD Apple TV output.

Based on whether the output is SD or HD, you can define the Aspect Ratio and Frame Rate in these pop-up menus, or you can select the automatic buttons and Compressor will define the settings for you.In this example, the automatic buttons are selected, so the pop-up menus are dimmed.

The default SD and HD data rates are the best choices for Apple TV content. You can also manually adjust the Bit Rate for custom output formats.

Frame Sync establishes the keyframe interval by setting the number of seconds between keyframes. Selecting the Automatic checkbox tells Compressor to determine the best interval based on the source media.

Selecting this checkbox creates an AAC audio track in the output movie file. Compressor encodes the audio at 128 Kbps with a sample rate of either 44.1 kHz or 48 kHz depending on the source media's sample rate.

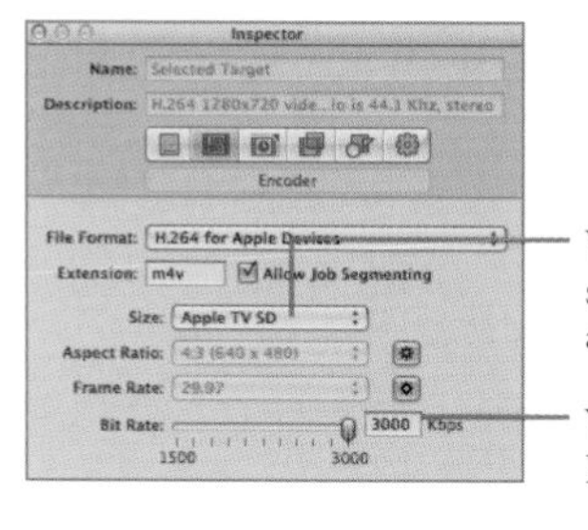
Inspector
Name:
Selected Target
Description:
Encoder
File Format:
H.264 for Apple Devices
Extension:
m4v
Allow Job Segmenting
Size:
Apple TV SD
Aspect Ratio:
4:3 (640 x 480)
Frame Rate:
29.97
Bit Rate:
3000
Kbps
1500
3000

When Apple TV SD is selected, the automatic settings for Aspect Ratio and Frame Rate adjust accordingly.

When Apple TV SD is selected, the ceiling for the Bit Rate is reduced to 3000 Kbps.

Encoding for Video iPods

The two Apple presets for iPod video encoding use H.264 as the video codec and AAC as the audio codec. When using H.264, the specifications are strict for iPod compliance. Therefore, you should apply one of the Apple presets instead of creating a custom H.264 preset. The Apple presets will consistently produce the best results.

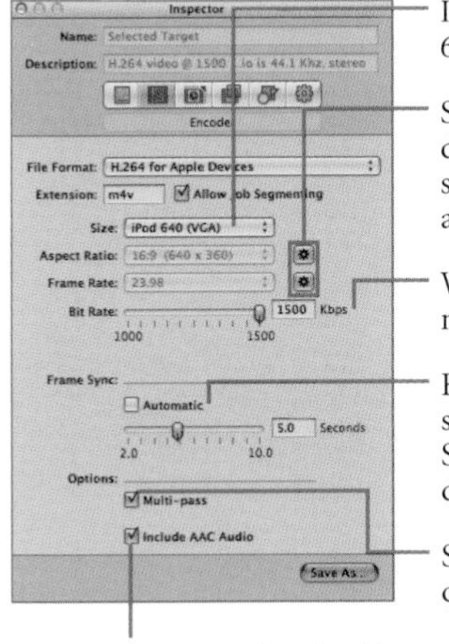
Inspector
Name:
Description:
File Format:
H.264 for Apple Devices
Extension:
m4v
Size:
iPod 640 (VGA)
Aspect Ratio:
Frame Rate:
Bit Rate:
1500
Kbps
1000
1500
Frame Sync:
Automatic
5.0
Seconds
2.0
10.0
Options:
Multi-pass
Include AAC Audio
Save As...

In the Size pop-up menu, choose between the iPod 640 (VGA) and iPod 320 (QVGA) settings.

Selecting the automatic buttons tells Compressor to determine the optimal Aspect Ratio and Frame Rate settings for iPod video output. You can deselect the automatic buttons and manually adjust the settings.

When iPod 640 (VGA) is selected in the Size pop-up menu, the maximum bit rate is set at 1500 Kbps.

Frame Sync establishes the keyframe interval by setting the number of seconds between keyframes. Selecting the Automatic checkbox tells Compressor to determine the best interval based on the source media.

Select the Multi-pass checkbox for higher encoding quality or deselect it for faster encoding speeds.

Selecting this checkbox creates an AAC audio track in the output movie file. Compressor encodes the audio at 128 Kbps with a sample rate of either 44.1 kHz or 48 kHz depending on the source media's sample rate.

iPod preset with 640 VGA settings.

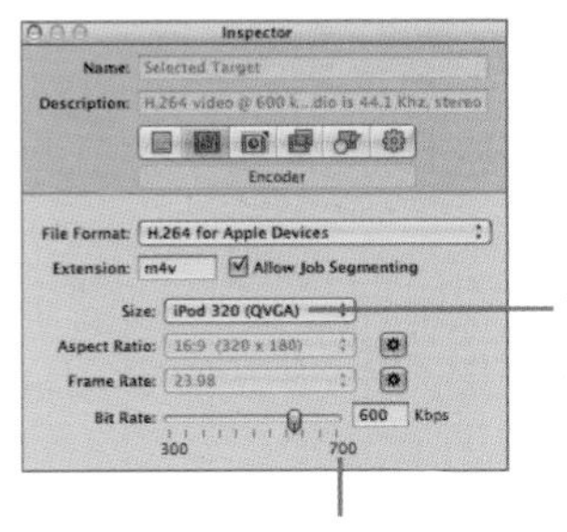
Inspector
Name:
Description:
Encoder
File Format:
H.264 for Apple Devices
Extension:
m4v
Allow Job Segmenting
Size:
iPod 320 (QVGA)
Aspect Ratio:
Frame Rate:
Bit Rate:
600
Kbps
300
700

When iPod 320 (QVGA) is chosen in the Size pop-up menu, the automatic Aspect Ratio and Frame Rate settings adjust accordingly.

When iPod 320 (QVGA) is selected, the maximum bit rate is 700 Kbps.

iPod preset with 320 QVGA settings.

MPEG-4 Encoding for Video iPods

An Apple iPod with video will also play media encoded with MPEG-4. The "Encoding for the Web" section of this chapter discusses steps to follow when using MPEG-4 to encode for the web; but you can follow those same steps to create a custom setting based on the following parameters to achieve smooth iPod video playback:

Option	Setting
Maximum Video Bit Rate	2.5 Mbps (2500 Kbps)
Maximum Video Frame Rate	30 fps
Maximum Video Frame Size	640 x 480 pixels
Profile	Basic (Simple)
Maximum Audio Sample Rate	48 kHz
Maximum Audio Data Rate	160 Kbps

Encoding for the Web

Internet-based distribution takes many forms and many formats. Compressor lets you directly encode most of them and indirectly encode to others using third-party plug-ins (see "Using QuickTime Components" in Chapter 9).

The balance between size and quality really comes to the fore when delivering content for the Internet because bandwidth is a constant consideration. Whether you are distributing a video podcast to high-speed broadband users or delivering a trailer to cell phones, the challenge is finding that sweet spot where the best quality is achieved within the delivery constraints. Experimenting with alternate encoders and employing test clip workflows (see Chapter 8) will greatly assist you in realizing optimal media quality for each Internet distribution scenario.

MPEG-4 Encoding for the Web

MPEG-4 is most commonly used to encode content for Internet distribution. It encodes more quickly than H.264, and intelligently manages the balance between file size and image quality. The MPEG-4 settings are located in four places in the Presets window:

- Apple > Formats > MPEG-4 (one setting)
- Apple > Other Workflows > Web > Download > QuickTime 6 Compatible (six settings)
- Apple > Other Workflows > Web > Streaming > QuickTime 6 Compatible (five settings)
- Apple > Other Workflows > Web > Web Videocast (one setting)

Encoding for the web requires some advance data-rate planning related to your target bandwidth. The data rate is the main factor that determines the suitability of media for playback within a given bandwidth. Files intended for dial-up-modem transmission, for example, will use a data rate quite different from the one you'd use to deliver broadband content.

Data rates are defined in kilobits per second (Kbps)—not to be confused with kilobytes (KB), the measurement that refers to media file size. MPEG-4–encoded content might have a data rate of 100 Kbps and occupy 2000 KB (2 MB) of disc space, for example.

The following table lists the most common delivery systems and their target bandwidths:

Delivery System	Target Bandwidth
Dial-up modem	40 Kbps
Cellular Connections (EDGE, GPRS)	100 Kbps
DSL (medium bandwidth)	300 Kbps
DSL (high bandwidth)	800 Kbps
Broadband: T1, T3, DSL, and cable modems	1.5 Mbps (megabits per second) and beyond

For example, for medium-bandwidth DSL distribution, apply the MPEG-4 300 Kbps setting from the Apple > Other Workflows > Web > Download > QuickTime 6 Compatible group.

To create a custom MPEG-4 setting, duplicate and modify an existing Apple setting. In the Presets window, duplicate an Apple MPEG-4 preset that is generally suitable for your target bandwidth (see Chapter 3 for information on duplicating a preset). Compressor places the copy in the Custom folder. Select the new setting to open it in the Inspector window.

Select the Video Enabled checkbox to enable video encoding; deselect it for audio-only output.

The ISMA (Internet Streaming Media Association) offers two profile choices: Basic and Improved. The Basic profile ensures greater compatibility with MPEG-4 playback devices. The Improved profile produces higher-quality output but may not be compatible with devices manufactured before the release of that profile.

Reducing the overall frame rate is a common strategy to reduce file size, most often employed by halving the source media's frame rate. You can enter the desired frame rate in the Frame Rate field or choose a rate from the pop-up menu.

The Key Frame Interval setting determines how often a keyframe appears in the data stream. A smaller number creates more keyframes, and a larger number creates fewer keyframes. The more keyframes in the data stream, the higher the image quality, but at the cost of increased file size.

The Bit Rate pop-up menu offers four choices: "Constant at" uses a fixed rate across the entire media. The three VBR options vary the rate depending on the source media: High VBR strives for quality at the expense of larger file sizes; Low VBR attempts to keep the overall file size down by varying a low bit rate across the source media; and Medium VBR balances between the two. When any of the VBR choices are used, the slider will be dimmed.

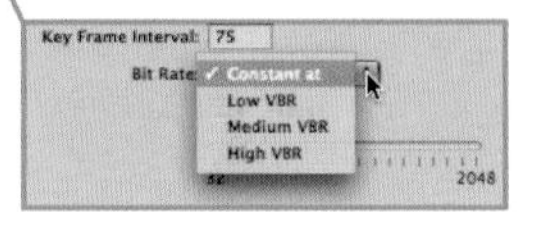
Key Frame Interval: 75
Bit Rate: ✓ Constant at
Low VBR
Medium VBR
High VBR
2048

When "Constant at" is chosen in the Bit Rate pop-up menu, enter a specific value into the Kbps field or use the slider to define a constant bit rate. Higher bit rates produce greater quality at increased file sizes.

Web-Encoding Tips

- When selecting frame rates, choose a rate that divides evenly into the source media's frame rate. If the source frame rate is 30 frames per second (fps), a choice of 5, 10, or 15 fps is acceptable. (Calculate by rounding up the NTSC frame rate of 29.97 fps to 30 fps and the PAL frame rate of 23.98 fps up to 24 fps.) Choosing frame rates that don't divide evenly into the source media's frame rate can produce choppy playback.
- When choosing keyframe intervals, find an interval that offers the best quality at the smallest output file size. If your source media content changes quickly from frame to frame, try a lower interval. If your source is primarily static, increase the interval value.
- Choosing constant bit rates provides more direct control when attempting to target a specific bandwidth. Choosing variable bit rates provides greater quality with more efficient use of the bandwidth, but the output file size and bandwidth will vary depending on the source media.

The MPEG-4 settings in Compressor use AAC to compress source audio. See Chapter 6 for more detailed information on using AAC audio in MPEG-4 containers.

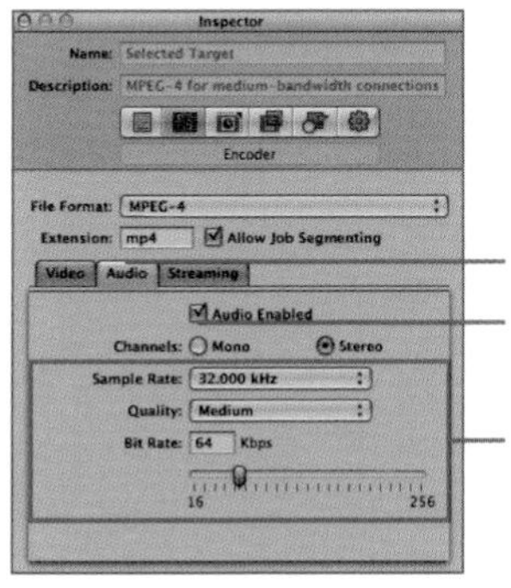
Inspector
Name: Selected Target
Description: MPEG-4 for medium-bandwidth connections
Encoder
File Format: MPEG-4
Extension: mp4
Allow Job Segmenting
Video
Audio
Streaming
Audio Enabled
Channels: Mono
Stereo
Sample Rate: 32.000 kHz
Quality: Medium
Bit Rate: 64 Kbps
16
256

Click the Audio tab to view the audio settings.

To encode audio, select the Audio Enabled option.

In general, higher Sample Rate and Bit Rate values produce higher quality at the cost of increased file sizes. See Chapter 6 for more information.

The Streaming tab performs one main function: flagging the output media with the proper metadata for hosting on a streaming server.

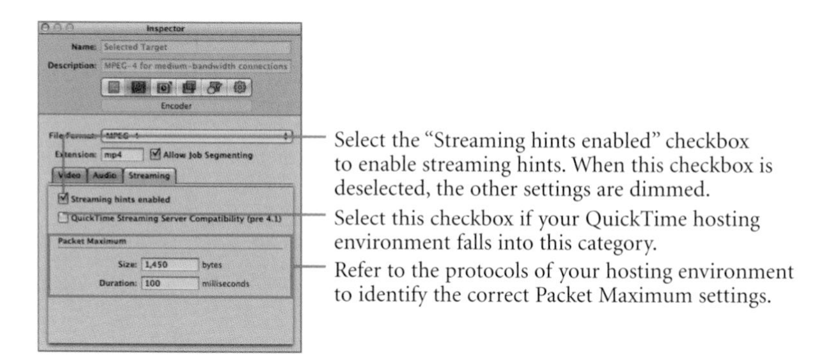
Inspector
Name: Selected Target
Encoder
Extension: mp4
Allow Job Segmenting
Video
Audio
Streaming
Streaming hints enabled
Packet Maximum
Size: 1,450 bytes
Duration: 100 milliseconds
Select the "Streaming hints enabled" checkbox to enable streaming hints. When this checkbox is deselected, the other settings are dimmed.
Select this checkbox if your QuickTime hosting environment falls into this category.
Refer to the protocols of your hosting environment to identify the correct Packet Maximum settings.

H.264 Encoding for the Web

H.264 represents a significant leap in compression technology. Compared with its MPEG-4 predecessor, H.264 scales much more efficiently, delivers up to four times the frame size at a comparable data rate, and achieves similar quality at almost one-third the MPEG-4 data rates.

The disadvantages of the H.264 codec are longer encoding times, greater playback processing demands, and some compatibility issues related to distribution (QuickTime 7 is required for H.264 playback).

Compressor has three Inspector-window interfaces for H.264 modification:

- H.264 for DVD Studio Pro, which controls the settings for high-definition disc encoding (see Chapter 5)
- H.264 for Apple devices (covered earlier in this chapter)
- H.264 for the creation of QuickTime container files, which is covered in this section

> **NOTE** ▶ When producing files for web delivery, use QuickTime movie settings instead of the presets designed for HD discs or Apple devices.

The H.264 settings that use QuickTime container files are located in four places in the Presets window:

- Apple > Formats > QuickTime (one setting)
- Apple > Other Workflows > Web > Download > QuickTime 7 Compatible (five settings)
- Apple > Other Workflows > Web > Streaming > QuickTime 7 Compatible (five settings)
- Apple > Other Workflows > Web > Web Videocast (one setting)

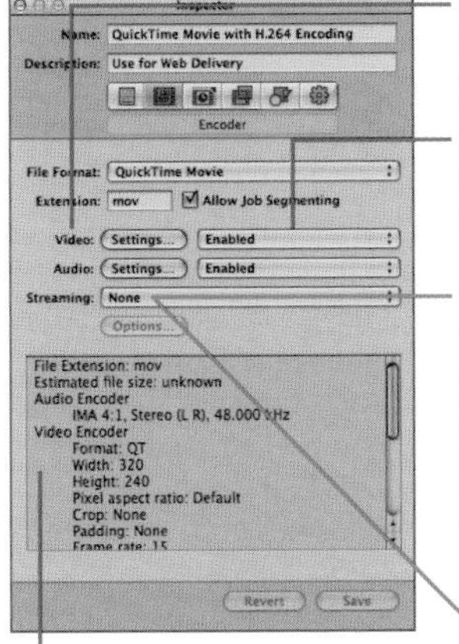
Name: QuickTime Movie with H.264 Encoding
Description: Use for Web Delivery
Encoder
File Format: QuickTime Movie
Extension: mov
Allow Job Segmenting
Video: Settings... Enabled
Audio: Settings... Enabled
Streaming: None
Options
File Extension: mov
Estimated file size: unknown
Audio Encoder
IMA 4:1, Stereo (L R), 48.000 kHz
Video Encoder
Format: QT
Width: 320
Height: 240
Pixel aspect ratio: Default
Crop: None
Padding: None
Revert
Save

The Video and Audio Settings buttons open the QuickTime windows where you can modify the parameters.

Choose Enabled or Disabled from the pop-up menus to independently turn video and audio encoding on and off.

The most common Streaming setting is Fast Start, which allows a movie to begin playing when enough data has been downloaded to permit uninterrupted playback. If you are hosting a movie on a QuickTime streaming server, choose Hinted Streaming, which will enable the Options button. Click Options to open a QuickTime dialog where you can modify the settings for your hosting provider.

The Summary pane is a quick reference for the audio and video settings defined in the QuickTime windows.

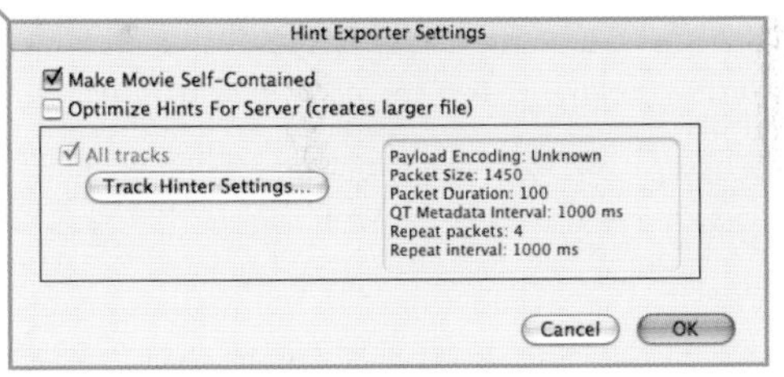
Hint Exporter Settings
Make Movie Self-Contained
Optimize Hints For Server (creates larger file)
All tracks
Track Hinter Settings...
Payload Encoding: Unknown
Packet Size: 1450
Packet Duration: 100
QT Metadata Interval: 1000 ms
Repeat packets: 4
Repeat interval: 1000 ms
Cancel
OK

Using H.264 for Video Encoding

In the Inspector, click the Settings button next to Video to open the QuickTime interface containing all of the H.264 video settings.

Set a value manually by selecting Every and entering a value in the frames field. The higher the value is, the fewer keyframes, and vice versa. Select Automatic to allow Compressor to determine the optimum number of keyframes based on an analysis of the source media. Select All to create a keyframe from every frame, producing pristine quality at very large output file sizes.

When selecting frame rates, choose a number that evenly divides into your source media's frame rate.

H.264 is the default Compression Type. Choosing another type from this pop-up menu will replace H.264 with another codec.

Define a Data Rate or select Automatic to allow the encoder to vary the data rate across the movie (see the following table).

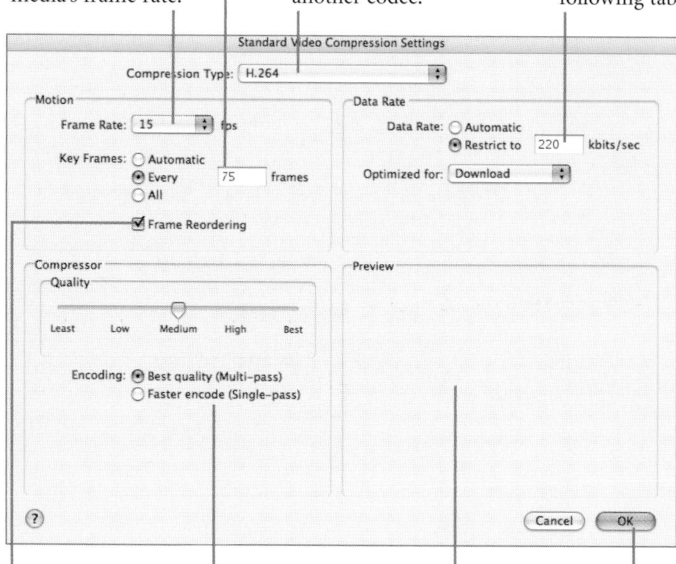
Standard Video Compression Settings
Compression Type: H.264
Motion
Frame Rate: 15 fps
Key Frames: Automatic
Every 75 frames
All
Frame Reordering
Data Rate
Data Rate: Automatic
Restrict to 220 kbits/sec
Optimized for: Download
Compressor
Quality
Least Low Medium High Best
Encoding: Best quality (Multi-pass)
Faster encode (Single-pass)
Preview
Cancel
OK

Frame Reordering is one of the innovations of the H.264 codec (see the following Note). Always keep this checkbox selected.

Unless speed is a paramount concern, always select "Best quality (Multi-pass)" for H.264 encoding. This allows Compressor to analyze the source media before the encoding pass.

The encoded video will not display in the Preview area. To preview the preset results, use the Preview window inside Compressor.

Click OK to save all settings and return to the Inspector window, or click Cancel to exit without modifying any settings.

NOTE ► H.264, like MPEG-4, employs an interframe compression scheme. Keyframes include all the data needed to reproduce an image, and delta frames contain only the interpreted image information between keyframes. Frame reordering allows the delta frames to look to any keyframe in the movie for relative information, which allows H.264 to encode high-quality media even more efficiently. The addition of a multi-pass option lets the H.264 codec intelligently calculate both keyframe and bandwidth when those parameters are set to Automatic.

The Quality and Data Rate settings work together to encode video. Use the following table to determine the best settings:

Encoding Objective	Settings
Highest-quality output	Set Data Rate to Automatic, and Quality to Best. In the "Optimized for" pop-up menu, choose Download, CD/DVD-ROM, or Streaming.
Smallest output file size	Set Data Rate to Automatic, and Quality to Low. In the "Optimized for" pop-up menu, choose the desired target delivery system.
Balancing output file size and quality	Set Data Rate to Automatic, and Quality to Medium. In the "Optimized for" pop-up menu, choose the desired target delivery system.
Specifying a data rate for a particular bandwidth	Set Data Rate to Restrict To, and enter a custom value in the corresponding data field. The Quality slider will be dimmed.

NOTE ► The Quality slider can be moved to any setting within its continuously-variable range.

Using H.264 for Audio Encoding

H.264 can use any QuickTime-compatible audio codec. The highest-quality encoder available to Compressor is AAC.

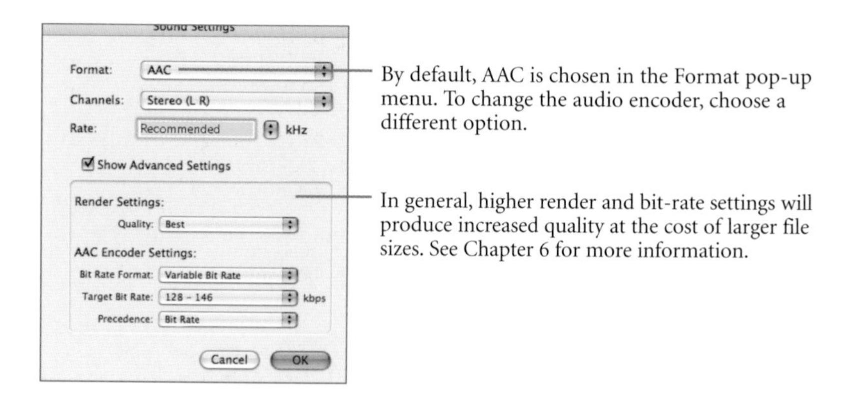
Format: AAC
Channels: Stereo (L R)
Rate: Recommended kHz
Show Advanced Settings
Render Settings:
Quality: Best
AAC Encoder Settings:
Bit Rate Format: Variable Bit Rate
Target Bit Rate: 128 - 146 kbps
Precedence: Bit Rate
Cancel
OK

By default, AAC is chosen in the Format pop-up menu. To change the audio encoder, choose a different option.

In general, higher render and bit-rate settings will produce increased quality at the cost of larger file sizes. See Chapter 6 for more information.

Encoding for Podcasting

Podcast is a term derived from the iPod and broadcasting. It describes content syndicated to its subscribers via the Internet and also describes the act of distributing that media. Podcasting has become synonymous with self-distributing content on the web. What makes podcasting unique is the RSS (Really Simple Syndication) technology that enables consumers to subscribe to and download episodes of content uploaded by podcast producers to content aggregators such as iTunes.

Podcasting comes in two forms: audio and video (sometimes referred to as videocasting). Compressor includes settings that support both forms:

The AAC setting works well for audio podcasts that will be syndicated via iTunes. For more information on AAC encoding, see Chapter 6.

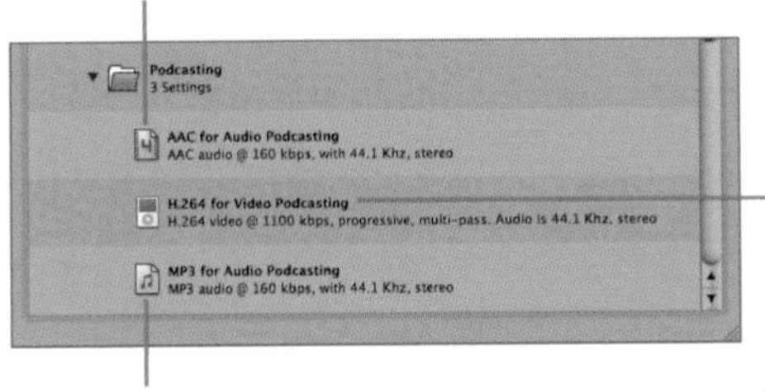
Podcasting
3 Settings
AAC for Audio Podcasting
AAC audio @ 160 kbps, with 44.1 Khz, stereo
H.264 for Video Podcasting
H.264 video @ 1100 kbps, progressive, multi-pass. Audio is 44.1 Khz, stereo
MP3 for Audio Podcasting
MP3 audio @ 160 kbps, with 44.1 Khz, stereo

The H.264 video setting is based on the iPod Video (VGA) setting. See "Encoding for Video iPods" earlier in this chapter for more information.

The MP3 setting works well for podcasts that require broad playback compatibility. For more information on MP3 encoding, see Chapter 6.

The Apple > Other Workflows > Web > Web Videocast group contains two more settings for video-based webcasting.

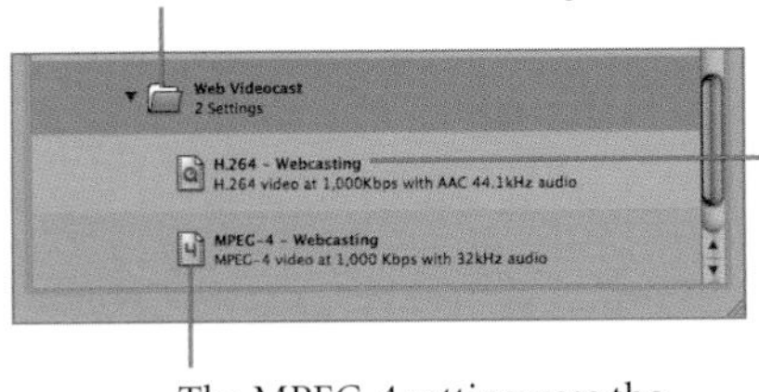
Web Videocast
2 Settings
H.264 - Webcasting
H.264 video at 1,000Kbps with AAC 44.1kHz audio
MPEG-4 - Webcasting
MPEG-4 video at 1,000 Kbps with 32kHz audio

The H.264 setting uses QuickTime container files encoded with H.264, instead of the H.264 for Apple devices format. Refer to "Using H.264 for Video Encoding" earlier in this chapter for more details.

The MPEG-4 setting uses the same options as covered in "MPEG-4 Encoding for the Web" earlier in this chapter.

Annotating Podcasts with Metadata

You can add metadata, such as a copyright notice or author information, to your source media. The metadata is embedded in the output file during encoding. This information will not be visible in the video stream, but it can be accessed when a viewer chooses Get Info in an application such as QuickTime Player.

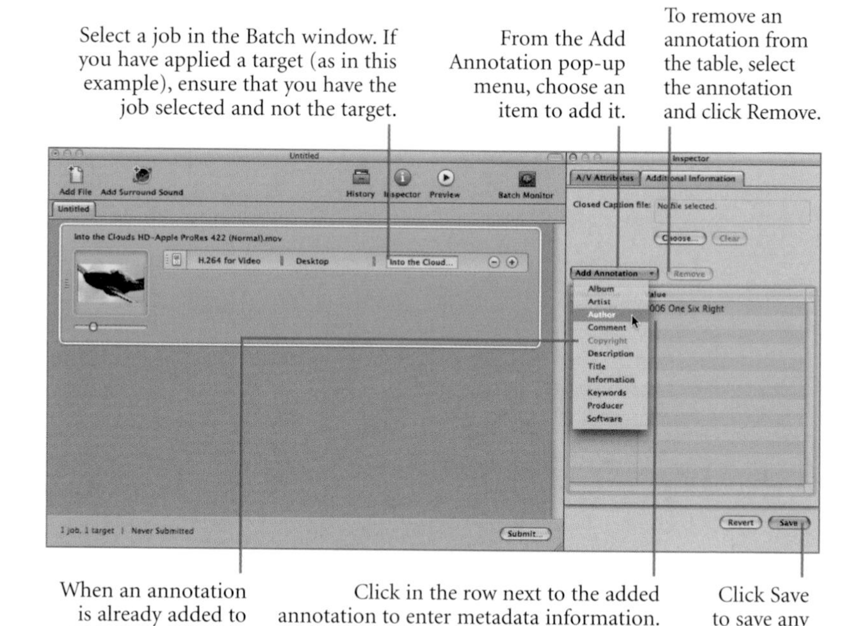
Select a job in the Batch window. If you have applied a target (as in this example), ensure that you have the job selected and not the target.
From the Add Annotation pop-up menu, choose an item to add it.
To remove an annotation from the table, select the annotation and click Remove.
When an annotation is already added to the list, it is dimmed in the pop-up menu.
Click in the row next to the added annotation to enter metadata information. In this example, a copyright annotation was added, and then the text "2006 One Six Right" was entered manually.
Click Save to save any changes.

NOTE ▸ Annotations are supported by the following output formats: H.264 for Apple devices, MP3, and QuickTime movie.

Adding URL Podcast Markers

You can add markers to the video stream, which will enable interactivity in Compressor's output files. For example, you can add an HTML link that will appear onscreen at a designated time and take the viewer to a website when clicked (if the client computer is connected to the Internet).

Load a job into the Preview window and follow these steps to add a URL podcast marker:

1 Find the frame in which you want the URL to appear, and press M to add a marker.

2 Without moving the playhead, choose Edit Marker from the Marker pop-up menu.

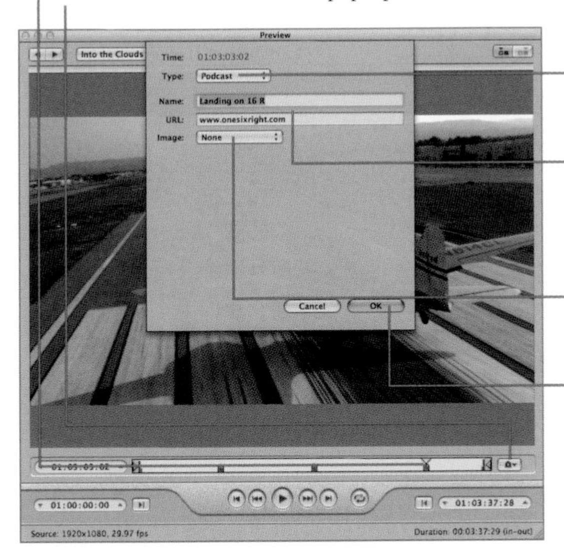
Preview
Into the Clouds
Time: 01:03:03:02
Type: Podcast
Name: Landing on 16 R
URL: www.onesixright.com
Image: None
Cancel
OK
01:00:00:00
01:03:37:28
Source: 1920x1080, 29.97 fps
Duration: 00:03:37:29 (in-out)

3 From the Type pop-up menu, choose Podcast.

4 Enter the desired onscreen text in the Name field, and then enter the web address in the URL field.

5 From the Image pop-up menu, choose None.

6 Click OK. Podcast markers are colored red in the timeline.

Add a video podcasting or webcasting target and then submit the job. Next, load the output movie into QuickTime player.

Into the Clouds.m4v
00:00:05

This clickable link will appear at the frame where you placed the marker.

TIP You can also use podcast markers to add image data to an audio-only podcast. Follow the preceding steps, but from the Image pop-up menu choose a still image that you want to appear in the data stream. Next, apply one of the audio podcasting settings in Apple > Other Workflows > Podcasting and submit the batch for encoding. The image markers will appear when the podcast is played in an application such as iTunes.

Adding Chapter Markers to QuickTime Content

You can add chapters markers to QuickTime files that will enable movie navigation interactivity when the file is played in QuickTime Player.

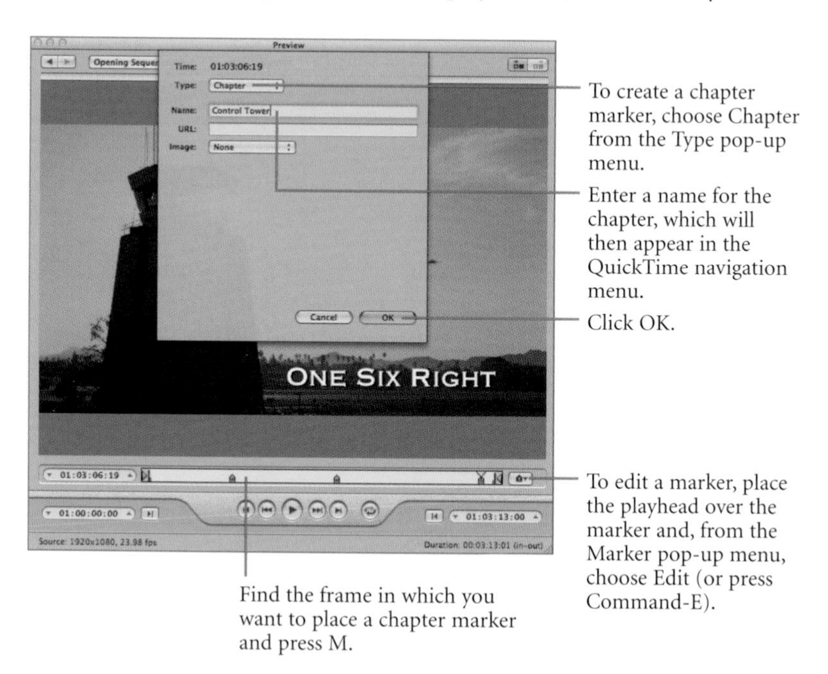
Preview
Opening Seque
Time: 01:03:06:19
Type: Chapter
Name: Control Tower
URL:
Image: None
Cancel
OK
ONE SIX RIGHT
01:03:06:19
01:00:00:00
01:03:13:00
Source: 1920x1080, 23.98 fps
Duration: 00:03:13:01 (in-out)

To create a chapter marker, choose Chapter from the Type pop-up menu.

Enter a name for the chapter, which will then appear in the QuickTime navigation menu.

Click OK.

To edit a marker, place the playhead over the marker and, from the Marker pop-up menu, choose Edit (or press Command-E).

Find the frame in which you want to place a chapter marker and press M.

Create a video podcast target by adding the H.264 for Video Podcasting setting contained in Apple > Other Workflows > Podcasting in the Presets window. Then submit the batch for encoding.

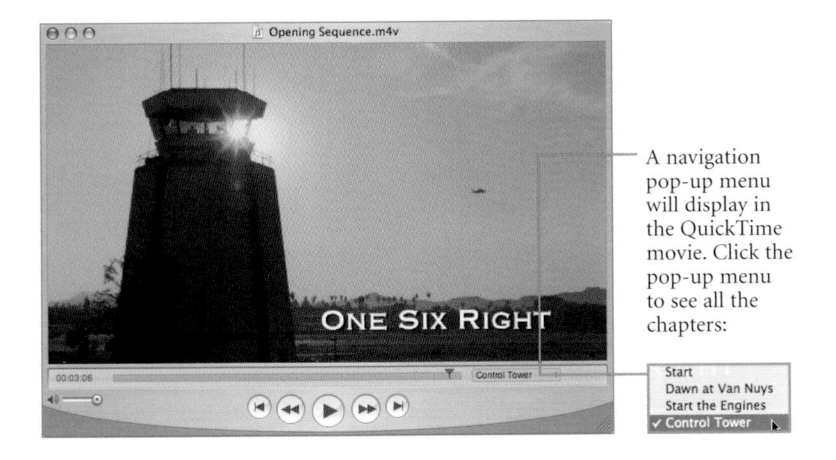
Opening Sequence.m4v
ONE SIX RIGHT
00:03:06
Control Tower
A navigation pop-up menu will display in the QuickTime movie. Click the pop-up menu to see all the chapters:
Start
Dawn at Van Nuys
Start the Engines
✓ Control Tower

NOTE ▶ Chapter markers are supported only for MPEG-2, MPEG-4 (audio only), QuickTime movies, H.264 for DVD Studio Pro, and H.264 for Apple devices.

Encoding Content for Cell Phones

Compressor includes multiple settings for encoding content for cellular carriers worldwide.

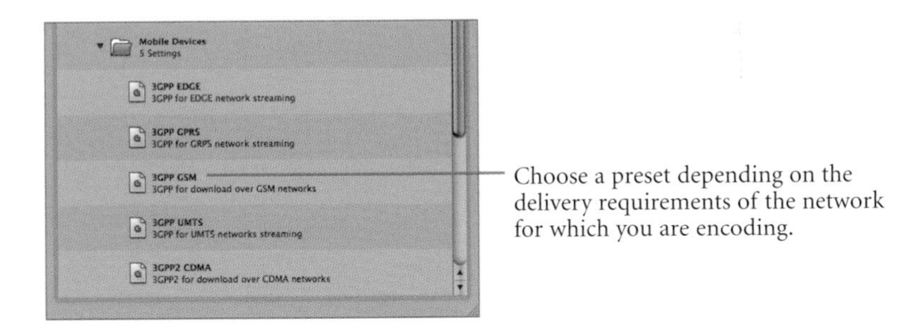
Mobile Devices
5 Settings
3GPP EDGE
3GPP for EDGE network streaming
3GPP GPRS
3GPP for GRPS network streaming
3GPP GSM
3GPP for download over GSM networks
3GPP UMTS
3GPP for UMTS networks streaming
3GPP2 CDMA
3GPP2 for download over CDMA networks
Choose a preset depending on the delivery requirements of the network for which you are encoding.

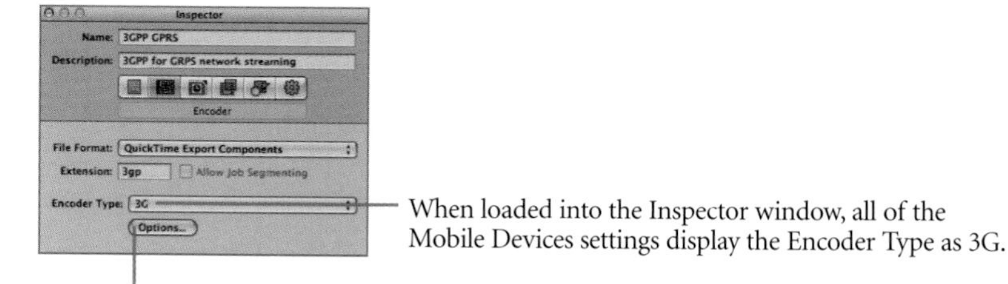
Inspector
Name: 3GPP GPRS
Description: 3GPP for GRPS network streaming
Encoder
File Format: QuickTime Export Components
Extension: 3gp
Allow Job Segmenting
Encoder Type: 3G
Options...

When loaded into the Inspector window, all of the Mobile Devices settings display the Encoder Type as 3G.

To manually adjust the encoder settings, click the Options button to open the QuickTime interface.

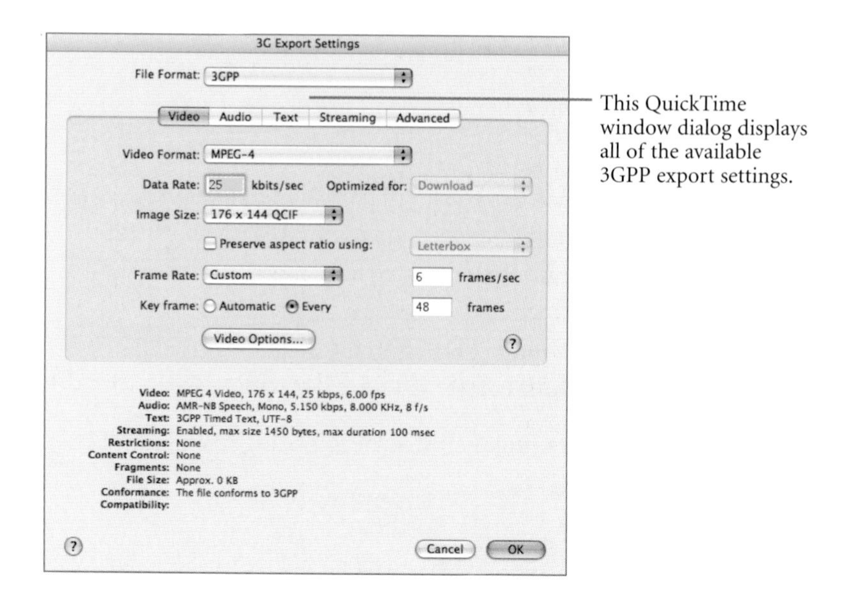
3G Export Settings
File Format: 3GPP
Video
Audio
Text
Streaming
Advanced
Video Format: MPEG-4
Data Rate: 25 kbits/sec
Optimized for: Download
Image Size: 176 x 144 QCIF
Preserve aspect ratio using:
Letterbox
Frame Rate: Custom
6 frames/sec
Key frame: Automatic Every
48 frames
Video Options...
Video: MPEG 4 Video, 176 x 144, 25 kbps, 6.00 fps
Audio: AMR-NB Speech, Mono, 5.150 kbps, 8.000 KHz, 8 f/s
Text: 3GPP Timed Text, UTF-8
Streaming: Enabled, max size 1450 bytes, max duration 100 msec
Restrictions: None
Content Control: None
Fragments: None
File Size: Approx. 0 KB
Conformance: The file conforms to 3GPP
Compatibility:
Cancel
OK

This QuickTime window dialog displays all of the available 3GPP export settings.

MORE INFO ▶ Although custom encoding for cell phones using 3GPP is outside the scope of this book, the *QuickTime Pro Quick-Reference Guide* from Peachpit Press covers this topic in depth.

8 Test Clip Workflows

Compressor allows you to create and efficiently organize a series of encoding jobs and then process them unattended. This works especially well if you are comfortable with your encoder settings and have confidence in the output file quality.

But what do you do when you are not sure of the final quality or you want to experiment with different targets to find the perfect match for your source media? Encoding multiple test compressions of a two-hour movie is not an efficient use of your time. Fortunately, Compressor supports real-time previews and test-render workflows that accurately represent the final output quality without requiring you to encode an entire movie.

Viewing Real-Time Previews

The Preview window displays real-time playback of source media originating from QuickTime files, Motion projects, or Final Cut Pro sequences. Additionally, target settings applied to source media will play back in real time with some limitations. Selecting source media or targets in the Batch window automatically loads the content into an active Preview window. If the Preview window is currently closed, choose Window > Preview or click the Preview button on the Batch window Toolbar.

Jump the playhead to a specific timecode by entering it into the timecode field. The up- and down-pointing triangles move the playhead forward and backward one frame at a time. See below for more details.

Click the Preview Scale pop-up menu to set the relative window size based on the pixel dimensions of the source media. Note that this setting has no effect on output file dimensions.

Blind Date.mov
100%
00:01:44:05
00:00:00:00
00:02:59:08
Source: 720x404, 23.98 fps
Duration: 00:02:59.27 (in-out)

Compressor displays the frame size and rate of the source media here.

Use the transport controls to preview the media. In addition to using the transport controls, you can press the Left or Right Arrow keys to move the playhead forward or backward one frame at a time.

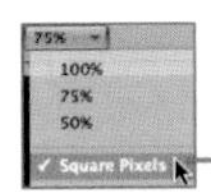
75%
100%
75%
50%
✓ Square Pixels

By default, the Preview window displays square pixels. If you want to display non-square pixels, deselect this option in the Preview Scale pop-up menu.

Placing the pointer over a specific interval value—hours, minutes, seconds, or frames—in the timecode field will display triangles above and below the value. Click the value and drag up or down to increase or decrease the value. For example, to advance the clip by seconds, drag up over the seconds value.

Click the Input/Output pop-up menu to choose among all the targets and media in the Batch window.

See Chapter 1 for a full explanation of the Source/Setting selection button.

Preview
MPEG-2 6.2Mbps 2-pass
100%
00:01:44:05
00:00:00:00
00:02:59:08
Source: 720x404, 23.98 fps
Duration: 00:02:59.27 (in-out)

Source media display

During playback, Compressor encodes frames on the fly and displays a real-time preview of the applied target settings on the right side of the split screen.

Drag the slider to the left or right to preview different sections of the media with the applied target. Move the slider during pause or playback. Compressor will dynamically adjust the real-time preview.

Preview
MPEG-2 6.2Mbps 2-pas
100%
Adjust the Source and Destination split
00:01:44:05
00:00:00:00
00:02:59:08
Source: 720x404, 23.98 fps
Duration: 00:02:59.27 (In-out)

The presence of the Split Screen slider indicates that a target is loaded into the Preview window.

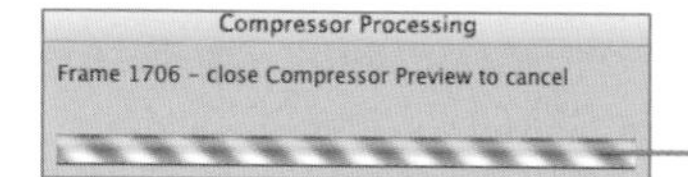
Compressor Processing
Frame 1706 – close Compressor Preview to cancel

If you exported a sequence directly from Final Cut Pro and have opened the sequence in the Preview window (or opened a target applied to the sequence), you will see this message in Final Cut Pro.

NOTE ▶ To release Final Cut Pro from sending the rendered frames to Compressor and re-enabling Final Cut Pro as an editor, close the Preview window.

Setting changes made in the Encoder pane of the Inspector window will update dynamically on the right side of the Preview window.

Source media

Source media with applied target

The Preview window updates dynamically to reflect any adjustments made in the Filters or Geometry panes, as well as changes made in the Encoder pane.

NOTE ▶ Changes made to parameters in the Frame Controls pane of any preset will not appear in the Preview window. Frame Controls options can be viewed only by encoding those settings into output media.

Encoding Test Clips

Viewing real-time previews on your computer screen is especially useful for testing presets destined for formats that use the RGB color space, such as movies for the web or CD-ROM. Non-RGB formats such as DVD, however, are often best tested in their native environments to verify output quality. During the authoring process, you can significantly improve your efficiency, as well as your quality control, by applying targets to small sections of the source media, encoding the batch, and then burning the results to DVD for playback. Test encoding 30 to 60 seconds of source media is often more than enough material to evaluate settings that, once approved, can then be applied to the entire source media—and it is much faster than processing a full 30- to 60-minute movie.

Testing a Single Section

The first step when creating test clips is to define the section of the imported source media that you want to encode with single or multiple target settings.

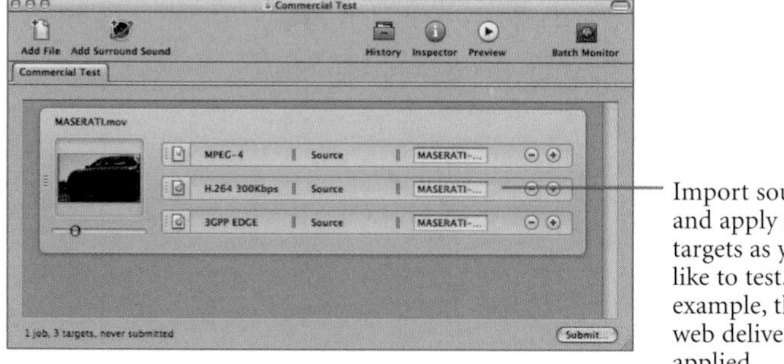
Commercial Test
Add File
Add Surround Sound
History
Inspector
Preview
Batch Monitor
Commercial Test
MASERATI.mov
MPEG-4
Source
MASERATI-...
H.264 300Kbps
Source
MASERATI-...
3GPP EDGE
Source
MASERATI-...
1 job, 3 targets, never submitted
Submit...

Import source media and apply as many targets as you would like to test. In this example, three different web delivery targets are applied.

Next, select the job—not any of the targets—to load it into the Preview window. Use the Preview window to set In and Out points that limit the duration of the test range; by default, all clips have their In and Out points set at the beginning and the end of the media.

The fastest way to set In and Out points is to scrub the playhead to your desired In point location and press I on the keyboard to set the In point. Set the Out point by scrubbing the playhead and pressing O at the desired end frame.

Use the following procedure as a more precise way to set In and Out points:

Use the Timecode field to find the exact frames for the In and Out points, either by manually entering the timecode or by clicking the triangles at each end of the field to move the playhead forward or backward one frame at at time.

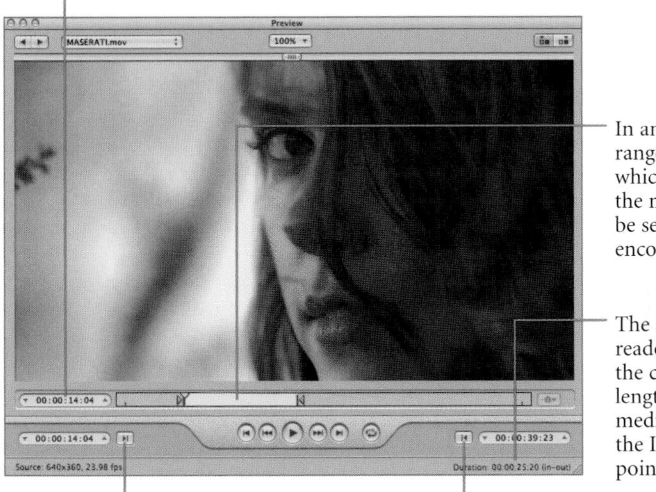
Preview
MASERATI.mov
100%
00:00:14:04
00:00:14:04
00:00:39:23
Source: 640x360, 23.98 fps
Duration: 00:00:25:20 (in-out)

In and Out range defines which section of the media will be sent to the encoder.

The Duration readout displays the current length of the media between the In and Out points.

When the playhead is parked on the desired start location, click this button to set an In point. The timecode field to the left will display the In point timecode.

When the playhead is parked on the desired end location, click this button to set an Out point. The timecode field to the right will display the Out point timecode.

The absence of the Split Screen slider indicates that source media is loaded into the Preview window.

Once you have applied targets to test in the Batch window and have defined the output clip's duration in the Preview window, you can submit the entire batch for encoding.

You may need to repeat the previous steps several times to find the best settings for your source media and output format.

When you have determined those final settings, re-import the job from the History window (for more information, see Chapter 1). Apply the target that produced the best output, and make sure that the In and Out points in the Preview window are placed at the beginning and end of the source media. Choose an output destination, make any desired adjustments to the filename, and submit the batch for encoding.

> **TIP** By default, Compressor does not delete batches after they are sent to the encoder. Instead, they remain open in the Batch window. You can resubmit the job with the best test output by modifying the settings of the original job and target in the open batch.

Testing Multiple Sections

You may have source media that changes significantly throughout the program, so testing just one section may not provide a broad enough sample for you to make an accurate determination of a specific target's performance quality.

The trick is to apply the same target to different sections of the source media and then encode the different samples as one batch.

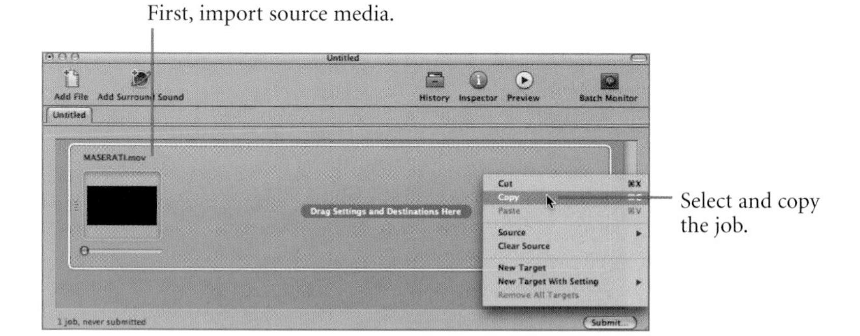
First, import source media.
Untitled
Add File
History
Inspector
Preview
Batch Monitor
MASERATI.mov
Drag Settings and Destinations Here
Cut
Copy
Paste
Source
Clear Source
New Target
New Target With Setting
Remove All Targets
1 job, never submitted
Submit...
Select and copy the job.

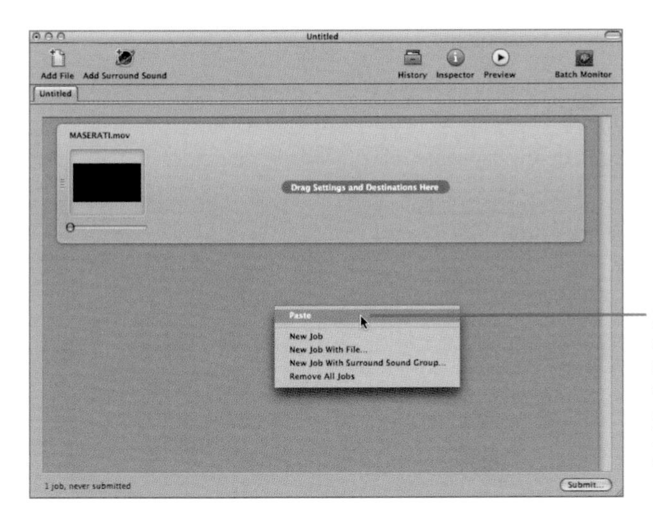
Untitled
Add File
Add Surround Sound
History
Inspector
Preview
Batch Monitor
Untitled
MASERATI.mov
Drag Settings and Destinations Here
Paste
New Job
New Job With File...
New Job With Surround Sound Group...
Remove All Jobs
1 job, never submitted
Submit...

Ensure that the original job is not selected, then Control-click in the Batch tab and choose Paste.

If you have more than two sections to test, continue pasting the source media into the active Batch tab until you've created enough jobs to satisfy all the sections.

Select the first job to open it in the Preview window and then set In and Out points for the first section you want to test. Repeat this process for as many jobs as you want to test, each time defining a different section of the source media.

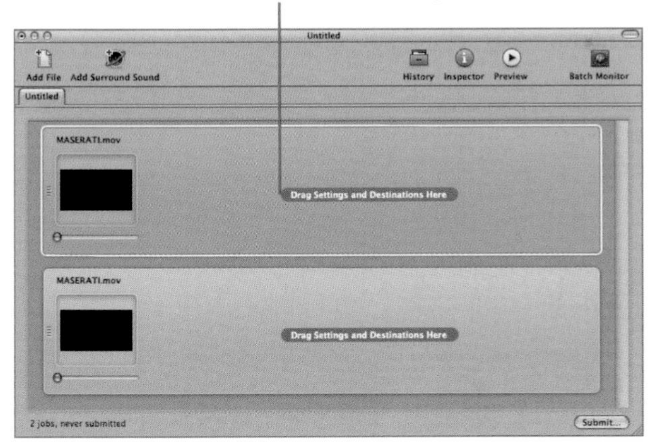
Untitled
Add File
Add Surround Sound
History
Inspector
Preview
Batch Monitor
Untitled
MASERATI.mov
Drag Settings and Destinations Here
MASERATI.mov
Drag Settings and Destinations Here
2 jobs, never submitted
Submit...

In this example, a high action shot and a static aerial shot were defined as the test samples.

You can quickly apply the same target to several jobs in the batch by Command-clicking each job and then choosing Target > New Target With Setting. From the drop-down window, select the target and choose Add. When the batch is ready to encode, click Submit.

Managing Test Clips

Compressor also lets you independently apply multiple targets to each of the test jobs. You could even apply multiple targets to one job and a single target to all the others. The options are many and varied.

Compressor lines up each job in the Batch tab and encodes all your tests one after the other.

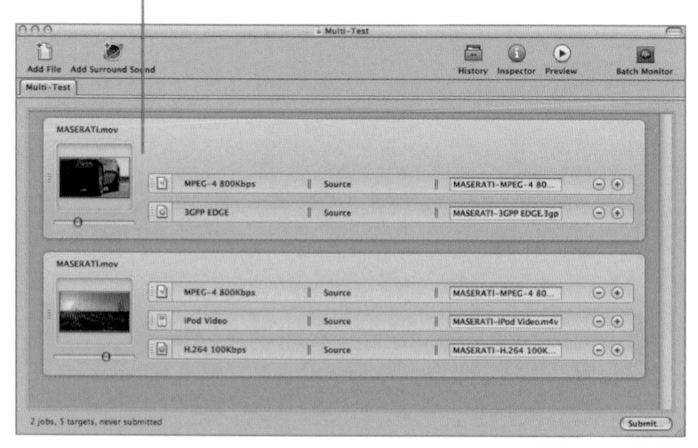
Multi-Test
Add File
Add Surround Sound
History
Inspector
Preview
Batch Monitor
Multi-Test
MASERATI.mov
MPEG-4 800Kbps
Source
MASERATI-MPEG-4 80...
3GPP EDGE
Source
MASERATI-3GPP EDGE.3gp
MASERATI.mov
MPEG-4 800Kbps
Source
MASERATI-MPEG-4 80...
iPod Video
Source
MASERATI-iPod Video.m4v
H.264 100Kbps
Source
MASERATI-H.264 100K...
2 jobs, 5 targets, never submitted
Submit...

Because only 30- to 60-second sections are sent to the encoder, even complex batches compress quickly.

After you find the best target for your delivery requirements, the challenge is managing all the test clips so that you can easily return to Compressor and apply that test clip's target to the entire movie.

You can easily accomplish this by creating custom destinations (see Chapter 4), custom presets (see Chapter 3) and modifying the output filenames so that each test is uniquely identified.

Click the output filename field within a target to modify the name manually.

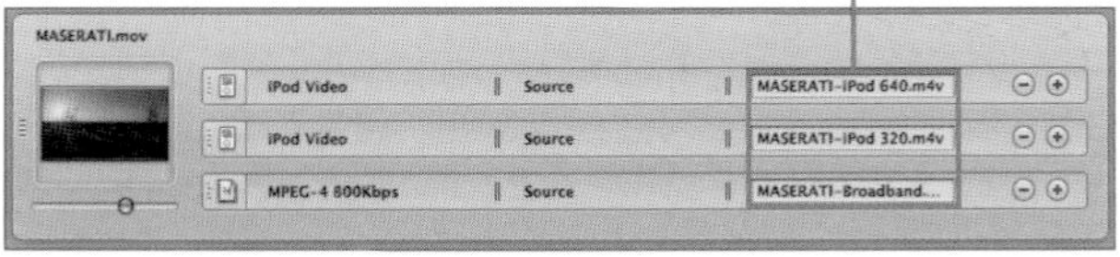

Using the History Window

The History window provides convenient access to previously-encoded jobs and is particularly handy when encoding multiple test clips because you can drag the job that rendered the most successful output back into the Batch window for resubmission. You can also click the Magnifying Glass icon next to a particular job to view the output media in the Finder.

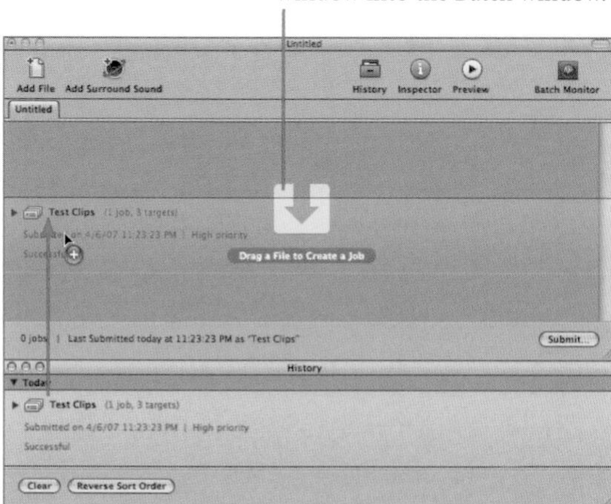
Drag batches directly from the History window into the Batch window.
Untitled
Add File
Add Surround Sound
History
Inspector
Preview
Batch Monitor
Untitled
Test Clips
Drag a File to Create a Job
Submit...
History
Test Clips
Clear
Reverse Sort Order

When the batch is re-imported, delete the targets that did not meet your requirements. When you're ready to export the full source media, make sure to select the job—not one of the targets—and reset the In and Out points of the source media to the beginning and end of the entire clip.

> **TIP** You can expand or collapse batches in the History window by clicking the disclosure triangles or double-clicking the entries in the list.

9

Format Conversions

Format conversions (also known as standards conversions) are the result of transcoding source media from one format into another format.

A golden rule of transcoding is: To achieve the highest quality output media, you should start with source media of equal or higher quality compared to your desired output. For example, you will produce significantly better format conversions when transcoding from HD to SD, from larger frames to smaller frames (such as 1280 x 720 to 320 x 240), and from uncompressed to compressed formats (such as 10-bit to DV) than when transcoding any of those examples in reverse.

Working with Production Codecs

Production codecs provide an intermediate format for transcoded media that lets you retain quality while conforming the media to a post-production workflow standard. In a digital workflow, production codecs perform the same function that dub masters perform in an analog workflow.

Final Cut Studio 2 installs with two very powerful production codecs: Apple ProRes 422 and Apple Intermediate Codec (AIC). Compressor includes four Apple settings for Apple ProRes 422 and three settings for AIC. The Apple ProRes codec was specifically designed for work within the Final Cut Studio 2 environment. It retains very high quality while reducing overall system demands compared to production codecs such as Animation or PhotoJPEG, or camera codecs like DVCProHD or HDV. Apple ProRes offers its highest-quality HD video at approximately 22 megabytes per second, a rate that rivals uncompressed SD video.

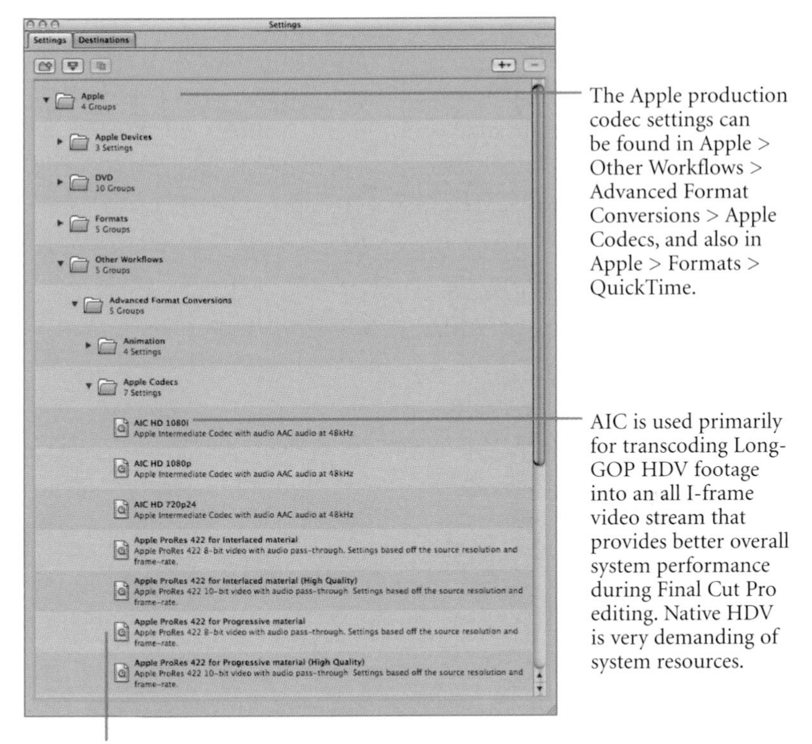
Settings
Settings
Destinations
Apple
4 Groups
Apple Devices
3 Settings
DVD
10 Groups
Formats
5 Groups
Other Workflows
5 Groups
Advanced Format Conversions
5 Groups
Animation
4 Settings
Apple Codecs
7 Settings
AIC HD 1080i
Apple Intermediate Codec with audio AAC audio at 48kHz
AIC HD 1080p
Apple Intermediate Codec with audio AAC audio at 48kHz
AIC HD 720p24
Apple Intermediate Codec with audio AAC audio at 48kHz
Apple ProRes 422 for Interlaced material
Apple ProRes 422 8-bit video with audio pass-through. Settings based off the source resolution and frame-rate.
Apple ProRes 422 for Interlaced material (High Quality)
Apple ProRes 422 10-bit video with audio pass-through. Settings based off the source resolution and frame-rate.
Apple ProRes 422 for Progressive material
Apple ProRes 422 8-bit video with audio pass-through. Settings based off the source resolution and frame-rate.
Apple ProRes 422 for Progressive material (High Quality)
Apple ProRes 422 10-bit video with audio pass-through. Settings based off the source resolution and frame-rate.

The Apple production codec settings can be found in Apple > Other Workflows > Advanced Format Conversions > Apple Codecs, and also in Apple > Formats > QuickTime.

AIC is used primarily for transcoding Long-GOP HDV footage into an all I-frame video stream that provides better overall system performance during Final Cut Pro editing. Native HDV is very demanding of system resources.

The Apple ProRes 422 codec has four settings differentiated by image bit depth—high quality 10-bit video or normal quality 8-bit video—and interlaced or progressive scan. Both settings support a 4:2:2 color space and pass-through audio. The high quality settings produce larger output file sizes than the normal settings.

Using the Apple Intermediate Codec

The Apple Intermediate Codec is specifically designed to create all I-frame video from Long GOP HDV source material. The benefit of working in AIC compared to HDV is better system performance within Final Cut Studio 2.

Apply one of the three AIC settings to an HDV job in the Batch window, and then select the target to open the settings in the Inspector window. The production codecs require little to no configuration and, by default, focus only on the video—the audio passes through unaltered.

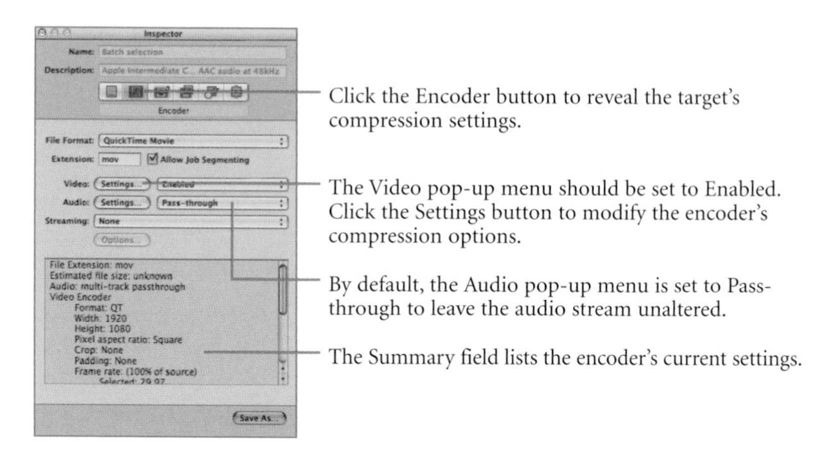
Inspector
File Format: QuickTime Movie
Extension: mov
Allow Job Segmenting
Video: Settings...
Audio: Settings... Pass-through
Streaming: None
Save As...
Click the Encoder button to reveal the target's compression settings.
The Video pop-up menu should be set to Enabled. Click the Settings button to modify the encoder's compression options.
By default, the Audio pop-up menu is set to Pass-through to leave the audio stream unaltered.
The Summary field lists the encoder's current settings.

When you click the Settings button next to the Video pop-up menu, the QuickTime interface window opens.

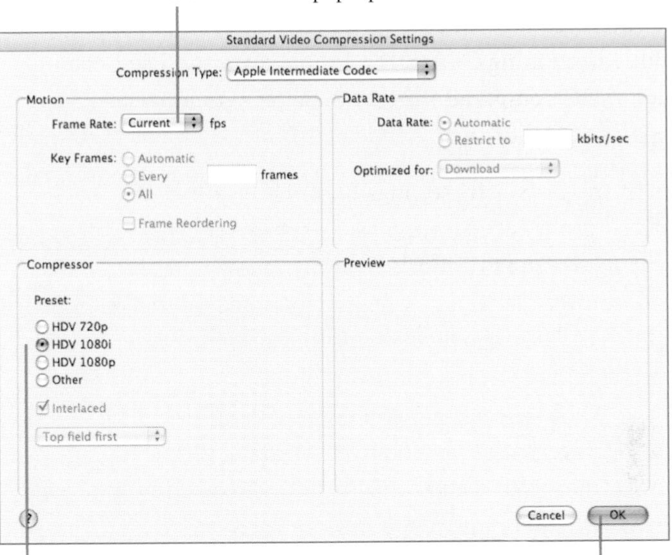
Unless you need to change the frame rate, leave the Frame Rate pop-up menu set to Current.
Standard Video Compression Settings
Compression Type: Apple Intermediate Codec
Motion
Frame Rate: Current fps
Key Frames: Automatic
Every frames
All
Frame Reordering
Data Rate
Data Rate: Automatic
Restrict to kbits/sec
Optimized for: Download
Compressor
Preset:
HDV 720p
HDV 1080i
HDV 1080p
Other
Interlaced
Top field first
Preview
Cancel
OK
The output Compressor settings are based on the source media. In this example, the source is HDV 1080i. If Compressor has not interpreted your source material properly, you can change the setting here.
Click OK when finished to return to the Inspector window.

The Geometry pane in the Inspector window controls the output frame size. The Apple settings automatically set the frame size when you apply the target, but you can manually adjust the dimensions, if necessary.

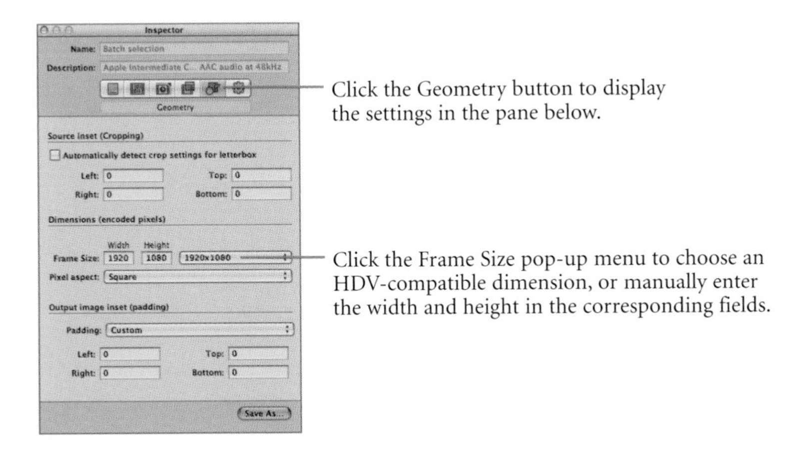
Inspector
Name: Batch selection
Geometry
Source Inset (Cropping)
Automatically detect crop settings for letterbox
Left: 0
Top: 0
Right: 0
Bottom: 0
Dimensions (encoded pixels)
Width Height
Frame Size: 1920 1080 1920x1080
Pixel aspect: Square
Output image inset (padding)
Padding: Custom
Left: 0
Top: 0
Right: 0
Bottom: 0
Save As...
Click the Geometry button to display the settings in the pane below.
Click the Frame Size pop-up menu to choose an HDV-compatible dimension, or manually enter the width and height in the corresponding fields.

Using Apple ProRes 422

Four Apple ProRes 422 settings are provided in Compressor: Interlaced, Interlaced (High Quality), Progressive, and Progressive (High Quality). The base settings encode to 8-bit video resolution while the high quality settings encode to 10-bit video. The high quality settings output larger files. As with AIC, the audio is passed unaltered through the encoding process by default.

When choosing an Apple ProRes 422 setting, base your choice on your desired output quality and whether you need interlaced or progressive video. For example, if you want to transcode camera-native progressive HD footage from production into the highest quality format for use when editing, you could apply the "Apple ProRes 422 for Progressive material (High Quality)" setting to all the footage. This would retain overall picture quality, frame size, and frame rate; but would create media requiring significantly less system overheard when editing in Final Cut Pro.

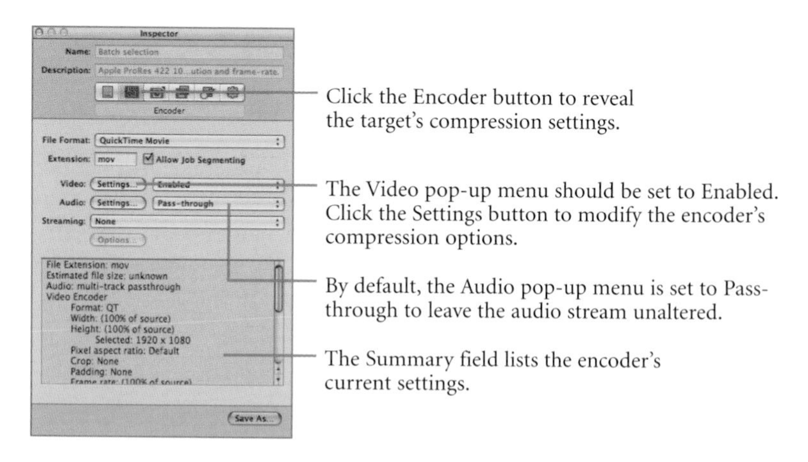
Inspector
Name: Batch selection
Encoder
File Format: QuickTime Movie
Extension: mov
Allow Job Segmenting
Video: Settings... Enabled
Audio: Settings... Pass-through
Streaming: None
Options...
File Extension: mov
Estimated file size: unknown
Audio: multi-track passthrough
Video Encoder
Format: QT
Width: (100% of source)
Height: (100% of source)
Selected: 1920 x 1080
Pixel aspect ratio: Default
Crop: None
Padding: None
Save As...
Click the Encoder button to reveal the target's compression settings.
The Video pop-up menu should be set to Enabled. Click the Settings button to modify the encoder's compression options.
By default, the Audio pop-up menu is set to Pass-through to leave the audio stream unaltered.
The Summary field lists the encoder's current settings.

When you click the Settings button next to the Video pop-up menu, the QuickTime interface window opens.

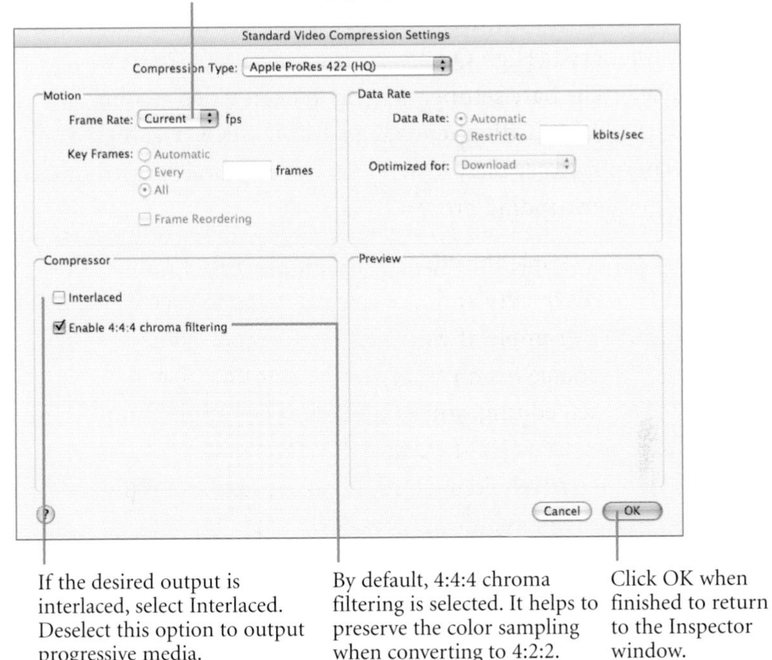
Unless you need to change the frame rate, leave the Frame Rate pop-up menu set to Current.
Standard Video Compression Settings
Compression Type: Apple ProRes 422 (HQ)
Motion
Frame Rate: Current fps
Key Frames: Automatic
Every frames
All
Frame Reordering
Data Rate
Data Rate: Automatic
Restrict to kbits/sec
Optimized for: Download
Compressor
Interlaced
Enable 4:4:4 chroma filtering
Preview
Cancel
OK
If the desired output is interlaced, select Interlaced. Deselect this option to output progressive media.
By default, 4:4:4 chroma filtering is selected. It helps to preserve the color sampling when converting to 4:2:2.
Click OK when finished to return to the Inspector window.

By default, all of the Apple ProRes 422 settings set the output frame size to 100% of the source media, meaning that output frame size will equal the input frame size. If you need to change the output frame size, you can do so in the Geometry pane.

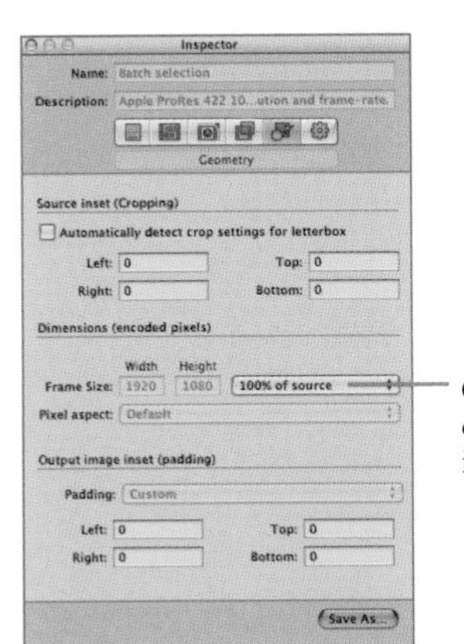
Inspector
Name: Batch selection
Geometry
Source inset (Cropping)
Automatically detect crop settings for letterbox
Left: 0
Top: 0
Right: 0
Bottom: 0
Dimensions (encoded pixels)
Width
Height
Frame Size: 1920 1080 100% of source
Pixel aspect: Default
Output image inset (padding)
Padding: Custom
Left: 0
Top: 0
Right: 0
Bottom: 0
Save As...

Click the Frame Size pop-up menu to choose the output dimensions. Choose Custom to manually input values in the Width and Height fields.

Creating HD to SD DVD Downconversions

Material shot in any HD format (including HDV) has stunning quality compared to SD video formats. The downside is that HD formats currently have far fewer distribution options than SD. However, Compressor can downconvert HD into SD formats destined for tape, digital, or DVD delivery.

Creating SD DVD assets from HD material follows most of the method for DVD creation outlined in Chapter 5, with just a few modifications.

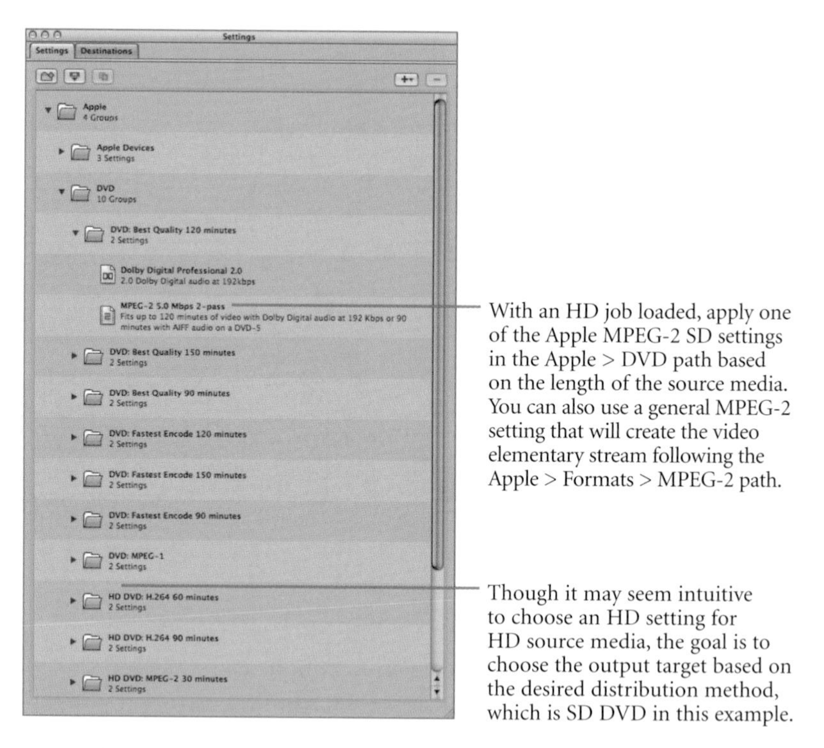
Settings
Settings
Destinations
Apple
4 Groups
Apple Devices
3 Settings
DVD
10 Groups
DVD: Best Quality 120 minutes
2 Settings
Dolby Digital Professional 2.0
2.0 Dolby Digital audio at 192kbps
MPEG-2 5.0 Mbps 2-pass
Fits up to 120 minutes of video with Dolby Digital audio at 192 Kbps or 90 minutes with AIFF audio on a DVD-5
DVD: Best Quality 150 minutes
2 Settings
DVD: Best Quality 90 minutes
2 Settings
DVD: Fastest Encode 120 minutes
2 Settings
DVD: Fastest Encode 150 minutes
2 Settings
DVD: Fastest Encode 90 minutes
2 Settings
DVD: MPEG-1
2 Settings
HD DVD: H.264 60 minutes
2 Settings
HD DVD: H.264 90 minutes
2 Settings
HD DVD: MPEG-2 30 minutes
2 Settings

With an HD job loaded, apply one of the Apple MPEG-2 SD settings in the Apple > DVD path based on the length of the source media. You can also use a general MPEG-2 setting that will create the video elementary stream following the Apple > Formats > MPEG-2 path.

Though it may seem intuitive to choose an HD setting for HD source media, the goal is to choose the output target based on the desired distribution method, which is SD DVD in this example.

Open the applied target in the Inspector window by selecting it from the job in the Batch window.

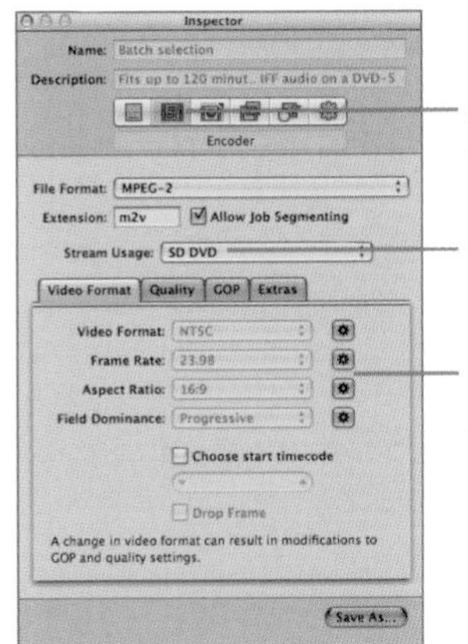
Inspector
Name: Batch selection
Description: Fits up to 120 minut...IFF audio on a DVD-5
Encoder
File Format: MPEG-2
Extension: m2v
Allow Job Segmenting
Stream Usage: SD DVD
Video Format
Quality
GOP
Extras
Video Format: NTSC
Frame Rate: 23.98
Aspect Ratio: 16:9
Field Dominance: Progressive
Choose start timecode
Drop Frame
A change in video format can result in modifications to GOP and quality settings.
Save As...

Click the Encoder button to reveal the MPEG-2 settings.

Note that the Stream Usage pop-up menu is set for SD DVD, the desired output platform.

Ensure that all of the Automatic buttons are selected.

When an Automatic button is selected, its corresponding pop-up menu will be dimmed. However, the menus will still display Compressor's assessment of the source media format.

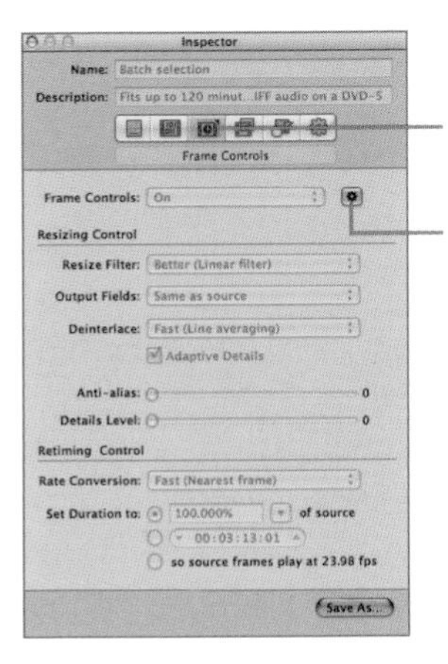
Inspector
Name: Batch selection
Description: Fits up to 120 minut...IFF audio on a DVD-5
Frame Controls
Frame Controls: On
Resizing Control
Resize Filter: Better (Linear filter)
Output Fields: Same as source
Deinterlace: Fast (Line averaging)
Adaptive Details
Anti-alias: 0
Details Level: 0
Retiming Control
Rate Conversion: Fast (Nearest frame)
Set Duration to: 100.000% of source
00:03:13:01
so source frames play at 23.98 fps
Save As...

Click the Frame Controls button to view the Optical Flow settings.

Ensure that the Automatic button is selected. When this button is selected, all the options below will be dimmed, but the menus will still display Compressor's assessment of how to apply Frame Controls to the source media during encoding.

Based on your encoding needs, you can add any Filters or Actions and then submit the batch for encoding.

HD material takes considerably longer to compress, compared to encoding SD material for SD DVD. In addition to applying the MPEG-2 codec, Compressor conforms the frame size of the HD source media to the standard 720 x 480 DVD resolution using Frame Controls.

Creating Advanced Format Conversions

In addition to downconverting HD material to SD DVDs, Compressor offers several presets that convert HD source media to SD media, and vice versa, using QuickTime container files.

Compressor also produces high-quality cross-conversions. For example, NTSC and PAL are SD formats that differ in frame rate and frame size. Converting from one to the other requires retiming and reframing—two operations that benefit greatly from the Optical Flow technology contained within Compressor's Frame Controls pane (see Chapter 10).

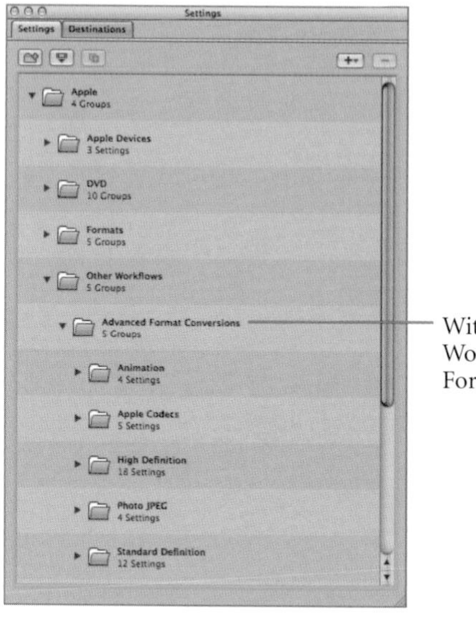
Settings
Settings
Destinations
Apple
4 Groups
Apple Devices
3 Settings
DVD
10 Groups
Formats
5 Groups
Other Workflows
5 Groups
Advanced Format Conversions
5 Groups
Animation
4 Settings
Apple Codecs
5 Settings
High Definition
18 Settings
Photo JPEG
4 Settings
Standard Definition
12 Settings

Within the Apple group, in the Other Workflows path, is the Advanced Format Conversion folder.

The following table describes each of the settings contained in the five Advanced Format Conversions groups:

Group	Setting	Use
Animation	Animation NTSC, PAL	Lossless, high-quality codec used in CGI, motion graphics, titles, and so on. Includes workflows in both the NTSC and PAL frame sizes and rates.
Animation	Animation NTSC, PAL (Alpha)	Adds an alpha channel for transparency.
Apple Codecs	AIC and Apple ProRes 422	Refer to the sections in this chapter that cover these production codecs.
High Definition	DVCPro HD: 1080i/50, 1080i/60, 720p/24 and 720p/60	Panasonic High Definition codec. Choose a setting based on the output frame size and frame rate. For example, choose the DVCPro HD 720p/24 setting to output a 1280 x 720 movie with 24 progressive frames per second, compressed using the DVCPro HD codec.
High Definition	HD Uncompressed 10-bit: 1080i/50, 1080i/60, and 1080p/24	Uncompressed high definition codec using 10-bit video. Choose a setting based on output frame size and rate.
High Definition	HD Uncompressed 8-bit: 1080i/50, 1080i/60, and 1080p/24	Uncompressed high definition codec using 8-bit video. Choose a setting based on output frame size and rate.
High Definition	HDV: 1080i/50, 1080i/60, 720p/30	High definition codec that uses Long GOP MPEG-2 compression. Used in Sony and JVC video cameras. Choose a setting based on frame size and output hardware compatibility.
Photo JPEG	JPEG 100 NTSC, PAL	High quality, intraframe compression codec used in post-production. Choose a setting based on output format: NTSC or PAL.
Photo JPEG	PEG 75 NTSC, PAL	Good quality with smaller output file sizes than JPEG 100. Choose a setting based on output format: NTSC or PAL.

Standard Definition	DV NTSC, PAL	Common production and post-production codec that provides good quality with low resource overhead. Choose a setting based on output format: NTSC or PAL.
Standard Definition	DV NTSC, PAL (Anamorphic)	Widescreen (16:9) version of the settings.
Standard Definition	DVCPro 50 NTSC, PAL	Panasonic codec with video quality similar to DigiBeta and double the file size and resource requirements of DV. Choose a setting based on output format: NTSC or PAL.
Standard Definition	DVCPro 50 NTSC, PAL (Anamorphic)	Widescreen (16:9) version of the settings.
Standard Definition	SD 10-bit Uncompressed NTSC, PAL	High quality post-production codec commonly used to digitize analog sources and as a common editorial format. Choose a setting based on output format: NTSC or PAL.
Standard Definition	SD 8-bit Uncompressed NTSC, PAL	Codec that balances good video quality with lower resource requirements than 10-bit. Choose a setting based on output format: NTSC or PAL.

All of the Advanced Format Conversion settings are modified in QuickTime windows via the Inspector window.

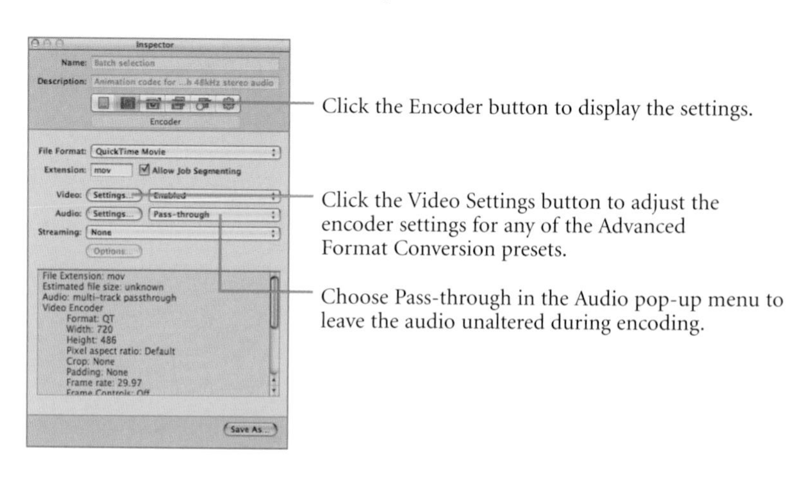
Inspector
Name:
Description:
Encoder
File Format:
QuickTime Movie
Extension:
mov
Allow Job Segmenting
Video:
Settings...
Audio:
Settings...
Pass-through
Streaming:
None
Options...
Save As...
Click the Encoder button to display the settings.
Click the Video Settings button to adjust the encoder settings for any of the Advanced Format Conversion presets.
Choose Pass-through in the Audio pop-up menu to leave the audio unaltered during encoding.

The QuickTime window provides access to all of the codec settings for the Advanced Format Conversion presets. The window is divided into four sections: Motion, Data Rate, Compressor, and Preview.

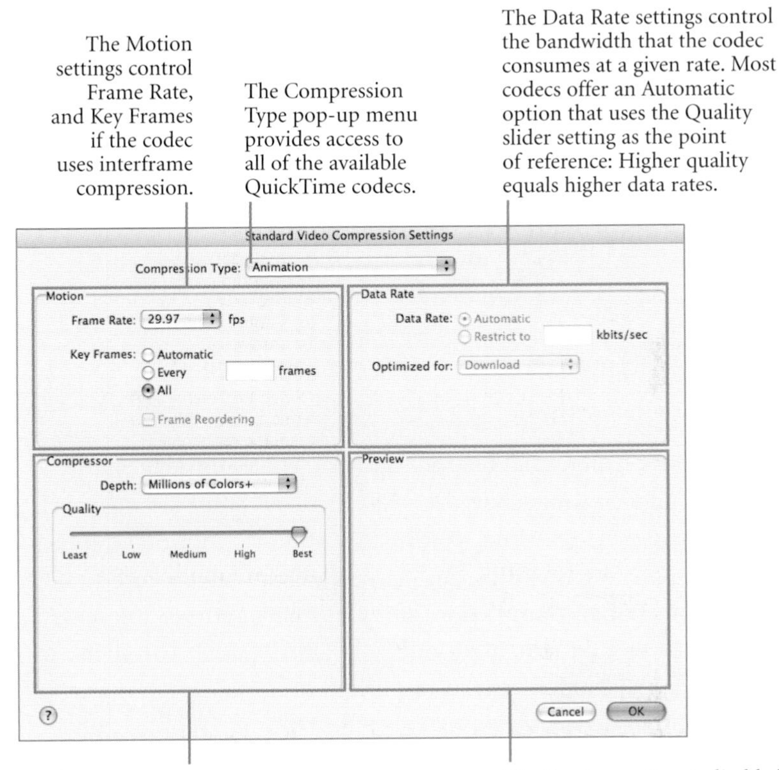
The Motion settings control Frame Rate, and Key Frames if the codec uses interframe compression.
The Compression Type pop-up menu provides access to all of the available QuickTime codecs.
The Data Rate settings control the bandwidth that the codec consumes at a given rate. Most codecs offer an Automatic option that uses the Quality slider setting as the point of reference: Higher quality equals higher data rates.
Standard Video Compression Settings
Compression Type: Animation
Motion
Frame Rate: 29.97 fps
Key Frames: Automatic
Every
frames
All
Frame Reordering
Data Rate
Data Rate: Automatic
Restrict to
kbits/sec
Optimized for: Download
Compressor
Depth: Millions of Colors+
Quality
Least
Low
Medium
High
Best
Preview
Cancel
OK

The Compressor section controls the primary encoder functions. Each Advanced Format Conversion codec may display different controls.

The Preview section is disabled when accessing the QuickTime window via Compressor. Use Compressor's Preview window for a real-time display.

TIP When working with the QuickTime encoder settings, two common rules apply: First, higher data rates produce greater quality at the expense of increased file size. Second, fewer keyframes produce greater quality but at the expense of increased file size.

Any format conversion that includes a change in frame rate or frame size—transcoding from HD to SD, for example—will benefit greatly from Compressor's Frame Controls.

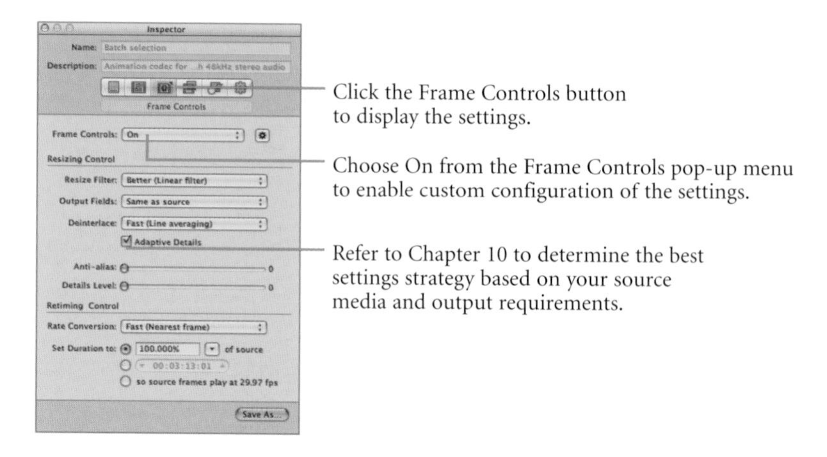
Inspector
Name:
Description:
Frame Controls
Frame Controls: On
Resizing Control
Resize Filter: Better (Linear filter)
Output Fields: Same as source
Deinterlace: Fast (Line averaging)
Adaptive Details
Anti-alias:
Details Level:
Retiming Control
Rate Conversion: Fast (Nearest frame)
Set Duration to: 100.000% of source
so source frames play at 29.97 fps
Save As...
Click the Frame Controls button to display the settings.
Choose On from the Frame Controls pop-up menu to enable custom configuration of the settings.
Refer to Chapter 10 to determine the best settings strategy based on your source media and output requirements.

In the Presets window, across the top level Apple setting groups, you will find that some codecs are repeated and some settings overlap. For example, the Apple > Other Workflows > Motion Graphics folder contains many of the same settings as the Advanced Format Conversions folder. Compressor provides many paths to the same settings that will ultimately produce the same results. Although each folder may contain settings found in other folders, it may also contain unique settings. For instance, the Motion Graphics folder contains two unique Pixlet settings, in addition to several settings also found in the Advanced Format Conversions folder. The Pixlet codec is used almost exclusively by animators and motion graphic artists as a production codec and is of little use elsewhere.

Converting Video into Image Sequences

In addition to transcoding video from one format to another, you can also use Compressor to create still images from motion video. When working on effects shots or complex composites, you may need to convert media into a series of individual frames—also known as an image sequence. Compressor does not contain an Apple setting for creating image sequences, so you'll have to create a custom setting for this purpose.

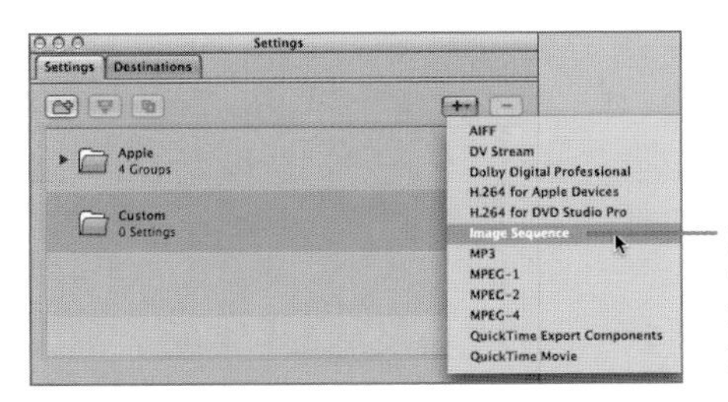
Settings
Settings
Destinations
Apple
4 Groups
Custom
0 Settings
AIFF
DV Stream
Dolby Digital Professional
H.264 for Apple Devices
H.264 for DVD Studio Pro
Image Sequence
MP3
MPEG-1
MPEG-2
MPEG-4
QuickTime Export Components
QuickTime Movie

In the Settings tab of the Presets window, choose Image Sequence from the "Create a new setting" pop-up menu.

A new custom setting will appear in the Custom folder. Select it to load it into the Inspector window.

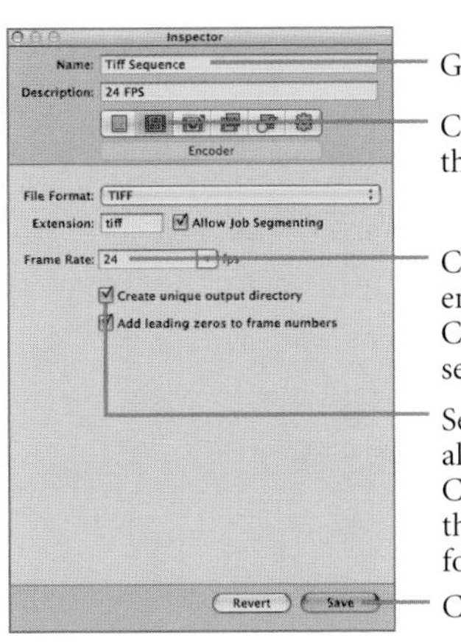
Inspector
Name: Tiff Sequence
Description: 24 FPS
Encoder
File Format: TIFF
Extension: tiff
Allow Job Segmenting
Frame Rate: 24
fps
Create unique output directory
Add leading zeros to frame numbers
Revert
Save

Give the new custom setting a name and description.

Click the Encoder button to display the settings for TIFF export.

Choose a frame rate from the pop-up menu or enter a specific value into the field. This value tells Compressor how many stills to make for each second of source video it processes.

Select "Create unique output directory" to place all stills (perhaps thousands) in a new folder that Compressor will create during processing. All the frames will be labeled with the word "frame" followed by the frame number.

Click to save the settings.

You can apply this custom setting to jobs just like any Apple setting.

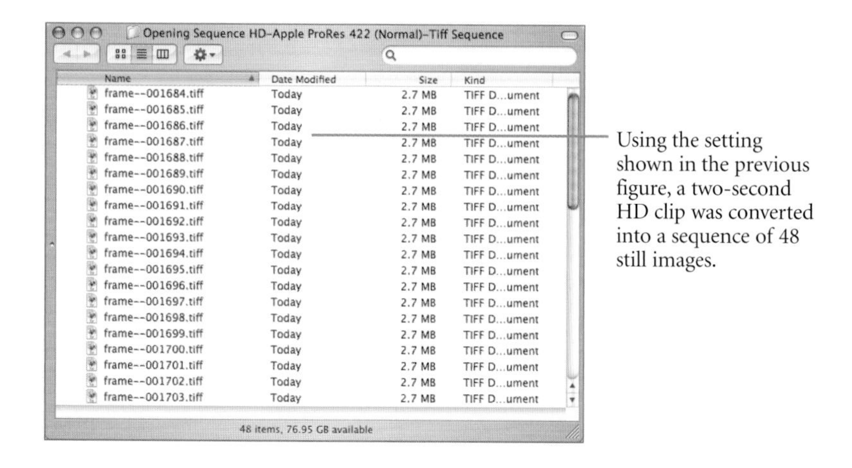
Opening Sequence HD-Apple ProRes 422 (Normal)-Tiff Sequence
Name
Date Modified
Size
Kind
frame--001684.tiff Today 2.7 MB TIFF D...ument
frame--001685.tiff Today 2.7 MB TIFF D...ument
frame--001686.tiff Today 2.7 MB TIFF D...ument
frame--001687.tiff Today 2.7 MB TIFF D...ument
frame--001688.tiff Today 2.7 MB TIFF D...ument
frame--001689.tiff Today 2.7 MB TIFF D...ument
frame--001690.tiff Today 2.7 MB TIFF D...ument
frame--001691.tiff Today 2.7 MB TIFF D...ument
frame--001692.tiff Today 2.7 MB TIFF D...ument
frame--001693.tiff Today 2.7 MB TIFF D...ument
frame--001694.tiff Today 2.7 MB TIFF D...ument
frame--001695.tiff Today 2.7 MB TIFF D...ument
frame--001696.tiff Today 2.7 MB TIFF D...ument
frame--001697.tiff Today 2.7 MB TIFF D...ument
frame--001698.tiff Today 2.7 MB TIFF D...ument
frame--001699.tiff Today 2.7 MB TIFF D...ument
frame--001700.tiff Today 2.7 MB TIFF D...ument
frame--001701.tiff Today 2.7 MB TIFF D...ument
frame--001702.tiff Today 2.7 MB TIFF D...ument
frame--001703.tiff Today 2.7 MB TIFF D...ument
48 items, 76.95 GB available

Using the setting shown in the previous figure, a two-second HD clip was converted into a sequence of 48 still images.

NOTE ▶ The output TIFFs will have the same frame size as the source media. So, if the source media is HD 1080p, the resulting TIFF images will be at a 1920 x 1080 pixel resolution.

Using QuickTime Components

Compressor can encode content using third-party codecs outside the QuickTime format via the QuickTime components plug-in architecture. This delivers huge time savings because you can stay within the Mac system environment, and also within Compressor, itself, when encoding for these alternative platforms.

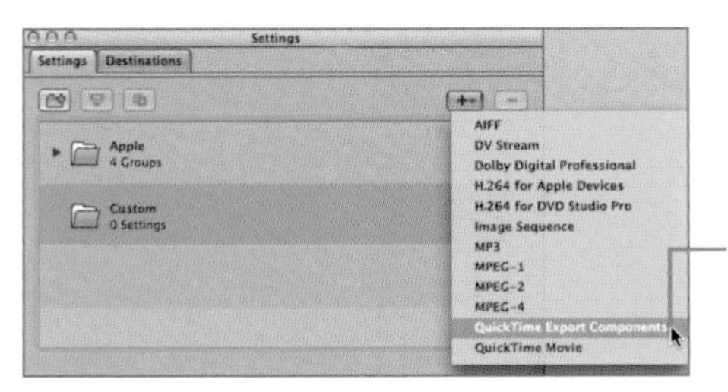
Settings
Settings
Destinations
Apple
4 Groups
Custom
0 Settings
AIFF
DV Stream
Dolby Digital Professional
H.264 for Apple Devices
H.264 for DVD Studio Pro
Image Sequence
MP3
MPEG-1
MPEG-2
MPEG-4
QuickTime Export Components
QuickTime Movie

In the Presets window, click the "Create a new setting" pop-up menu, and choose QuickTime Export Components.

In addition to using the Mobile Devices (3GPP) presets in the Apple folder, you can create custom QuickTime component presets.

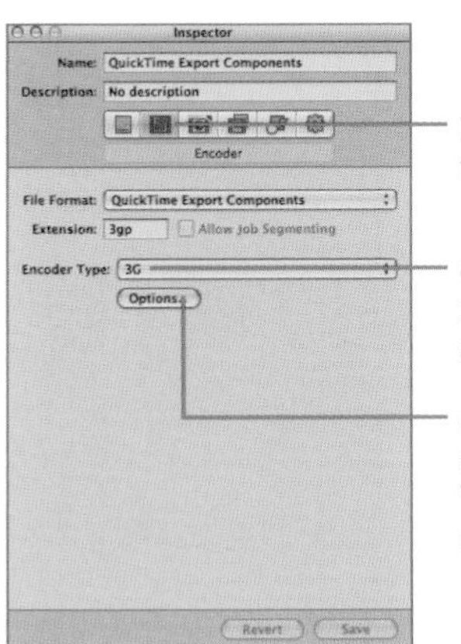
Inspector
Name: QuickTime Export Components
Description: No description
Encoder
File Format: QuickTime Export Components
Extension: 3gp
Allow Job Segmenting
Encoder Type: 3G
Options...
Revert
Save

Load a custom preset into the Inspector window to make changes to the settings.

Compressor installs three Encoder Type components: 3G (for cell phones), iPod (for iPods with video), and AVI (for Windows-based content).

Click the Options button to open the QuickTime settings interface for the individual components. When you're using third-party plug-ins, the interface may vary greatly from component to component.

Because you set all the options in the third-party codec's separate interface, none of the settings are available in the Frame Controls or Geometry panes.

Encoding with Flip4Mac

You can install the Flip4MacQuickTime plugin from Telestream (www.flip4mac.com) and create a custom QuickTime component setting in Compressor. The Flip4Mac codec will appear in the Inspector window in the Encoder Type pop-up menu as "Windows Media". Just as with the other QuickTime components, you can access all of the Flip4Mac settings by clicking the Options button.

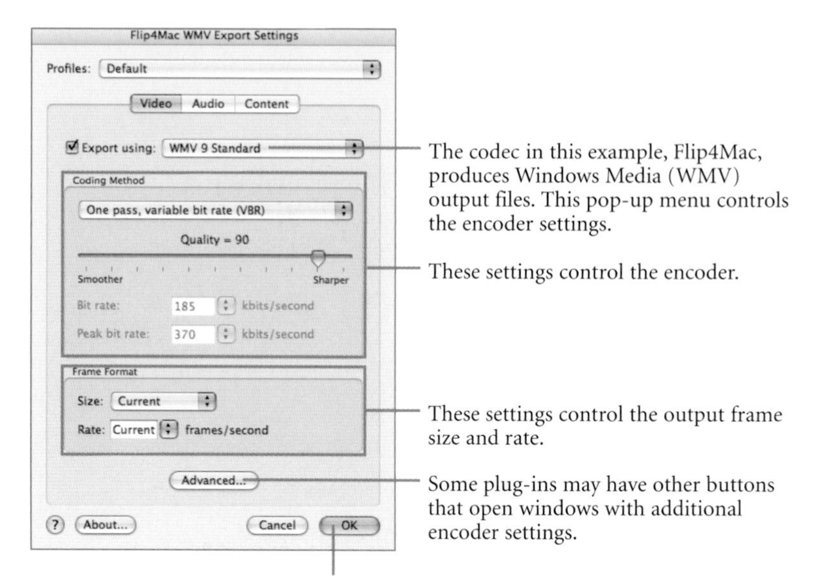
Flip4Mac WMV Export Settings
Profiles: Default
Video
Audio
Content
Export using: WMV 9 Standard
Coding Method
One pass, variable bit rate (VBR)
Quality = 90
Smoother
Sharper
Bit rate: 185 kbits/second
Peak bit rate: 370 kbits/second
Frame Format
Size: Current
Rate: Current frames/second
Advanced...
About...
Cancel
OK
The codec in this example, Flip4Mac, produces Windows Media (WMV) output files. This pop-up menu controls the encoder settings.
These settings control the encoder.
These settings control the output frame size and rate.
Some plug-ins may have other buttons that open windows with additional encoder settings.
When you finish modifying the settings, click OK to save the settings and return to the Inspector window.

Apply QuickTime component presets just as you would apply any other preset to a job in the Batch window.

NOTE ▸ QuickTime component settings may create files that encode correctly for the target platform but do not play in QuickTime Player.

Consult the Compressor support pages on the Apple website (www.apple.com/support/compressor) to verify the compatibility of third-party plug-ins.

Encoding with Episode

Telestream's Episode (www.flip4mac.com) encodes to a wide range of codecs like Flash, VC1, and Windows Media. Compressor can use Episode's presets when you create custom settings.

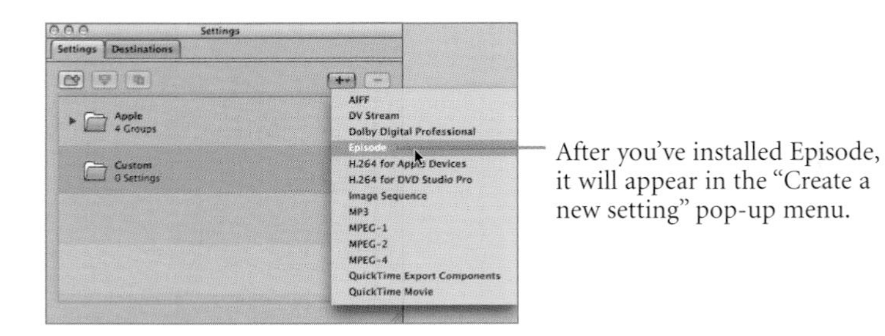
Settings
Settings
Destinations
Apple
4 Groups
Custom
0 Settings
AIFF
DV Stream
Dolby Digital Professional
Episode
H.264 for DVD Studio Pro
Image Sequence
MP3
MPEG-1
MPEG-2
MPEG-4
QuickTime Export Components
QuickTime Movie

After you've installed Episode, it will appear in the "Create a new setting" pop-up menu.

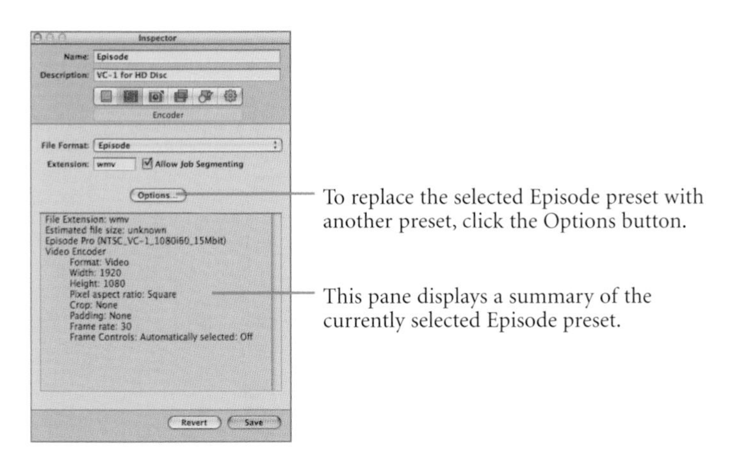
Inspector
Name: Episode
Description: VC-1 for HD Disc
Encoder
File Format: Episode
Extension: wmv
Allow Job Segmenting
Options...
File Extension: wmv
Estimated file size: unknown
Episode Pro (NTSC_VC-1_1080i60_15Mbit)
Video Encoder
Format: Video
Width: 1920
Height: 1080
Pixel aspect ratio: Square
Crop: None
Padding: None
Frame rate: 30
Frame Controls: Automatically selected: Off
Revert
Save

To replace the selected Episode preset with another preset, click the Options button.

This pane displays a summary of the currently selected Episode preset.

After you click Options, the following drop-down window appears:

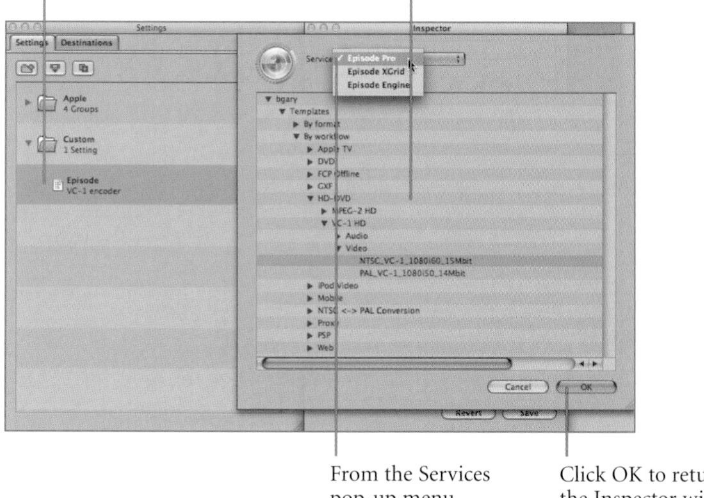
A customized Episode setting in the Custom folder of the Presets window.
In the Presets table, choose a preset from the “By format” or “By workflow” lists.
From the Services pop-up menu, choose Episode Pro.
Click OK to return to the Inspector window.

You can add custom Episode settings to jobs in the Batch window just as you can add any Apple or custom setting.

> **NOTE ▸** To modify the Episode presets or to create custom Episode presets, you will need to work within Episode, itself.

10

Working with Frame Controls and Filters

Frame controls and filters let you augment the encoding process performed by individual codecs. Frame controls implement more advanced technology when converting video formats. Filters can add visual elements, such as watermarks and timecode burns, and can also perform general modifications to the video image. Frame controls and filters function as separate tasks during encoding, apart from the target's codec. You can control this added layer of processing by implementing the job chaining tactics discussed in Chapter 4.

Using Frame Controls

Frame controls employ optical flow technology (also used in Apple's Shake), which calculates motion tracking for every pixel vector as it goes from one movie frame to the next. When that calculation is completed for a given frame rate and frame size, Compressor can more intelligently place those pixels in different frame rates and sizes during a conversion. Compared to inferior conversion techniques like blending and scaling, optical flow produces amazing results, but the massive increases in quality come at the expense of lengthy encoding times.

Frame controls are most useful when converting from one video format (standard) to another requires a conversion of frame size and/or rate, such as converting NTSC footage (720 x 480 at 29.97fps) to PAL (720 x 546 at 25fps). Frame controls can also improve conversions between interlaced and progressive video. You can achieve broadcast-level transcoding in Compressor at levels of quality previously reserved for hardware-only converters. As a general rule, though, when working with frame controls, you have to choose between higher quality and faster encoding.

You access frame controls in the Inspector window by selecting a target from the Batch window.

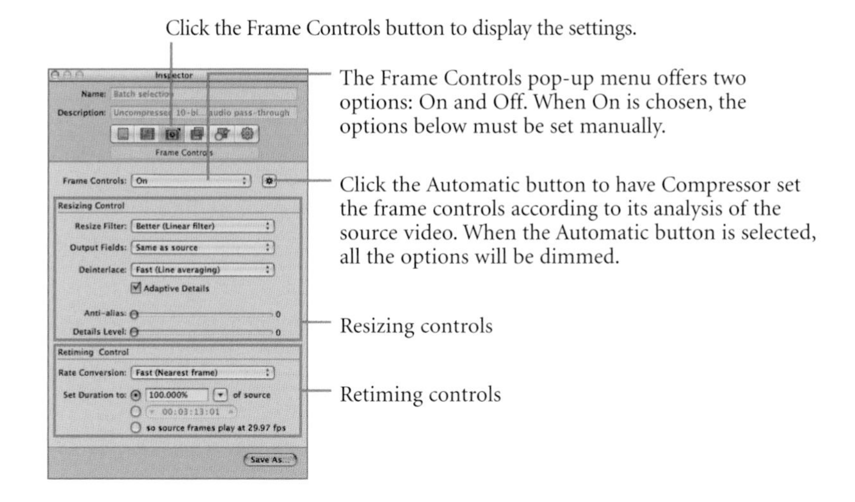
Click the Frame Controls button to display the settings.
The Frame Controls pop-up menu offers two options: On and Off. When On is chosen, the options below must be set manually.
Click the Automatic button to have Compressor set the frame controls according to its analysis of the source video. When the Automatic button is selected, all the options will be dimmed.
Resizing controls
Retiming controls
Inspector
Frame Controls:
On
Resizing Control
Resize Filter:
Better (Linear filter)
Output Fields:
Same as source
Deinterlace:
Fast (Line averaging)
Adaptive Details
Anti-alias:
Details Level:
Retiming Control
Rate Conversion:
Fast (Nearest frame)
Set Duration to:
100.000%
of source
so source frames play at 29.97 fps
Save As...

NOTE ▸ The Automatic option works in only three instances: HD to SD MPEG-2 downconversions, H.264 encoding for Apple devices, and H.264 encoding for DVD Studio Pro. For all other instances you will need to create custom settings. From the Frame Controls pop-up menu, choose On and deselect the Automatic button.

Resizing Controls

When source media is transformed from one frame size to another—in converting HD footage to SD, for example—the resizing controls can significantly increase the conversion quality.

The Output Fields and Deinterlace pop-up menus work together to control conversions between interlaced and progressive footage. If you choose "Same as source" in the Output Fields pop-up menu, for example, no conversion will occur, and Compressor will ignore the Deinterlace option. If you choose Progressive in the Output Fields pop-up menu and the source media is interlaced, the selection in the Deinterlace pop-up menu is applied. Generally, the best choice in the Deinterlace pop-up menu is Better (Motion adaptive).

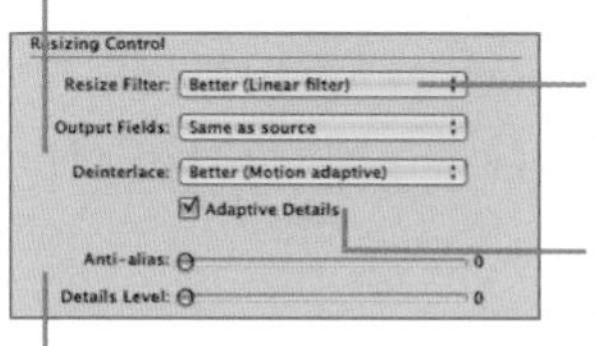
Resize Filter:
Better (Linear filter)
Output Fields:
Same as source
Deinterlace:
Better (Motion adaptive)
Adaptive Details
Anti-alias:
Details Level:

The Resize Filter pop-up menu dictates the method that Compressor will use to resize the source media (see the table on next page).

Select the Adaptive Details box to have the encoder delineate carefully between noise and edge detail.

The Anti-alias and Details Level sliders increase smoothness and sharpness within the frame size conversion. When source media is scaled up or down, jagged artifacting or detail blurring can occur in the transcoded media. Use the Anti-alias slider to smooth jagged edges, and use the Details Level slider to adjust image sharpness. Use the sliders independently or in tandem to achieve the desired results. The effects are subtle, so begin with a setting of at least 20, because lower settings produce limited results.

TIP Deselect the Adaptive Details box when encoding for iPods with video, the web, or any media that will be viewed on progressive-scan displays. Deselecting this box allows Compressor to utilize the same deinterlacing algorithms used by Apple's DVD Player. The resulting encoding times will be significantly shorter with the box deselected.

Quality versus Encoding Time	Resize Filter Choice
Fastest encoding	Fast (Nearest pixel). Encoding calculations are based on a blending of relative pixel positions from frame to frame.
Balance between speed and quality	Better (Linear filter). This option adds a weighted-average calculation to the Fast method that produces much smoother results at the cost of increased encoding time. Use this option if motion artifacting is present when Fast is used.
Best quality	Best (Statistical Prediction). This option kicks optical flow into high gear, as it analyzes each frame pixel by pixel and reconstitutes frames mathematically by repositioning each pixel relative to the new frame size.

Reverse Telecine

When 24-frame film is transferred to video, it undergoes a process called *telecine.* During that process, extra frames are added to conform the 24 fps progressive footage into 29.97 fps interlaced video for playback in the NTSC format. This process is commonly referred to as a 3:2 pulldown. You can use frame controls to reverse that process (reverse telecine) and output 23.98-frame media from NTSC media for editorial in Final Cut Pro.

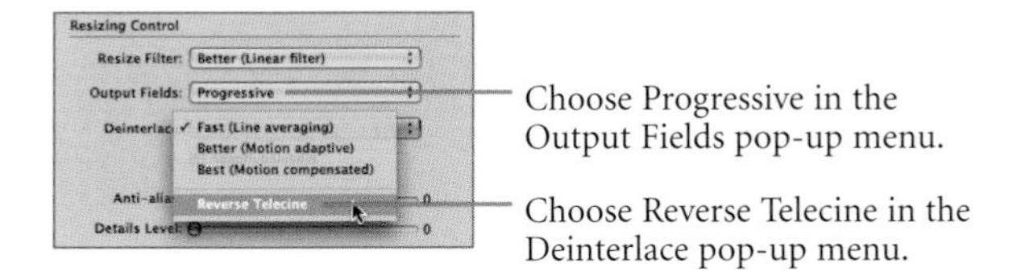
Resizing Control
Resize Filter: Better (Linear filter)
Output Fields: Progressive
Fast (Line averaging)
Better (Motion adaptive)
Best (Motion compensated)
Reverse Telecine
Details Level
Choose Progressive in the Output Fields pop-up menu.
Choose Reverse Telecine in the Deinterlace pop-up menu.

NOTE ▶ When Reverse Telecine is selected, the other frame controls options are disabled.

Retiming Controls

When changes in frame rate are introduced into a conversion—such as in converting 29.97 fps NTSC to 25 fps PAL—the retiming controls can be used to increase the output quality significantly.

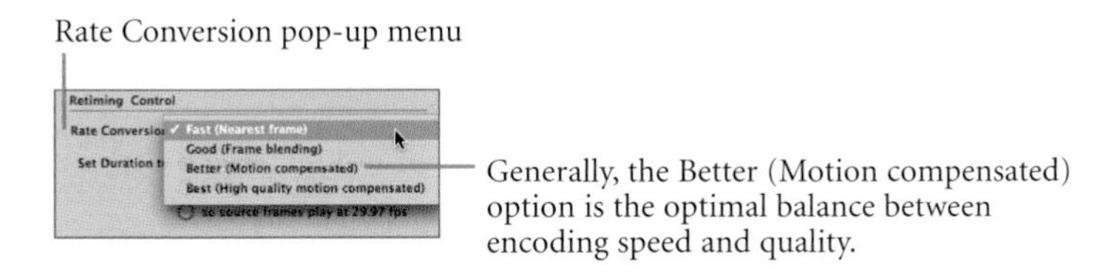
Rate Conversion pop-up menu
Retiming Control
Fast (Nearest frame)
Good (Frame blending)
Better (Motion compensated)
Best (High quality motion compensated)
Generally, the Better (Motion compensated) option is the optimal balance between encoding speed and quality.

Quality versus Encoding Time	Rate Conversion Choice
Fastest encoding	Fast (Nearest frame). Depending on the format conversion, Compressor removes or adds frames by copying the neighboring frames on either side. This setting will introduce stuttering playback (frame judder) except when used with mostly static content, such as interview footage. Use it only when encoding speed is paramount and the source media can bear the compromise.
Good quality with faster conversion time	Good (Frame blending). Compressor blends the average picture data of neighboring frames to smooth the removal of frames or to cover the addition of frames to the frame-rate conversion.
Better quality with slower conversion time	Better (Motion compensated). Compressor uses optical flow to determine the vector path of each pixel from frame to frame and completely reinterprets the source media in the new frame rate.
Best quality	Best (High quality motion compensated). This setting increases the detail value of the optical flow motion calculations, placing each pixel more precisely in the reconstructed frame rate. Consider this option only when you are increasing the frame rate (adding frames). The significant increase in encoding time is not offset by greater quality when you use this option for frame-rate reductions.

Speed Changes

By default, the "Set Duration to" field in the Retiming Controls is set to 100.000% of source. With that setting, no changes in speed will occur even if the frame rate changes from one rate to another—for example, 29.97 fps NTSC to 25 fps PAL.

> **NOTE ▶** When applying speed changes to media that contains audio, or audio-only media, the pitch will not shift because Compressor will automatically use Mac OS X's Core Audio technology during the conversion.

You can use frame controls in one of three ways to make constant speed changes to the output media:

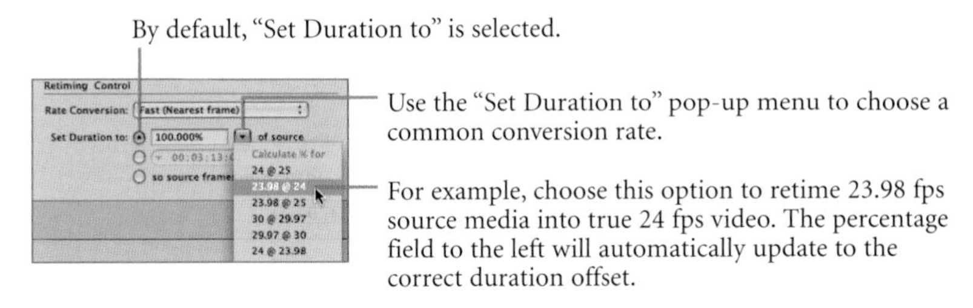
By default, “Set Duration to” is selected.
Retiming Control
Rate Conversion: Fast (Nearest frame)
Set Duration to: 100.000% of source
so source frame
Calculate % for
24 @ 25
23.98 @ 24
23.98 @ 25
30 @ 29.97
29.97 @ 30
24 @ 23.98
Use the “Set Duration to” pop-up menu to choose a common conversion rate.
For example, choose this option to retime 23.98 fps source media into true 24 fps video. The percentage field to the left will automatically update to the correct duration offset.

Using timecode to determine the speed change is very similar to a fit to fill edit in Final Cut Pro, whereby you set an edit duration and the source clip either speeds up or slows down to fill into the edit.

The percentage field automatically updates to the correct duration offset. Values greater than 100.000% will cause the output movie to slow down, and values less than 100.000% will speed up the output.

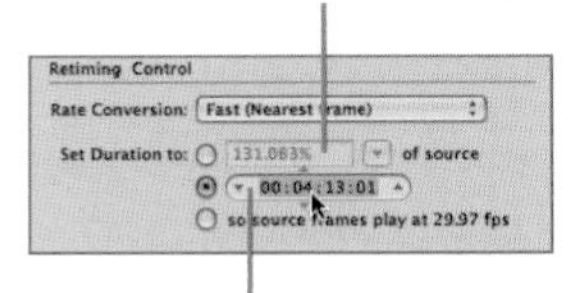
Retiming Control
Rate Conversion: Fast (Nearest frame)
Set Duration to: 131.083% of source
00:04:13:01
so source frames play at 29.97 fps

Select the radio button next to the timecode field and enter a new duration into the field. When you hold the pointer over the individual hours, minutes, seconds, and frames values, up and down triangles appear above and below the field. You can click the up and down arrows to move the values forward or backward.

Selecting the last “Set Duration to” option is similar to the way Cinema Tools retimes media by conforming the source frame rate into the target frame rate. With this option selected, Compressor will not employ optical flow in the conversion.

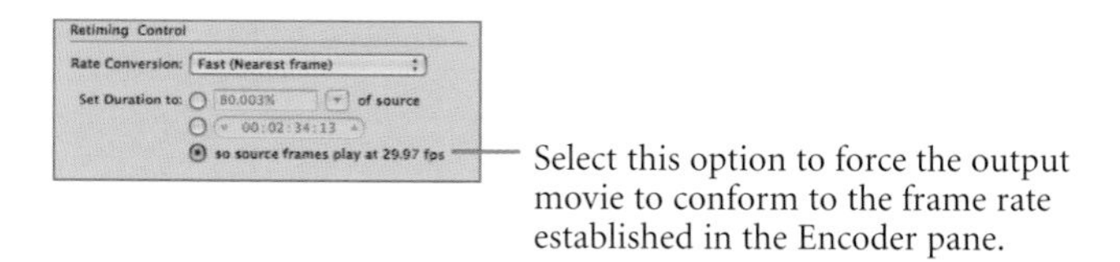
Retiming Control
Rate Conversion: Fast (Nearest frame)
Set Duration to:
80.003%
of source
00:02:34:13
so source frames play at 29.97 fps
Select this option to force the output movie to conform to the frame rate established in the Encoder pane.

TIP It's common to have a video or audio clip that is a few seconds (or frames) too long or too short. You can use the retiming controls to fit the output clip exactly into your time constraints.

Frame Controls in the Real World

The results of settings made in the Frame Controls pane do not appear in the Preview window, so a real-time preview of their impact is not available. However, because of the potentially lengthy encoding times when frame controls are applied, you will want to use a test-clip workflow (see Chapter 8) on small sections of the source media to audition the settings. This carries a two-fold benefit: You will not waste time encoding the entire media with an unsatisfactory setting, and you can estimate encoding times for the entire media based on the test time. If one minute of footage is encoded in ten minutes, it will take roughly ten hours to encode one hour of footage with the same settings.

Applying Filters

Compressor includes a series of video and audio filters that you can combine with Apple and custom settings to modify the look of encoded media. You can preview the results of all the filters in real time in the Preview window (see Chapter 8).

Both audio and video filters are applied in the same manner, but this chapter focuses only on the video filters. The four audio filters are covered in Compressor's user manual.

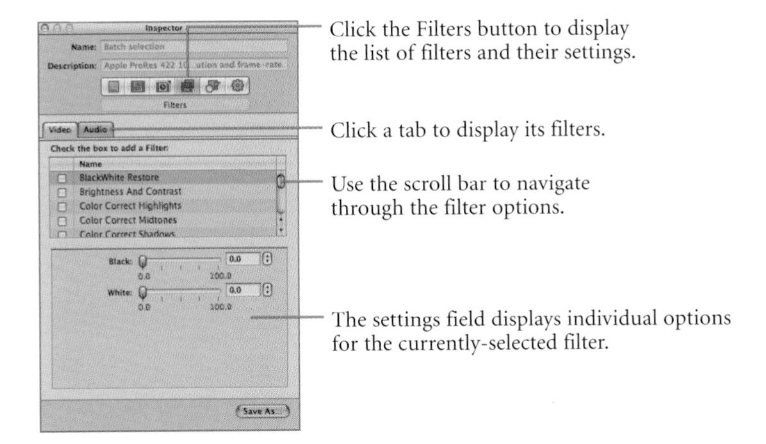
Click the Filters button to display the list of filters and their settings.
Click a tab to display its filters.
Use the scroll bar to navigate through the filter options.
The settings field displays individual options for the currently-selected filter.
Inspector
Filters
Video
Audio
Name
BlackWhite Restore
Brightness And Contrast
Color Correct Highlights
Color Correct Midtones
Black:
White:
Save As...

TIP Compressor initially lists filters alphabetically, but you can change the order by dragging filters in the list. This is useful when you want to change the render order of multiple activated filters; Compressor renders filters in this list from top to bottom.

Additive Filters

Several filter options add image elements to the data stream during encoding.

Timecode Filter

A common request during postproduction is to display reference timecode within the video. You can easily add this element during encoding.

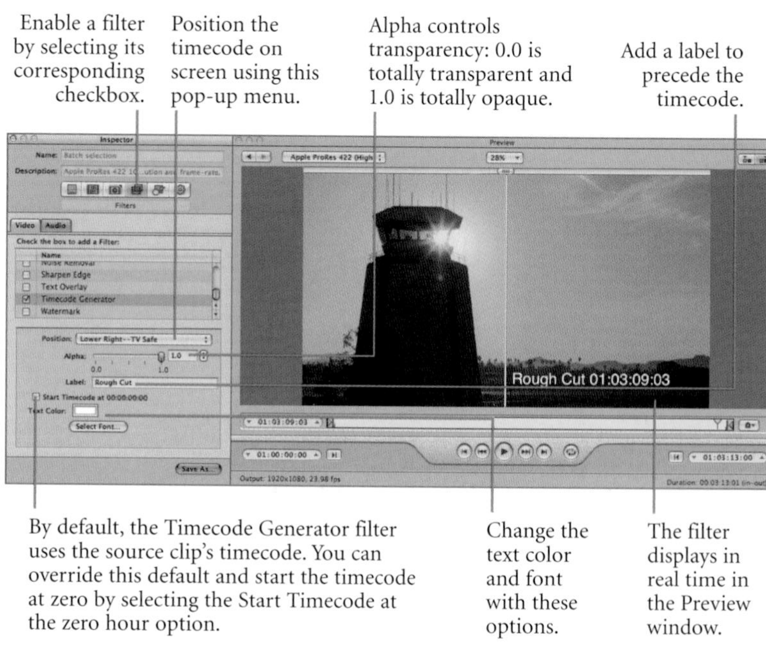
Enable a filter by selecting its corresponding checkbox.
Position the timecode on screen using this pop-up menu.
Alpha controls transparency: 0.0 is totally transparent and 1.0 is totally opaque.
Add a label to precede the timecode.
Rough Cut 01:03:09:03
By default, the Timecode Generator filter uses the source clip's timecode. You can override this default and start the timecode at zero by selecting the Start Timecode at the zero hour option.
Change the text color and font with these options.
The filter displays in real time in the Preview window.

Opening the Preview window during filter adjustment makes the process easier because you can see changes update in real time.

Watermark Filter

The Watermark filter lets you add both static and animated graphics to the video stream. For instance, you could add your company logo or copyright notice to your video, or insert an animated station identification (often referred to as a "bug").

You can import any graphic file that QuickTime can open, but you'll achieve the best visual results with files that have transparency (or an alpha channel) because the source video will show through areas of the graphic that are entirely transparent. Image formats like TIFF, PICT, and Photoshop PSD files can contain transparency. JPEG files are not the best choice because they do not contain transparency or alpha channels. Any areas that you originally created with transparency will display white in the watermark.

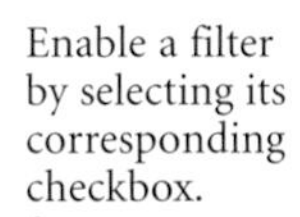

Enable a filter by selecting its corresponding checkbox.
Use the Scale By controls to adjust the relative size of the graphic.
The Alpha settings control the tranparency of the graphic. If your file contained transparency, Compressor automatically removes those sections of the image. This setting adjusts the opaque or semitransparent areas of the image.
Position the timecode on screen using this pop-up menu.
Click the Choose button and navigate to the graphic file you want to import.
The watermark displays in real time in the Preview window.

Animated graphics can also be used as watermarks. You could use a Motion project file or QuickTime movie encoded using the Animation codec (with an alpha channel) as watermark sources. The same transparency rules apply to motion graphics as they do to still images, and the Watermark filter uses the same controls. Motion graphics start at the beginning of the source clip and play through their entire media duration. If the Repeat option is selected in the Watermark filter controls, the motion graphic will keep looping for the entire duration of the source media. If you only want the motion graphic to play once and stop, deselect the Repeat option.

TIP Working with motion graphics using Motion project files will give you the most flexibility when timing your motion graphic on screen. For example, if you want a motion graphic to display after 60 seconds of the source media has elapsed, you can create a Motion project that has no content for 60 seconds before the motion graphic animation begins.

Fade In/Out Filter

You can use the Fade In/Out filters in both the Video and Audio tabs to create standalone content that fades the sound and picture in and out of the encoded clip.

In the Video tab, select the Fade In/Out filter.

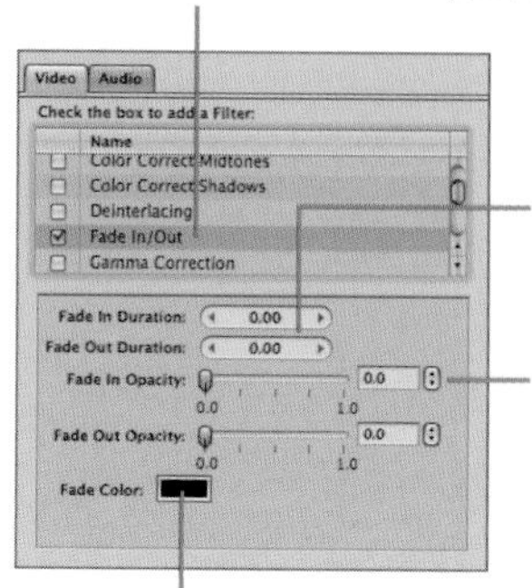
Video
Audio
Check the box to add a Filter:
Name
Color Correct Midtones
Color Correct Shadows
Deinterlacing
Fade In/Out
Gamma Correction
Fade In Duration:
0.00
Fade Out Duration:
0.00
Fade In Opacity:
0.0
0.0
1.0
Fade Out Opacity:
0.0
0.0
1.0
Fade Color:

Set the fade in and out durations by entering the time in seconds and frames, or by clicking the arrows to increase or decrease the duration.

Set the opacity of the fades with these sliders. If you want the media to fade up from total black (or any color you choose in the Fade Color box), set the slider to 0.0. A setting of 1.0 has the same result as not applying the filter.

Click the Fade Color box to open the color picker and choose the color that the exported media will both fade in from and fade out to.

In the Audio tab, select the Fade In/Out filter.

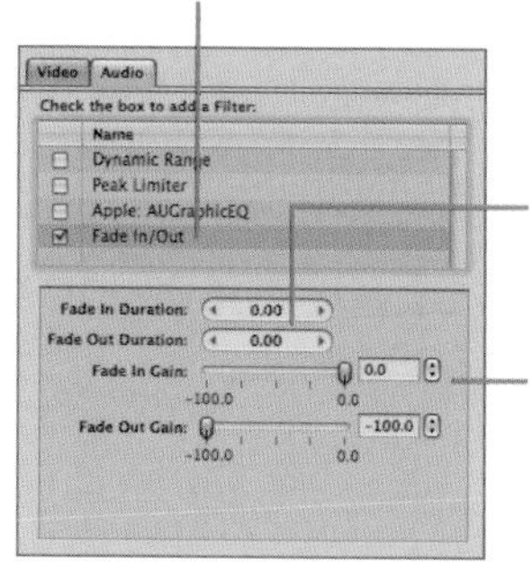
Video
Audio
Check the box to add a Filter:
Name
Dynamic Range
Peak Limiter
Apple: AUGraphicEQ
Fade In/Out
Fade In Duration:
0.00
Fade Out Duration:
0.00
Fade In Gain:
0.0
-100.0
0.0
Fade Out Gain:
-100.0
-100.0
0.0

Set the fade in and out durations by entering the time in seconds and frames, or by clicking the arrows to increase or decrease the duration.

Set the gain of the fades with these sliders to control the volume of the source media when the fade is complete.

In this example, the audio fades up to full volume and fades out to silence.

Corrective Filters

In addition to content filters, corrective filters can adjust specific visual aspects of the output media. When encoding an MPEG-4 job for the web, for example, you may find that the resulting image appears too soft. A Sharpen Edge filter could counteract the apparent loss of detail that the encoding process is introducing.

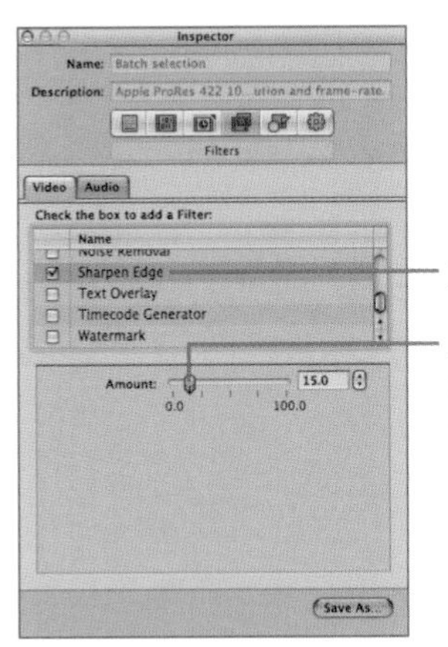
Inspector
Name:
Batch selection
Description:
Filters
Video
Audio
Check the box to add a Filter:
Name
Sharpen Edge
Text Overlay
Timecode Generator
Watermark
Amount:
15.0
0.0
100.0
Save As...

Enable a filter by selecting its corresponding checkbox.

Adjust the Amount setting by using the slider, manually entering a value, or by clicking the up and down arrows to the right of the Amount field.

When using the Sharpen Edge filter, or any of the corrective filters for that matter, ease into the adjustment. For the most part, a little of each filter goes a long way. Setting the Sharpen Edge filter to a value greater than 25 can create fairly severe looking video (although that could be the creative look you are trying to achieve). Just as color correction is not only the science of achieving optimal color values but also an artistic technique, the corrective filters can be used artistically and aesthetically to manipulate the output image.

TIP To view descriptions of each of the available filters in the Filters pane, choose Help > Compressor User Manual or press Command-?.

11

The Geometry and Actions Panes

While you'll use Inspector's Encoder pane for the "heavy lifting" in Compressor, in the other panes you'll fine-tune and finesse encoding jobs. In the Geometry and Actions panes, you'll change the output frame size, adjust the aspect ratio of the output movie, pad the source movie inside the output frame size, and assign actions to jobs in the batch table that will run an AppleScript or send an email when the job is completed.

Using the Geometry Pane

The Geometry pane settings control the frame size and aspect ratio of the output media and also determine how the source media displays within the output frame.

Although aesthetic or logistical considerations are key when choosing frame dimensions, scaling down to a smaller output frame size is a common strategy for reducing overall file size. For example, a DV NTSC movie with a 720 x 480 frame size can be reduced to a 320 x 240 frame, creating a smaller file that is still large enough for acceptable computer playback. This size reduction has a direct correlation to a decrease in output file size; smaller frame sizes require less data.

In some instances, Compressor will dictate the output frame size and dim the options in the Geometry pane. The SD DVD specification, for example, requires a fixed frame size of 720 x 480 pixels. Therefore, the Geometry options are shadowed and unavailable for all DVD settings, including HD settings.

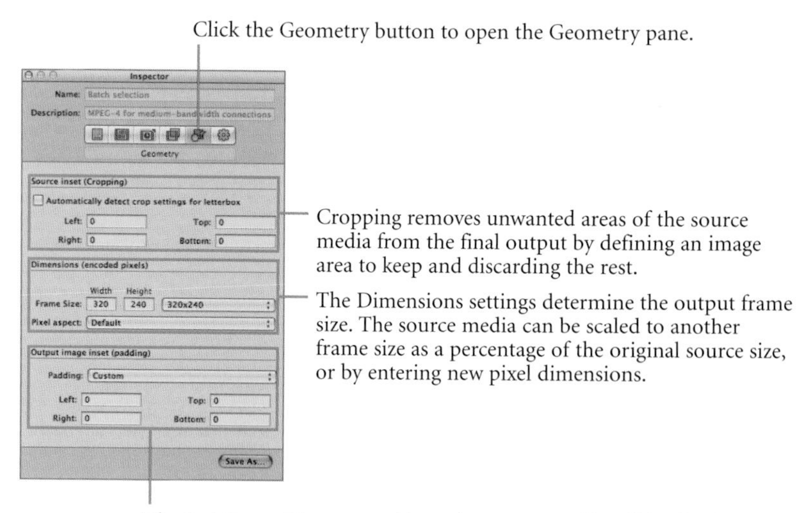
Click the Geometry button to open the Geometry pane.
Inspector
Name: Batch selection
Description: MPEG-4 for medium-bandwidth connections
Geometry
Source inset (Cropping)
Automatically detect crop settings for letterbox
Left: 0
Top: 0
Right: 0
Bottom: 0
Dimensions (encoded pixels)
Width
Height
Frame Size: 320 240 320x240
Pixel aspect: Default
Output image inset (padding)
Padding: Custom
Left: 0
Top: 0
Right: 0
Bottom: 0
Save As...
Cropping removes unwanted areas of the source media from the final output by defining an image area to keep and discarding the rest.
The Dimensions settings determine the output frame size. The source media can be scaled to another frame size as a percentage of the original source size, or by entering new pixel dimensions.
The Padding settings control how the source media will be displayed within the frame size established by the Dimensions controls.

Changing Frame Dimensions

Many Apple settings have predetermined or fixed frame sizes. If the Dimensions options are dimmed, that particular output format's frame size cannot be changed.

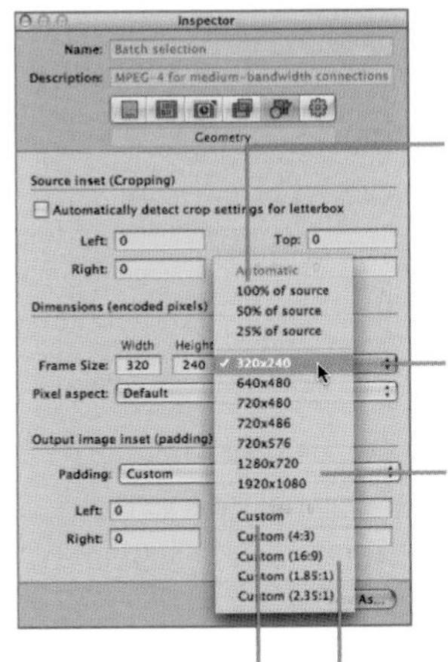
Inspector
Name:
Batch selection
Description:
MPEG-4 for medium-bandwidth connections
Geometry
Source inset (Cropping)
Left: 0
Top: 0
Right: 0
100% of source
50% of source
25% of source
Dimensions (encoded pixels)
Width
Frame Size: 320 240
320x240
640x480
720x480
720x486
720x576
1280x720
1920x1080
Pixel aspect: Default
Padding: Custom
Left: 0
Right: 0
Custom

The percentage options change the output frame size based on a percentage of the source media size. For example, applying a 50% of source option to a DV NTSC source clip at 720 x 480 will create an output frame size of 360 x 240.

Click the Frame Size pop-up menu to define the output dimensions.

The fixed frame size options set output dimensions to the values in the list. If you choose a frame size with an aspect ratio that's different from your source, the source media will be scaled during encoding.

The Custom option displays whenever you input values directly into the Frame Size Width and Height fields.

The Custom options with common aspect ratios affect only the source's Height value. For example, if 320 x 240 is the current frame size and you choose Custom (16:9), Compressor will adjust the Height to 180 and leave the Width unchanged.

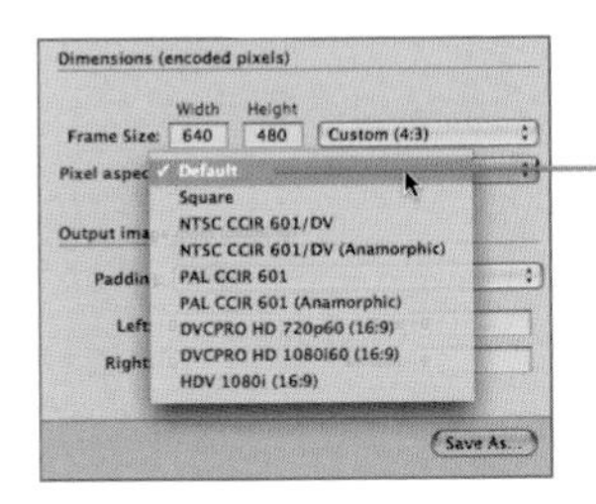
Dimensions (encoded pixels)
Width
Height
Frame Size: 640 480
Custom (4:3)
Default
Square
NTSC CCIR 601/DV
NTSC CCIR 601/DV (Anamorphic)
PAL CCIR 601
PAL CCIR 601 (Anamorphic)
DVCPRO HD 720p60 (16:9)
DVCPRO HD 1080i60 (16:9)
HDV 1080i (16:9)
Save As...

Click the Pixel aspect pop-up menu to force the output media's pixels into one of the listed aspect ratios. Choosing Default will leave the source media's aspect ratio unchanged. When encoding media intended for playback on computer displays, choose Square.

When choosing options other than the default, base your decision on the final playback destination. For example, if the output movie is intended for playback on HD progressive displays, you could choose DVCPRO HD 720p60 (16:9).

Cropping Media

By default, Compressor uses the entire source media frame during the encoding process. You can redefine which part of the image will be encoded by creating a source inset.

Compressor offers two ways to crop media: a visual method using the Preview window, and a numerical method using the Geometry pane.

To crop using the Preview window, select a target in the Batch window or click the Input/Output pop-up menu and choose a target.

Drag the Split Screen slider to the left to see the entire cropped image.

If you cannot see the cropping boundaries, make sure that the Preview window's display is relative to the source media (not the output) and that the preset (not the source) is loaded into the Preview screen area.

MPEG-4 300Kbps
50%
L:340 T:150 R:260 B:
01:04:05:20
01:00:00:00
01:12:40:04

Red cropping boundaries surround the source media. You can adjust all four sides of the image by dragging those boundaries to define the part of the image to be encoded.

While dragging a boundary, Compressor displays the numeric values of the crop.

You can drag the sides of the cropping boundaries independently, or constrain the entire crop to the aspect ratio of the source media by holding down Shift while dragging one of the corner handles. The cropping boundaries' values will update automatically in the Geometry pane. You can also reposition the entire box by clicking in the center of the box and dragging it to a new location.

Cropping in the Preview window

If your source media contains a letterbox (black bars at the top and bottom of the clip), select this option to detect the letterbox and automatically determine the top and bottom crop values.

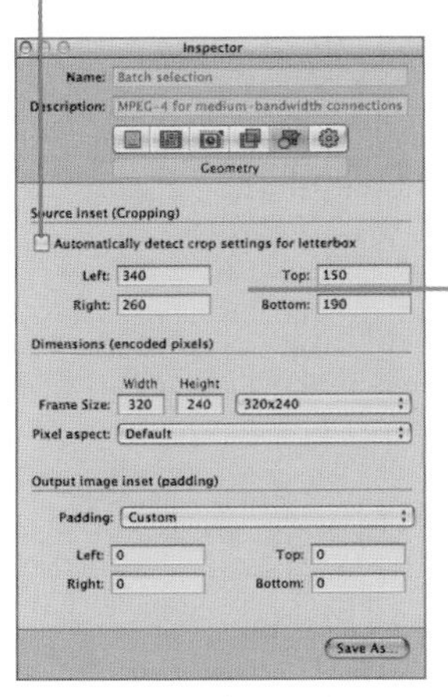
Inspector
Name: Batch selection
Description: MPEG-4 for medium-bandwidth connections
Geometry
Source Inset (Cropping)
Automatically detect crop settings for letterbox
Left: 340
Top: 150
Right: 260
Bottom: 190
Dimensions (encoded pixels)
Width
Height
Frame Size: 320
240
320x240
Pixel aspect: Default
Output image inset (padding)
Padding: Custom
Left: 0
Top: 0
Right: 0
Bottom: 0
Save As...

You can enter crop values directly in the Source Inset section.The values entered will limit the viewable portion of the source media. A value of zero in all fields will use the entire source media.

Cropping in the Geometry pane of the Inspector window

The Source Inset (Cropping) controls work in tandem with the Dimensions (encoded pixels) controls. For example, if you crop a movie and have a fixed output dimension, the cropped source media will be scaled to fit inside the fixed-frame dimensions.

To apply a crop and not scale the output media, in the Frame Size pop-up menu, choose 100% of Source, or manually enter the frame-size values based on the resulting reduction of the crop. For example, if a 720 x 480 frame was cropped 40 lines from the top and 40 lines from the bottom, enter a custom frame size of 720 x 400.

Padding the Output

If cropping limits which part of the visual image Compressor will encode, then padding dictates which part of the output frame the source media will occupy. For instance, if you have a DV NTSC clip that's 720 x 480 and you apply an HD frame size (1280 x 720) target, by default, the DV source clip will be scaled up to fill the entire frame size. Using padding, you can maintain the DV's actual frame size of 720 x 480 and play it *within* the output HD frame size of 1280 x 720.

The following example uses the Padding controls to retain the DV frame size of 720 x 480 within the HD output dimensions.

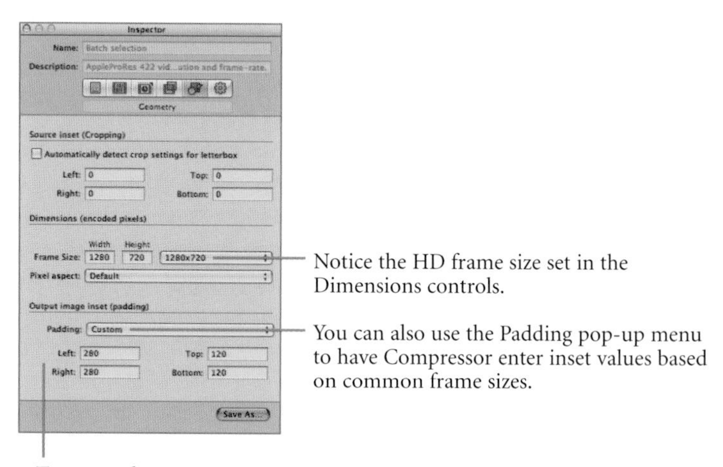
Inspector
Name:
Description:
Geometry
Source inset (Cropping)
Automatically detect crop settings for letterbox
Left: 0
Top: 0
Right: 0
Bottom: 0
Dimensions (encoded pixels)
Width
Height
Frame Size: 1280 720 1280x720
Pixel aspect: Default
Output image inset (padding)
Padding: Custom
Left: 280
Top: 120
Right: 280
Bottom: 120
Save As...
Notice the HD frame size set in the Dimensions controls.
You can also use the Padding pop-up menu to have Compressor enter inset values based on common frame sizes.

To center the DV movie without altering the aspect ratio, enter the values as seen in this image.

Here's how the values were derived:

To calculate the width: 1280 – 720 = 560; 560 ÷ 2 = 280.

Therefore, to center the image, enter 280 in the Left and Right fields.

To calculate the Height: 720 – 480 = 240; 240 ÷ 2 = 120

Therefore, to center the image, enter 120 in the Top and Bottom fields.

TIP You can quickly find the source media's frame size by selecting it in the Batch window and reviewing the clip information in the Inspector window.

MASERATI-Framed.mov
00:00:00
Compressor fills the padded areas of the frame size with black.
The full-frame, unscaled DV movie is centered within the HD frame.

This output movie used the previous settings for export.

NOTE ▶ It's good practice to export a test clip (see Chapter 8) to ensure that the proper aspect ratio and final positioning are produced accurately.

Padding, in essence, creates a matte around the source media inside the output frame size, much as you would frame a painting or photograph. This can be used in several practical and creative situations. For example, a network might want you to deliver a full HD-framed movie of standard definition source media. You could use padding to have your SD content play back in its original frame size and aspect ratio within a 16:9 HD frame. The black, empty areas of the border could later be filled with commercial content from the network or additional content of your own (think of Bloomberg Television).

Another example would occur in a post-production workflow where you are building elements for HD delivery and are responsible for only one element in the frame. You could inset your content into the frame and leave the rest of the frame available for others.

TIP Using the Apple ProRes 422 codec is a good choice for this type of work.

Exploring the Math Behind the Numbers

All the functions in the Geometry pane can significantly alter the presentation of your output video, so it is essential to understand why certain values produce certain results. For example, if you start with HD source media at 1920 x 1080 and choose the MPEG-4, 300K Apple setting, the default output frame size will be 320 x 240. Houston, we have a problem! Compressor will do exactly what you tell it to do: It will squeeze the 16:9 footage into a 4:3 box and your movie will look like the opening sequence of Kung-Fu Theatre—the image is pushed in at the sides to make everything look tall and thin.

Video frame sizes ranging from web delivery to SD to HD are all governed by width and height proportions called aspect ratios. For example, DV NTSC has a frame size of 720 pixels wide by 480 pixels high (720 x 480). The aspect ratio for that frame size is 3:2, meaning that for every 3 pixels in width, the image is 2 pixels tall. That's why, when you look at a DV NTSC image, it's not a square, it's a rectangle.

The following table lists basic calculations for the most common frame sizes. You can use this information in the Geometry pane to correct display problems in your output movies and also to creatively produce unconventional frame sizes.

Using the table, you can quickly deduce the proper frame size if you have just one of the output dimensions. For example, a common task is creating web-ready versions of 16:9 movies. The common 320 x 240 web output frame size represents a 4:3 aspect ratio. It will not accurately display 16:9 content because the source is scaled to fit (which changes the aspect ratio). But, using the 16:9 calculation in the table, you can derive the proper widescreen height for a 320-pixel width by multiplying 320 by .5625, which equals 180 pixels. Granted, Compressor addresses this common output issue in the Dimensions settings where you can easily set the widescreen aspect using the pop-up menus, but the calculations listed in the following table can address any custom situation you may encounter.

Frame Size	Aspect Ratio	Width Calculation	Height Calculation
DV NTSC 720 x 480	3:2	Multiply the height by 1.5	Multiply the width by .667
Widescreen DV 720 x 480 (squeezed)	16:9	Multiply the height by 1.778	Multiply the width by .5625
HD 1280 x720	16:9	Multiply the height by 1.778	Multiply the width by .5625
HD 1920 x 1080	16:9	Multiply the height by 1.778	Multiply the width by .5625
HDV 1440 x 1080	16:9	Multiply the height by 1.333	Multiply the width by .75
Web 320 x 240	4:3	Multiply the height by 1.333	Multiply the width by .75
N/A	Academy 1:85:1	Multiply the height by 1.851	Multiply the width by .5403
N/A	Panavision 2:35:1	Multiply the height by 2.351	Multiply the width by .425

NOTE ▶ Some equations may not produce whole numbers. Screen dimensions cannot include fractions, so you must round off fractional values. For example, if the height equals 319.23, round up the height value to 320 pixels.

Using the Actions Pane

The Actions pane controls two tasks that Compressor can perform after processing a job: Sending a notice to an email address, and running an AppleScript.

To enable email notification, you must configure Compressor's preferences properly by choosing Compressor > Preferences.

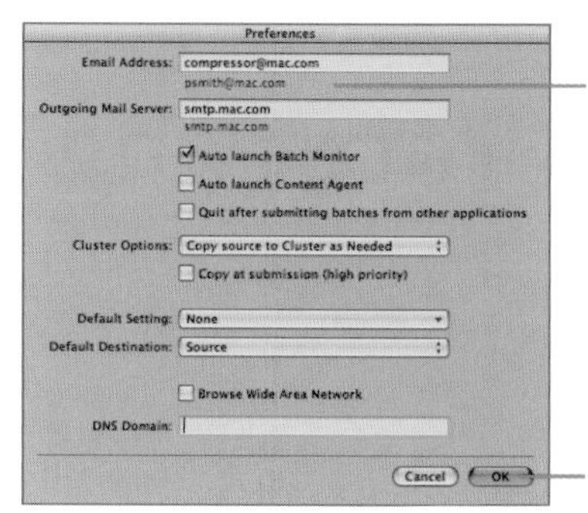
Preferences
Email Address: compressor@mac.com
Outgoing Mail Server: smtp.mac.com
Auto launch Batch Monitor
Auto launch Content Agent
Quit after submitting batches from other applications
Cluster Options: Copy source to Cluster as Needed
Copy at submission (high priority)
Default Setting: None
Default Destination: Source
Browse Wide Area Network
DNS Domain:
Cancel
OK

In the Preferences dialog, enter an email address and outgoing mail server information. Note that email notification works only with mail servers that do not require authentication.

Click OK to save the settings.

Click this button to open the Actions pane of any Apple or custom setting.

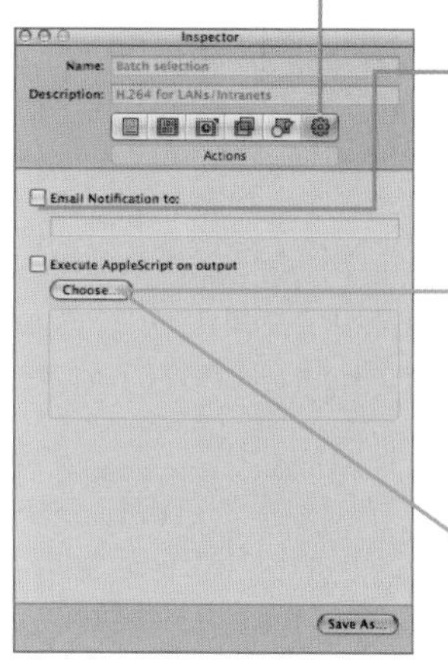
Inspector
Name: Batch selection
Description: H.264 for LANs/Intranets
Actions
Email Notification to:
Execute AppleScript on output
Choose...
Save As...

Select the Email Notification to checkbox and Compressor will automatically enter the address into this field from the Preferences dialog.You can also manually enter any valid email address to receive email notification.

Compressor can also run a single AppleScript (which includes Automator workflows) at the end of processing. When you select the Execute AppleScript on output checkbox, Compressor opens a dialog in which you can choose an AppleScript. Once selected, the path to the script appears in the field below.

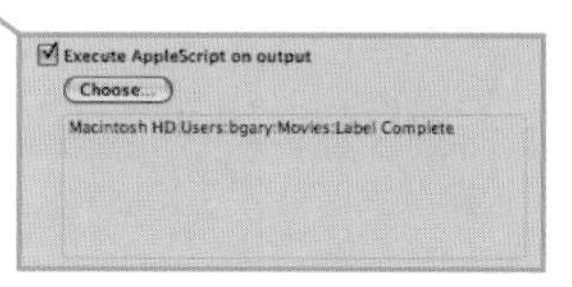
Execute AppleScript on output
Choose...
Macintosh HD:Users:bgary:Movies:Label Complete

If you need to change the path to the script or select a new path, click the Choose button and navigate to the new location or script.

TIP You can set email notification or script execution for each job in a batch by configuring the Actions pane for each individual preset. As Compressor completes each job in the list, it sends an email or runs a script.

12

Distributed Processing

Distributed processing harnesses the collective encoding power of two or more computers on the same local area network (LAN)—sometimes referred to as a *render farm.* By spreading the encoding load across multiple computers, you can reduce processing time compared to using a single computer that must shoulder the entire job.

Before performing the tasks in this chapter, familiarize yourself with the Distributed Processing Setup PDF document in Compressor's Help Menu > Distributed Processing Setup. Distributed processing works best with robust hardware environments in which the media is centralized on XSAN-controlled RAIDs (redundant array of independent disks) and the computers are connected to a high-speed fiber channel network.

Installing Distributed Processing in Final Cut Studio

During the Final Cut Studio installation, the following screen appears that allows you to create an AutoCluster.

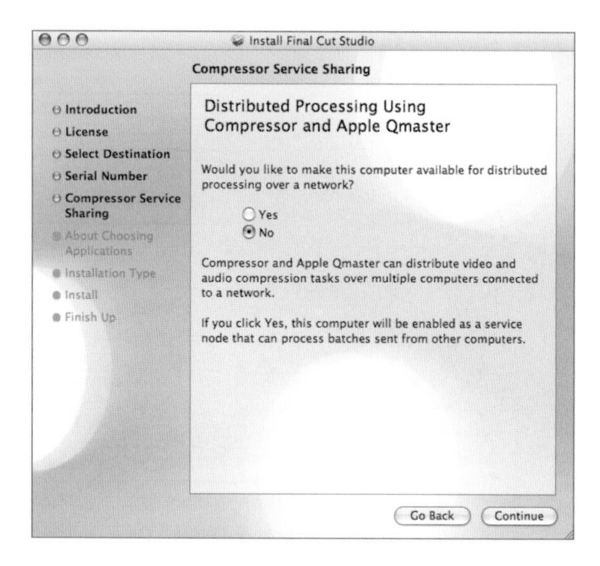
Install Final Cut Studio
Compressor Service Sharing
Introduction
License
Select Destination
Serial Number
Compressor Service Sharing
About Choosing Applications
Installation Type
Install
Finish Up
Distributed Processing Using Compressor and Apple Qmaster
Would you like to make this computer available for distributed processing over a network?
Yes
No
Compressor and Apple Qmaster can distribute video and audio compression tasks over multiple computers connected to a network.
If you click Yes, this computer will be enabled as a service node that can process batches sent from other computers.
Go Back
Continue

This window allows you to quickly set up distributed processing on the target computer by automatically designating it as a *node*—a computer available to encode network jobs. By default, the Compressor Service Sharing option is set to No. So, if you want the target computer to process batches on the network, choose Yes, then click Continue.

Creating a QuickCluster

Apple Qmaster, used in conjunction with Mac OS X and Compressor, allows you to create a simple, easily-configured distributed processing network referred to as a QuickCluster. Before creating a network, consult the following table to verify that your hardware meets the minimum requirements:

Component	Hardware/Software Requirements
Network	All computers must be physically connected to a local network. (Gigabit Ethernet, Fiber Channel, and so on are suitable. Wireless connections are not recommended.)
	All computers must be on the same subnet of the local network.
Computer	All computers must be running the same version of Macintosh OS X, version 10.4.x or higher.
	All computers must be running the same version of QuickTime, version 7 or higher.
	Final Cut Studio must be installed on each system to ensure that all Compressor presets are available to the QuickCluster.

Setting Up the Cluster Controller

You need to designate one computer as the cluster controller. This computer will send the encoding instructions with all the frames to the rest of the computers—the node computers—during processing.

On the computer designated as the cluster controller, click Apple Qmaster in System Preferences.

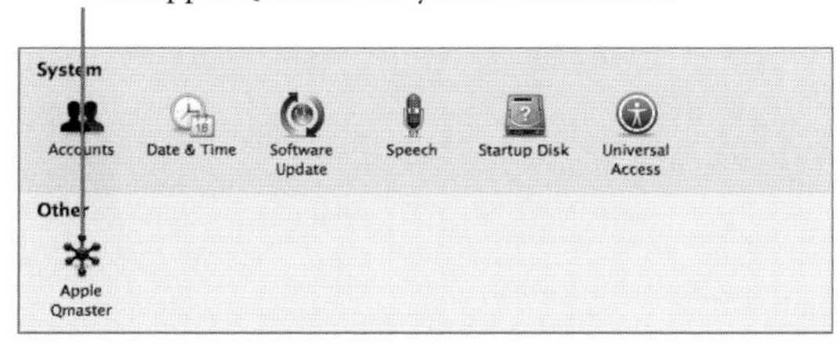
System
Accounts
Date & Time
Software Update
Speech
Startup Disk
Universal Access
Other
Apple Qmaster

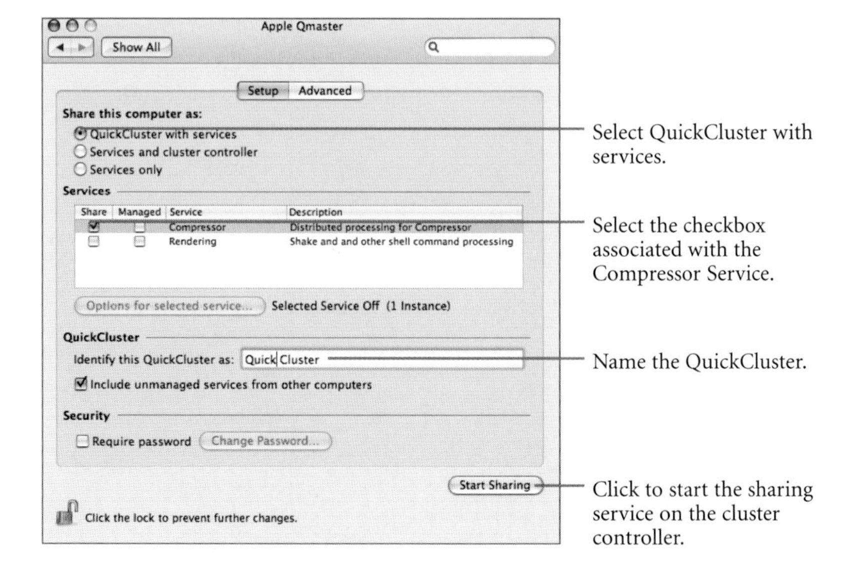

Apple Qmaster
Show All
Setup
Advanced
Share this computer as:
QuickCluster with services
Services and cluster controller
Services only
Services
Share
Managed
Service
Description
Compressor
Distributed processing for Compressor
Rendering
Shake and and other shell command processing
Options for selected service...
Selected Service Off (1 Instance)
QuickCluster
Identify this QuickCluster as:
Quick Cluster
Include unmanaged services from other computers
Security
Require password
Change Password...
Start Sharing
Click the lock to prevent further changes.
Select QuickCluster with services.
Select the checkbox associated with the Compressor Service.
Name the QuickCluster.
Click to start the sharing service on the cluster controller.

Setting Up the Node Computer

If you selected Yes on the Distributed Processing Screen during the Final Cut Studio installation (see "Installing Distributed Processing in Final Cut Studio"), then your computer will already be configured as an available node.

If you did not, you can easily configure your computer as a node by matching the following settings in the Qmaster Preference pane:

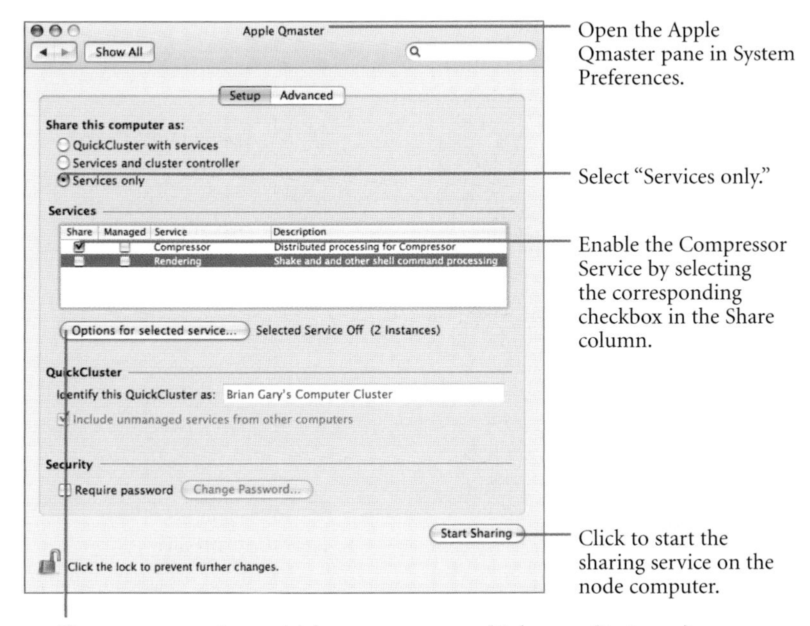
Apple Qmaster
Show All
Setup Advanced
Share this computer as:
QuickCluster with services
Services and cluster controller
Services only
Services
Share Managed Service Description
Compressor Distributed processing for Compressor
Rendering Shake and and other shell command processing
Options for selected service... Selected Service Off (2 Instances)
QuickCluster
Identify this QuickCluster as: Brian Gary's Computer Cluster
Include unmanaged services from other computers
Security
Require password Change Password...
Start Sharing
Click the lock to prevent further changes.
Open the Apple Qmaster pane in System Preferences.
Select "Services only."
Enable the Compressor Service by selecting the corresponding checkbox in the Share column.
Click to start the sharing service on the node computer.
If your computer has multiple processors or multiple cores (Instances), you can limit the number of resources that will be shared by clicking this button. (See the next figure for more details.)

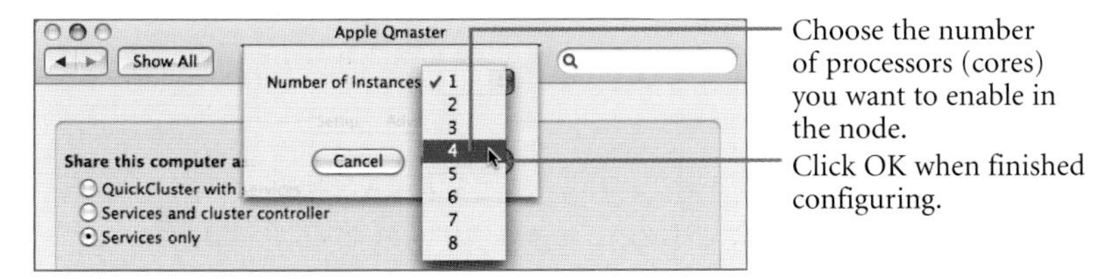
Apple Qmaster
Show All
Number of Instances
1
2
3
4
5
6
7
8
Cancel
Share this computer a
QuickCluster with
Services and cluster controller
Services only
Choose the number of processors (cores) you want to enable in the node.
Click OK when finished configuring.

A drop-down window appears after clicking the "Options for selected service" button.

NOTE ▸ You might want to limit the available processors to retain computing power on your local computer. For example, you could make one processor in a computer available for distributed Compressor processes and leave the other processor available for local Final Cut Pro editing.

Qmaster can display the status of active services in the menu bar alongside the clock, AirPort status, Spotlight, and so on.

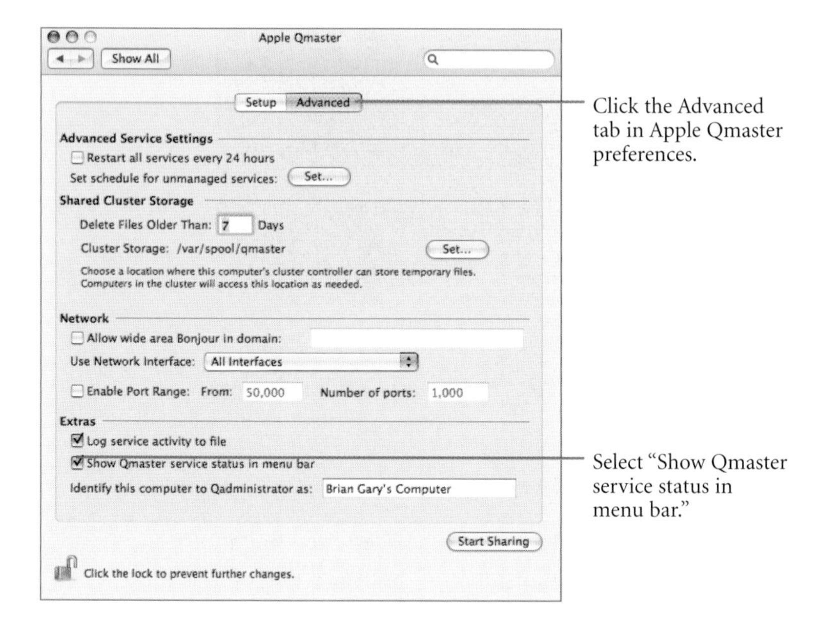
Apple Qmaster
Show All
Setup
Advanced
Advanced Service Settings
Restart all services every 24 hours
Set schedule for unmanaged services:
Set...
Shared Cluster Storage
Delete Files Older Than: 7 Days
Cluster Storage: /var/spool/qmaster
Set...
Choose a location where this computer's cluster controller can store temporary files.
Computers in the cluster will access this location as needed.
Network
Allow wide area Bonjour in domain:
Use Network Interface: All Interfaces
Enable Port Range: From: 50,000 Number of ports: 1,000
Extras
Log service activity to file
Show Qmaster service status in menu bar
Identify this computer to Qadministrator as: Brian Gary's Computer
Start Sharing
Click the lock to prevent further changes.
Click the Advanced tab in Apple Qmaster preferences.
Select "Show Qmaster service status in menu bar."

Submitting a Batch to a QuickCluster

After clicking Submit in the Batch window, Compressor lets you decide where to send the batch for encoding. You do not have to create a separate workflow for distributed processing.

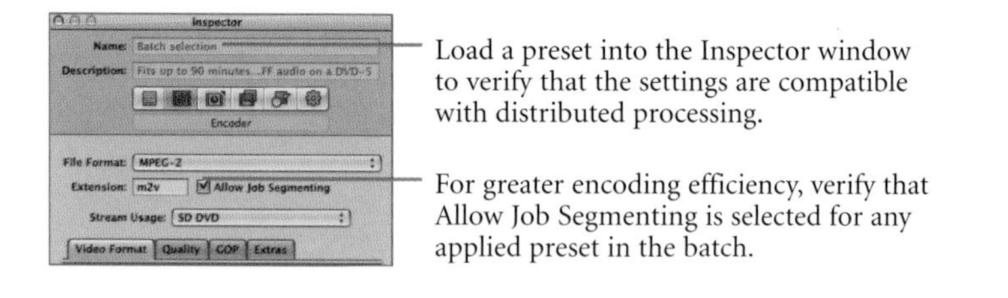
Inspector
Name:
Description:
Encoder
File Format: MPEG-2
Extension: m2v
Allow Job Segmenting
Stream Usage: SD DVD
Video Format
Quality
GOP
Extras
Load a preset into the Inspector window to verify that the settings are compatible with distributed processing.
For greater encoding efficiency, verify that Allow Job Segmenting is selected for any applied preset in the batch.

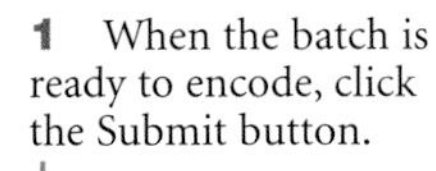

1 When the batch is ready to encode, click the Submit button.

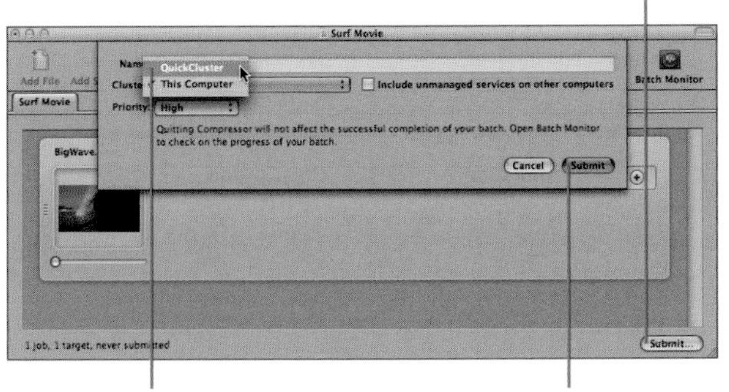
Surf Movie
QuickCluster
This Computer
Include unmanaged services on other computers
Batch Monitor
Surf Movie
Priority: High
Quitting Compressor will not affect the successful completion of your batch. Open Batch Monitor to check on the progress of your batch.
Cancel
Submit
Submit...

2 In the drop-down window, click the Cluster pop-up menu and choose the desired cluster.

3 When finished, click Submit.

Monitoring a QuickCluster

You can use the Batch Monitor to oversee encoding jobs on a QuickCluster, just as you monitor jobs processing on a local computer.

Choose your QuickCluster from the list in the left pane to display currently-encoding jobs in the right pane.

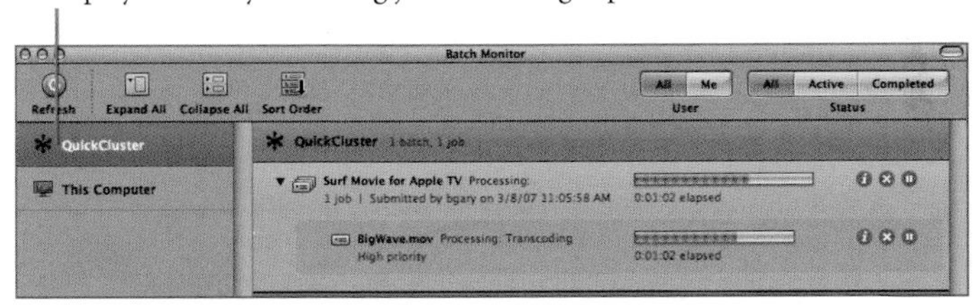
Batch Monitor
Expand All
Collapse All
Sort Order
All
Me
User
All
Active
Completed
Status
QuickCluster
This Computer
QuickCluster
Surf Movie for Apple TV Processing:
0:01:02 elapsed
BigWave.mov Processing: Transcoding
High priority
0:01:02 elapsed

Troubleshooting QuickClusters

Distributed processing adds multiple variables to the encoding mix. Use the following table to troubleshoot some common issues:

Problem	Solution
Sequences exported directly from Final Cut Pro are not encoding in the QuickCluster.	When exporting sequences directly from Final Cut Pro to Compressor, you must install Final Cut Pro on each node computer for the QuickCluster to work properly. All the nodes must have access to the media referenced in the Final Cut Pro project—that is, the volume with the assets must be mounted on each computer. Note that every running network instance of Final Cut Pro must have a unique product serial number.
Node computers do not have access to some or all of the components of a QuickTime reference movie.	Use self-contained source media by having Final Cut Pro (or any other application creating the source media) write the entire contents of a movie to a single file, or consolidate the media on shared storage such as an XSAN.
Unsatisfactory quality issues arise from multipass encoding jobs sent to the QuickCluster.	Allowing Compressor to segment the job produces faster encoding times because different nodes are working concurrently on separate sections of the job. A potential problem arises with multipass presets. With unsegmented encoding, a single computer will analyze the whole media on the first pass to inform its compression decisions. When a job is segmented, each node reviews only a portion of the media on the first pass, so overall compression decisions are based only on that source segment. This may not produce the best results for source media that changes visual style considerably during its length—for example, a documentary that has static interviews and dynamic B-roll. Clearing the Allow Job Segmenting checkbox will output more consistent quality on multipass jobs, but will also reduce the overall distributed processing speed.

Creating a Local Virtual Cluster

With any multiprocessor or multicore Mac, you can create a local cluster that treats each of your processors (or cores) as if it were a separate node computer. On a computer with robust resources, this can offer significant speed advantages during encoding, especially for codecs like H.264 that are not multi-threaded, because Qmaster will segment the job and send work to the separate processors as if they were different nodes on the network.

For example, if you want to encode a movie for iPods with video (using, by default, the H.264 codec) and you submit the job to "This Computer," the Compressor engine will only be able to harness one of your processors (cores) because H.264 is not multi-threaded. However, if you create a virtual cluster, submit the job to "This Computer," and allow Compressor to harness any unmanaged services, then all of the processors (cores) that you've made available will be tasked to the job.

To create a virtual cluster, follow the steps in "Setting Up the Node Computer" to configure your system as an unmanaged node. Also ensure that the target has Job Segmenting enabled (see "Submitting a Batch to a QuickCluster").

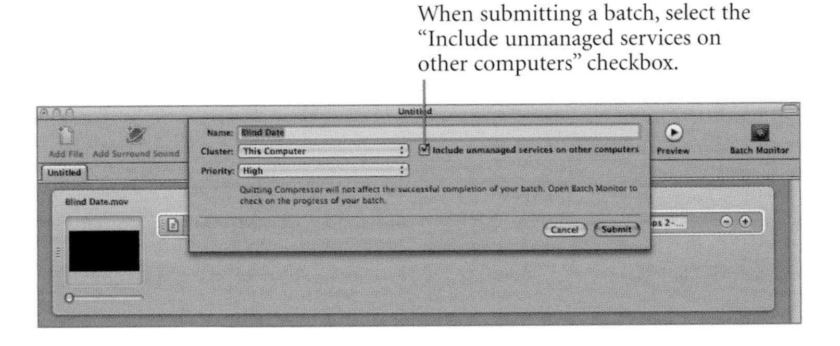
Untitled
Name: Blind Date
Cluster: This Computer
Include unmanaged services on other computers
Priority: High
Quitting Compressor will not affect the successful completion of your batch. Open Batch Monitor to check on the progress of your batch.
Cancel
Submit
Preview
Batch Monitor
Blind Date.mov

When submitting a batch, select the "Include unmanaged services on other computers" checkbox.

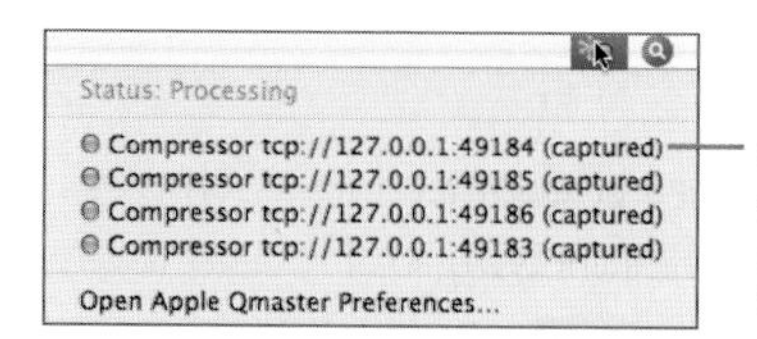
Status: Processing
Compressor tcp://127.0.0.1:49184 (captured)
Compressor tcp://127.0.0.1:49185 (captured)
Compressor tcp://127.0.0.1:49186 (captured)
Compressor tcp://127.0.0.1:49183 (captured)
Open Apple Qmaster Preferences...

Compressor will then capture all of the available local services as if they were nodes on the network. In this example, four services were created from eight cores.

The job will segment and encode across the available services. In this example, five segments are currently encoding: one for the local computer and one for each of the four services.

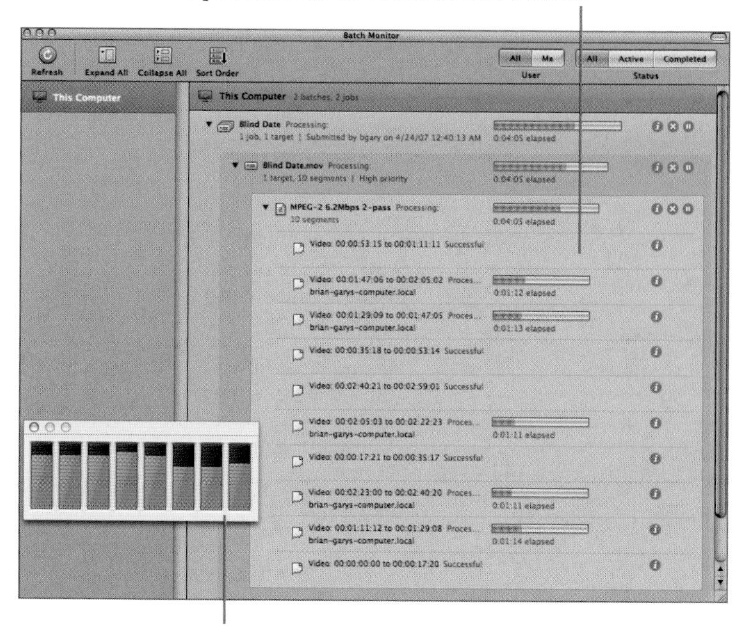
Batch Monitor
Refresh
Expand All
Collapse All
Sort Order
All
Me
User
All
Active
Completed
Status
This Computer
This Computer

This is the floating CPU window from Activity Monitor. Notice that all eight cores are processing the job.

NOTE ▶ Local Clusters can have very high hardware requirements because each service must have full RAM available to it as if it were a standalone computer—meaning that if a node requires 2 GB of RAM, then four instances in a Local Cluster would require 8 GB of RAM.

Technical Considerations

Distributed processing in Compressor adds a layer of technical complexity to the process of encoding media. Use the following table to guide you when submitting encoding jobs to a virtual or remote cluster.

Codec	Distributed Processing Considerations
AIC, Apple ProRes	These codecs are multi-threaded and will take advantage of all available processors (cores). There is no minimum clip duration for job segmenting.
MPEG-2	This codec is multi-threaded. The best performance for local clusters will be achieved when using half of the available services. For example, on an eight core machine, use four services.
H.264	This codec is not multi-threaded. You must have job segmenting enabled for this codec to take advantage of distributed processing. The minimum clip duration for segmenting is two minutes.
Any codec used in an Episode custom setting	The Episode workflow in Compressor does not take advantage of distributed processing. You will need to use the proprietary Episode Engine as an alternative to Apple QMaster. Refer to the Episode documentation for more information.

NOTE ▶ For more information on distributed processing, visit the Compressor website (www.apple.com/finalcutstudio/compressor).

Glossary

1:37:1 Aspect ratio of 35mm film, commonly referred to as *Academy ratio.*

1:85:1 Widescreen version of the Academy aspect ratio.

2:35:1 Aspect ratio common to widescreen, theatrical-release motion pictures.

3:2 Aspect ratio common to digital video (DV) and DVD.

3:2 pulldown A process for converting film-footage frame rates to video-footage frame rates.

4:3 Aspect ratio of a standard-definition NTSC television set.

16:9 Aspect ratio of a high-definition television set and HD video formats. Also referred to as 1:78:1.

16-bit A standard bit depth for digital audio recording and playback.

A

alpha channel A channel that exists in some file formats along with the color channels. Used to store transparency information for compositing purposes. Formats that support an alpha channel include Targa, TIFF, PICT, PSD, and the QuickTime Animation codec.

animation codec Lossless codec used for the real-time playback of uncompressed RGB video.

AppleScript Scripting language developed by Apple Computer that sends commands to scriptable applications and creates simple instruction sets that can be packaged into executable files.

Apple Intermediate Codec A high-quality video codec developed by Apple as an alternative to native MPEG-2 HDV editing in an HDV workflow. Instead of editing the MPEG-2 HDV data directly, video is captured from a tape source and transcoded by the codec to optimize the video data for playback performance and quality.

Apple ProRes 422 Codec A high-quality production codec designed for use in Final Cut Studio workflows. Uses 4:2:2 chroma sampling, 8- or 10-bit sample depth, full frame width up to 1920, and all I-frame encoding.

aspect ratio The ratio of the width and height of an image. For example, standard-definition TV has an aspect ratio of 4:3; high-definition TV has a 16:9 aspect ratio.

B

bandwidth A measurement of the amount of data delivered from a source to a destination within a period of time. Generally stated in kilobits per second (kbps) or megabits per second (Mbps).

bit budgeting The process of calculating the required data rates of media to determine if that media will fit within a specific bandwidth or within the storage limitations of a distribution format.

bit rate (also *bitrate*) A measurement of the quantity of data transmitted over time. See also *bandwidth.*

Blu-ray Disc A high-density (up to 50 GB) optical media format that can hold data, SD video, and HD video.

broadband A relative term used to identify the faster data delivery options provided by Internet service providers.

C

chroma sampling The process of storing more luminance information relative to the color information in a video signal. Commonly represented as a ratio of three numbers, such as 4:2:2 or 4:4:4, where the first number represents the luminance value, and the next two numbers represent the color values.

codec Abbreviation for *compression/decompression.* A program used to compress and decompress data such as audio and video files.

color correction (also *color grading*) The process of modifying or correcting the color reproduction of film or video assets by digital or chemical means.

compression A process by which data files (often video, graphics, and audio data) are reduced in size. Size reduction of an audio or video file that is implemented by removing perceptually-redundant image data is referred to as *lossy* compression. *Lossless* compression uses a mathematical process to reduce file size by consolidating redundant information without discarding it. wSee also *codec.*

D

data rate The speed at which data is transferred, often described in megabytes per second (Mbps). Higher video data rates usually exhibit increased visual quality, but higher data rates also require more system resources (such as processor speed and hard disk space) for processing. Some codecs allow you to specify a maximum data rate for a media capture. See also *bandwidth, bit rate.*

deinterlace Combining video frames composed of two interlaced fields into a single unified frame.

Digital Cinema A system to capture, distribute, and display motion pictures in either 2k resolution (2048 horizontal pixels) or 4k resolution (4096 horizontal pixels). The format is independent of SD or HD video.

digital intermediate (DI) High-resolution digital media created from film footage for the purpose of color correction and other creative picture adjustments.

digital video Video that has been captured, manipulated, and stored in a digital format, and that can be easily imported into a computer. Digital video formats include Digital-8, DVC PRO, DVCAM, and DV.

DV A standardized digital video format created by a consortium of camcorder vendors that uses Motion JPEG compression in a 720 x 480 pixel resolution running at 29.97 frames per second in NTSC format or 720 x 546 pixel resolution running at 25 fps in PAL format. DV content is stored at a bit rate of 25 Mbps with a compression of 4:1:1.

F

field dominance The choice of whether field 1 or field 2 will first be displayed on a monitor. The default value should be lower (field 2) for DV and Targa captures.

floating point A system of calculation that allows otherwise fixed incremental measurements within a bit depth to change in relative fashion so that a higher degree of accuracy can be achieved at the widest dynamic ranges.

frame rate The playback speed of individual images in a moving sequence, either film or video, measured in frames per second (fps). Film in 16mm or 35mm is usually shot at 24 fps; NTSC video at 29.97 fps; and PAL video at 25 fps. HD content can employ a variety of frame rates depending on the format.

H

HD (high-definition) Formats created to increase the number of pixels (resolution) of video images, and to solve many of the frame rate and cadence problems that exist between film and video. The two most common pixel resolutions for HD footage are 1080 with a native resolution of 1920 x 1080; and 720 with a native resolution of 1280 x 720. Both formats can be recorded at various frame rates and can be interlaced or progressive.

HD DVD A high-density (up to 30 GB) optical disc format that can hold data, SD video, and HD video.

I

I frame See *keyframe.*

interlaced video A video scanning method that first scans odd-numbered picture lines (field 1) and then scans the even-numbered picture lines (field 2). The two fields are combined to constitute a single frame of video.

K

keyframe (also *I frame*) A frame encoded with the entire image data and no reference to any other frame. In intra-frame compression, all frames are keyframes. In inter-frame compression, an interval of keyframes is separated by delta frames that interpolate their image data by referencing multiple keyframes.

L

lossless compression See *compression.*

lossy compression See *compression.*

M

metadata Information in a digital file that includes additional data in the content or context of the media.

MPEG (Moving Pictures Experts Group) A group of compression standards for video and audio developed by that group, which includes MPEG-1, MPEG-2, MPEG-1 Layer 3 (MP3), and MPEG-4.

multiplexed (also *muxing*) The interleaving of audio and video into one stream.

muxing See *multiplexed.*

N

NTSC (National Television Systems Committee) A standard format for color TV broadcasting developed by the committee and used mainly in North America, Mexico, and Japan. The NTSC format consists of 525 scan lines per frame of 720 x 486 pixel resolution (720 x 480 for DV), running at a 29.97 fps rate.

P

PAL (phase alternating line) A color TV broadcasting standard used primarily in Europe and consisting of 625 lines per frame of 720 x 546 pixel resolution, and running at a 25 fps rate.

pixel Abbreviation for *picture element.* One dot in a digital video or still image.

pixel aspect ratio The width-to-height ratio for the pixels that compose an image. Pixels on computer screens and in high-definition video signals are square (1:1 ratio); pixels in standard-definition video signals are not square (0.9:1 ratio).

progressive frame video (also *progressive scan*) A format for delivering video in which all lines are drawn in sequence. Its presence is commonly denoted by the letter *p*, such as *720p* or *1080p*.

progressive scan See *progressive frame video.*

R

RGB (red-green-blue) The three primary colors that make up a color video image.

S

sample rate The frequency at which analog audio is measured and converted into digital data. The sampling rate of an audio stream specifies how often digital samples are captured. Higher sample rates yield higher-quality audio. Standard audio sampling rates are usually measured in kilohertz (kHz). The standard CD sampling rate is 44.1 kHz. A rate of 48 kHz is also common in professional audio production.

SD (standard definition) The term used to differentiate traditional television resolutions from those of the high-definition formats. Standard-definition resolutions are 720 x 486 (NTSC) or 720 x 576 (PAL). See also *HD*.

SDI (Serial Digital Interface) Broadcast-grade interface used for transmission of uncompressed video signals. HD-SDI is a higher bandwidth version of the same format.

T

telecine The process of transferring film footage to video media. Can also refer to the machine that performs the process.

TIFF (tagged image file format) A bitmapped graphics file format for monochrome, grayscale, and 8- and 24-bit color images. There are two types of TIFF images: with an alpha channel and without an alpha channel.

timecode A numbering system of electronic signals placed onto video content and used to identify individual video frames. Each video frame is labeled with hours, minutes, seconds, and frames, expressed in the format: 01:00:00:00. Timecode can be drop frame, non-drop frame, or time of day (TOD) timecode, or EBU (European Broadcast Union) for PAL projects.

X

Xsan Apple Computer's branded, cross-platform SAN (storage area network) solution that offers both high speed and large storage capacity.

Y

YUV The three-channel PAL video signal with one luminance (Y) and two chrominance color difference signals (UV).

Index

ONE SIX RIGHT
THE ROMANCE OF FLYING
TERWILLIGER PRODUCTIONS presents a BRIAN J. TERWILLIGER film "ONE SIX RIGHT"
original music by NATHAN WANG director of photography STEVEN R. MILES edited by KIM FURST
visual effects by ALAN CHAMBERLAIN aerial director KEVIN LAROSA original guitar music by FREDDY CLARKE
aerial director of photography CARSTON BELL and DOUG HOLGATE
produced and directed by BRIAN J. TERWILLIGER
WWW.ONESIXRIGHT.COM
TERWILLIGER

Footage used in this book is from the feature documentary "One Six Right".
Learn more about this independent film's journey from conception to distribution at:
www.apple.com/pro/profiles/terwilliger

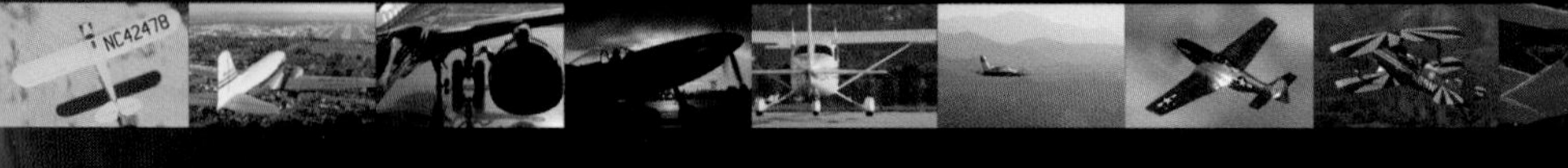
NC42478

WWW.ONESIXRIGHT.COM